International Investment Law and Policy in Africa

This book studies the international investment law regime in Africa and provides a comprehensive analysis of the current treaty practices in Africa from global, regional and domestic perspectives. It develops a public interest regulation theory to highlight the role of investment regulation in sustainable development and the protection of human rights. In doing so, the book identifies seven factors that should be considered by arbitrators in resolving international investment disputes that affect the public interest. It considers how corporations can be held accountable through investment treaties in the absence of a global treaty on business and human rights while protecting the rights of investors and their investments. Furthermore, the book explores the current objectives and features of investor-state dispute settlement (ISDS) as well as the deficiencies and its intersection with the rule of law. It identifies alternatives for ISDS and the extent to which these alternatives address the objectives of attracting investment, depoliticise investment disputes, promote the rule of law and offer remedies to investors. These solutions are offered in relation to the protection of human rights, the promotion of sustainable development and the right of states to introduce domestic public interest regulation. Finally, the book takes a prospective stance and discusses future trends for dispute settlement and investment rulemaking in Africa.

Fola Adeleke is a Visiting Senior Researcher at University of Witwatersrand and a fellow on social and economic inequalities at the London School of Economics. In preparing this book, he was a Fulbright scholar at Columbia University and Harvard Law School. He holds a PhD in international investment law. Some sections of this book were adapted from his doctorate.

Routledge Research in International Economic Law

Available titles in this series include:

International Investment Law and Policy in Africa

Exploring a Human Rights Based
Approach to Investment Regulation and
Dispute Settlement

Fola Adeleke

Routledge
Taylor & Francis Group

LONDON AND NEW YORK

First published 2018 by Routledge

2 Park Square, Milton Park, Abingdon, Oxfordshire OX14 4RN
52 Vanderbilt Avenue, New York, NY 10017

Routledge is an imprint of the Taylor & Francis Group, an informa business

First issued in paperback 2019

British Library Cataloguing in Publication Data
A catalogue record for this book is available from the British Library

Library of Congress Cataloging in Publication Data
Names: Adeleke, Fola, author.
Title: International investment law and policy in Africa : exploring a human rights based approach to investment regulation and dispute settlement / Fola Adeleke.
Description: Abingdon, Oxon [UK] ; New York : Routledge, 2017. | Series: Routledge research in international economic law | Includes bibliographical references and index.
Identifiers: LCCN 2017022762| ISBN 9781138240629 (hbk) | ISBN 9781315277264 (ebk)
Subjects: LCSH: Investments, Foreign--Law and legislation--Africa. | Investments--Law and legislation--Africa. | Arbitration and award--Africa. | Dispute resolution (Law)--Africa. | Human rights--Africa. | Social responsibility of business--Law and legislation--Africa. | Investments, Foreign--Economic aspects. | Investments, Foreign (International law)
Classification: LCC KQC747 .A34 2018 | DDC 346.6/092--dc23
LC record available at https://lccn.loc.gov/2017022762

ISBN: 978-1-138-24062-9 (hbk)
ISBN: 978-0-367-88474-1 (pbk)

Typeset in Galliard
by Fish Books Ltd.

This book is dedicated to my father, Olufemi, who encouraged me to be a man of letters from my childhood. And to my mother, Moyoade, who has given me a life of love and endless prayers.

Contents

List of cases

List of tables

List of acronyms and abbreviations

ACHPR	African Court on Human and People's Rights
ADR	Alternative Dispute Resolution
AU	African Union
BEE	Black Economic Empowerment
BIT	Bilateral Investment Treaty
CEMAC	Economic and Monetary Community of Central Africa
CEN-SAD	Community of Sahel-Saharan States
CFA	Communauté Financière Africaine
CFTA	Continental Free Trade Area
CIFA	Cooperation and Investment Facilitation Agreement
COMESA	Common Market for Eastern and Southern Africa
DRC	Democratic Republic of Congo
EAC	East African Community
ECCAS	Economic Community of Central African States
ECCHR	European Center for Constitutional and Human Rights
ECGLC	Economic Community of Great Lakes Countries
ECHR	European Court of Human Rights
ECOWAS	Economic Community of West African States
EU	European Union
FET	Fair and Equitable Treatment
FDI	Foreign Direct Investment
FIP	Finance and Investment Protocol
GATT	General Agreement on Tarriffs and Trade
GDP	Gross Domestic Product
IACHR	Inter-American Court of Human Rights
ICC	International Criminal Court
ICSID	International Centre for Settlement of Investment Disputes
ICESCR	International Convention on Economic, Social and Cultural Rights
ICJ	International Court of Justice
IGAD	Inter-Governmental Authority on Development
IIA	International Investment Agreement

IISD	International Institute for Sustainable Development
ILC	International Law Commission
IMF	International Monetary Fund
IOC	Indian Ocean Commission
ISDS	Investor–State Dispute Settlement
MFN	Most Favoured Nation
MIGA	Multilateral Investment Guarantee Agency
MNC	Multi-National Corporation
MRU	Mano River Union
NAFTA	North American Free Trade Agreement
NGO	Non-Governmental Organisation
NIPC	Nigerian Investment Promotion Commission Act
NPM	Non Precluded Measure
NT	National Treatment
OAU	Organisation of African Unity
OECD	Organisation for Economic Co-operation and Development
OPIC	Overseas Private Invesment Corporation
PIA	Protection of Investment Act
PRI	Political Risk Insurance
REC	Regional Economic Community
SACU	Southern African Customs Union
SADC	Southern African Development Community
SDG	Sustainable Development Goal
SME	Small and Medium Sized Enterprises
TFTA	Tripartite Free Trade Area
TPP	Trans-Pacific Partnership
TRIPS	Trade-Related Aspects of Intellectual Property Rights
TTIP	Trans-Atlantic Trade and Investment Partnership
UEMOA	West African Economic and Monetary Union
UK	United Kingdom
UMA	Arab Maghreb Union
UN	United Nations
UNCITRAL	United Nations Commission on International Trade Law
UNCTAD	United Nations Conference on Trade and Development
UNECA	United Nations Economic Commission for Africa
UNESCO	United Nations Educational, Scientific and Cultural Organization
USA	United States of America
VCLT	Vienna Convention on the Law of Treaties
WTO	World Trade Organization

Acknowledgements

I am indebted to a number of people and institutions whose support and guidance made this book possible. I would like to thank Professor Jonathan Klaaren of the University of Witwatersrand, Professor Tyler Giannini of Harvard Law School, Professor Lisa Sachs and Lise Johnson of Columbia Centre for Sustainable Investment, Fulbright Scholars Program, Oppenheimer Memorial Trust, and the Mandela Institute, University of Witwatersrand.

I also wish to thank the researchers who worked with me on this project: Roland Nzanzu, John Sabet and Amandla Makhongwana. I would like to thank four students of the Harvard international human rights clinic, fall semester 2016, whose research shaped Chapter 4 of this book: Katelyn Cioffi, Adam Savitt, Julia Cortez da Cunha Cruz and Malo Gall Gurvan.

I am also highly indebted to my wife, Chiedza Caroline – my source of encouragement – and my siblings, Durotolu, Oluseyi and Olusanmi – my sources of inspiration.

1 Introduction

Introduction

International investment agreements (IIAs), with their neoliberal origins and favourable protections for investors and their investments, may appear to be an unlikely place to protect human rights and promote inclusive and sustainable development that addresses social and economic inequalities between global north and south states and within individual states. IIAs have gained notoriety for preferencing the interests of corporate foreign investors, limiting state regulation that can advance public interests and adopting secretive dispute resolution processes that erode the rule of law. However, IIAs have tremendous potential to help states in imposing human rights obligations on non-state actors and in the realisation of economic policies that will tackle global challenges.

There are currently over 3,304 IIAs, with 150 economies negotiating 57 new IIAs by the end of May 2016.[1] A large number of these IIAs are Bilateral Investment Treaties (BITs) with 2946 in existence at the end of May 2016. Given the recent backlash across the globe against multilateral treaties it is possible that we may see an increase in the conclusion of BITs between states.[2] Furthermore, the number of active BITs with long periods of enforcement means that BITs will continue to substantially impact global financial activity for a considerably long time.

The role of IIAs in the implementation of a sustainable development agenda and in the protection of human rights have not received sufficient attention. If IIAs are to become a useful tool to ensure inclusive and integrated economic development, states must find ways to integrate stronger protections for human rights and sustainable development objectives into the language of IIAs themselves.

1   United Nations Conference on Trade and Development (UNCTAD), 2016, *World Investment Report 2016*, viewed (20 March 2016), from http://unctad.org/en/PublicationsLibrary/wir2016_en.pdf, p. 101.
2   These include the decision of the USA to withdraw from the negotiation of the Trans-Pacific Partnership and Britain's withdrawal from the European Union.

IIAs have experienced major developments over the last few years and have become the governing framework for foreign direct investment (FDI) particularly through BITs. The proliferation of BITs in the 1990s was as a result of the acceptance of the ideology of neo-liberalism, which was driven by the USA and international financial institutions of the time.[3] However, more recently, there has been a retreat from neo-liberalism, which has also resulted in a decline in the number of BITs being concluded by states on an annual basis after the explosion of this phenomenon during the 1990s.[4] In addition, recent developments in the international investment regime show that there is a greater emphasis on the sovereign right to regulate of states and the protection of national interests.[5]

The roots of the proliferation of BITs can be traced back to the end of colonialism. Shortly after the decolonisation period of the 1960s, countries concluded BITs with their former colonies – a process that was instigated by these countries to protect their interests in the new independent states.[6] Following the wave of trans-continental BITs signed by newly independent African countries, African countries also embraced the conclusion of BITs with each other in recognition of common interests in the regulation of investment as well as 'a means to attract greater investment and to deepen regional integration'.[7] This led to a period of globalisation, which gained momentum in the 1990s for several reasons. These included the dissolution of the Soviet Union, the increase in a large number of developing countries opening up for foreign investment, and the rise in investors from advanced economies seeking ways to reduce costs and gain market access abroad.[8] BITs were seen as the signal that a state has liberalised and as a result, most countries signed a few BITs within a decade between 1990 and 2000.[9]

It has been suggested that African countries continued to sign BITs that negatively affected their interests due to a lack of awareness and understanding of the financial implications in the event of breach of an agreement.[10] Furthermore, a lack of understanding of the consequences of

---

3   Sornarajah, M., 2010, *The International Law on Foreign Investment*, 3rd edn., Cambridge University Press, New York, p. 174.

4   *Id.*

5   For instance, the recent 2012 model BIT of the USA shows a retreat towards 'a sovereignty-centered approach born out of their experience of being at the wrong end of several NAFTA arbitrations' (Sornarajah, *supra* note 3, at p. 175).

6   *Id.*

7   United Nations Economic Commission for Africa (UNECA), 2016, *Investment Policies and Bilateral Investment Treaties in Africa: Implications for Regional Integration*, viewed (15 March 2017) from www.uneca.org/sites/default/files/PublicationFiles/eng_investment_landscaping_study.pdf, p. 21.

8   United Nations Conference on Trade and Development (UNCTAD), 2015, *World Investment Report 2015*, viewed (15 March 2016), from http://unctad.org/en/PublicationsLibrary/wir2015_en.pdf, p. 123.

9   *Id.*

10 UNECA, *supra* note 7 at p. 24.

change in government or any other external factor that made compliance with BITs difficult, poor knowledge of treaty language that increased the liability of states in terms of the protections offered to investors continued to affect the interests of African states.[11]

Notwithstanding the problems BITs created for states, BITs have continued to fill the space of investment regulation in the absence of a multilateral treaty on foreign investment protection.[12] BITs are popular among states under the false premise that they promote FDI and that foreign investments are beneficial to the economic development of host states.[13] However, emerging empirical evidence is increasingly showing that not all foreign investments contribute to economic development or alternatively, have a positive impact on public policy considerations of states.[14] As a result, recent BITs are introducing screening tests to 'keep out investments that do not promote the economic objectives of the state'.[15] In cases where BITs do increase FDI, it has been suggested that the benefits do not outweigh the costs of lost policy space and investor–state litigation risks.[16] Given the lack of concrete evidence to link the conclusion of investment treaties with FDI, a rethink of the role of IIAs such as BITs in advancing FDI is necessary.

FDI trends in Africa

While a large number of BITs form the core of regulation of investment in Africa, within the last decade there have been regulatory developments in sub-regional institutions such as the Common Market for Eastern and Southern Africa (COMESA) and the Southern African Development Community (SADC) aimed at making the Southern African and East African regions investor friendly with the aim of developing a harmonised regional approach towards FDI regulation.[17]

Recent data on trade in Africa show that only 17.9 per cent of international trade in goods and services takes place between African countries.[18] However, these data do not capture the informal trade that takes place between African countries which constitute 55 per cent of Africa's gross

---

11 *Id*, p. 26.
12 Sornarajah, *supra* note 3 at p. 183.
13 *Id*, p. 190.
14 Wei, D., 2012, 'Bilateral investment treaties: An empirical analysis of the practices of Brazil and China', *European journal of Law and Economics*, 33(3), p. 10.
15 Sornarajah, *supra* note 3 at p. 195.
16 UNECA, *supra* note 7 at p 12.
17 These developments are discussed in Chapter 6 of this book.
18 United Nations Conference on Trade and Development (UNCTAD), *Key Statistics and Trends in International Trade in Goods 2015*, viewed (15 March 2017), from http://unctad.org/en/PublicationsLibrary/ditctab2015d1_en.pdf; World Trade Organisation, *International Trade Statistics 2015*, viewed (15 March 2017), from www.wto.org/english/res_e/statis_e/its2015_e/its2015_e.pdf

domestic product (GDP).[19] With such informal trades going undetected and regulation measures not taking them into consideration, African economic integration has a long way to go.[20]

While FDI was exclusively the playground of western investors, multinational companies (MNCs) in Africa are also playing an increasing role. African companies have driven growth in the telecommunications, mining and retail, as well as financial services industry.[21] For example, South Africa is currently the largest outward investing economy within Africa.[22]

There are also signs of diversification with the services sector recording the largest growth in Africa in 2015 moving away from the extractive industry.[23] Drivers that have shaped FDI into Africa according to United Nations Conference on Trade and Development (UNCTAD) include the rise in intra-African FDI, the expansion by emerging-market firms and non-traditional actors such as private equity, as well as growing consumer markets.[24] Despite the growth in Africa and the liberal economic policies adopted by states, the global share of FDI into Africa remains low with only 6 per cent of such flows occurring between 2007 and 2013.[25] Some of the reasons for this include poor infrastructure availability and regulatory uncertainties, which limit business confidence.

In the past, FDI mainly originated from advanced economies; as a result, BIT approaches in African states have mainly developed from that perspective. The Canada and US model BITs are said to 'represent the broader, Western Hemisphere approach, while the model BITs of European countries stand for the narrower, European approach'.[26] While both approaches protect FDI flows, the Western Hemisphere approach also covers the liberalisation of investment. One important feature of the Western Hemisphere approach is that it prohibits performance requirements. These requirements are imposed by host states to ensure foreign investors export a percentage of their production, buy local products and services as well as employ local labour among other requirements. These requirements enhance the value of foreign investment in developing countries.[27] The debate on the value of

---

19   African Development Bank (AfDB), *Recognising Africa's Informal Sector*, viewed (15 March 2017), from www.afdb.org/en/blogs/afdb-championing-inclusive-growth-across-africa/post/recognizing-africas-informal-sector-11645/

20   Though FDI flows have risen to US$54 billion, this represents only 4.4 per cent of global FDI flows.

21   UNCTAD, *supra* note 8 at p. 6.

22   *Id*, pp. 8–9; South Africa has an intense FDI flow with neighbouring countries such as Swaziland, Zimbabwe, Mozambique, Lesotho, Malawi, Botswana, Namibia, Ghana and Kenya.

23   *Id*, pp. 32 and 35; the sector increased by four-fold between 2001 and 2012 and accounted for 48 per cent of the total stock of FDI.

24   UNCTAD, *supra* note 8 at p. 34.

25   UNECA, *supra* note 7 at p. 8.

26   UNCTAD, 2005, *South-South cooperation in international investment agreements*, viewed (31 March 2017) from http://unctad.org/en/docs/iteiit20053_en.pdf, p. 31.

27   Sornarajah, *supra* note 3 at p. 205.

performance requirements is unsettled and arguments such as the distortion of international trade have been used by advanced economies to argue against the use of performance requirements. However, performance requirements aid the developmental goals of host states and it was on the basis of policy approaches such as these that developed countries built their economies.

IIAs are often concluded between unequal partners, particularly, when developed and developing states are involved. Developing states, in expectation of investment flows,[28] cede part of their sovereignty to offer external protection from investor–state dispute settlement (ISDS) mechanisms, which are often insulated from the reach of domestic laws.[29]

However, there has also been an increase in the conclusion of BITs between developing states.[30] This is occurring at a period where there is an increase of FDI flows between South–South countries, which is taking place as a result of growth opportunities in developing markets, procurement of raw materials and extractives, demand for lower labour costs as well as geographic proximity.[31] South–South economies, such as China, have also become a strong player in FDI outflows into Africa, with China's demand for mineral resources to build its economy growing exponentially.[32]

In the light of these considerations where new interests are coming into play in doing business in Africa, it is necessary to examine the origins of investment regulation in Africa and the extent to which these origins inform the negotiation and content of such treaties today.

Origins and development of international investment law in Africa

Africa has been described as a birthplace of statecraft, peace-craft, treaty-craft as well as an innovator of international law.[33] It has been suggested that international rules on the protection of foreign-owned property originated in Europe where there were reciprocal arrangements by European states to secure similar standards of treatment for their citizens investing in other European states.[34] With colonialism came the application of these standards

28   *Id*, p. 177.
29   *Id*, p. 178.
30   Ismail M., 2016, *International Investment Arbitration: Lessons from Developments in the MENA Region*, Routledge, p. 95.
31   UNCTAD, *supra* note 26 at p. 13.
32   *Id*, p. 9; China's strongest bilateral FDI flows in Africa are with Burundi, Zimbabwe, Angola, Guinea-Bissau and the Democratic Republic of Congo.
33   Levitt, Jeremy I., 2015, 'African origins of international law: Myth or reality?', *UCLA Journal of International Law and Foreign Affairs*, 19, p. 159.
34   Miles, K., 2010, 'International investment law: Origins, imperialism and conceptualizing the environment', *Colorado Journal of International Environmental Law & Policy*, 21(1), p. 3.

to protect commercial interests and 'foreign investment protection law moved from a base in reciprocity to one of imposition'.[35] As a result, former colonialists and capital-exporting states ensured that international investment law developed towards the protection of investors only.[36]

Arguably, international law was used to facilitate the advancement of colonialism.[37] For Sornarajah, the transition of European investment rules into principles of international law is embedded in colonialism and legal norms were manipulated to suit vested commercial interests where the interests of capital-exporting states were protected in the advancement of exploitation and imperialism.[38] In consequence, host states were unable to rely on international investment law to address damages suffered as a result of foreign investor conduct.

In a bid to restructure the unbalanced nature of international investment law, Latin American states led the charge for the introduction of the national treatment rule, which later became known as the Calvo doctrine.[39] This doctrine sought to prohibit states from intervening in the affairs of other states by asserting the doctrine of state sovereignty. It also sought to ensure that foreign nationals of other states received the same treatment as citizens and could only seek redress through the national judicial systems.[40] The adoption of this doctrine was resisted by developed states creating a pathway for the internationalisation of the current investment rules that are applicable and feature in most BITs.

Sornarajah argues that it was due to the dissolution of empires after the colonial period that 'the need for a system of protection of foreign investment came to be felt by the erstwhile imperial powers which now became the exporters of capital to the former colonies and elsewhere'.[41] He identifies four periods during the post-colonialist period that shaped the development of the law on foreign investment. In the first period, he argues that there was antagonism towards foreign investment driven by 'a nationalist fervour'.[42] This arose as a result of the desire of newly independent states to take control of their economies and as a result, there was a wave of nationalisations of foreign property.[43] In the second period, Sornarajah describes a period of rationalisation and pragmatism where states had rearranged their economies, and international and domestic positions were taken that suited a state's interests.[44] During this period, there was a

35   *Id.*
36   *Id*, p. 4.
37   Sornarajah, supra note 3 at p. 51.
38   *Id*, pp. 54–57.
39   *Id*, p. 102.
40   *Id.*
41   *Id*, p. 21.
42   *Id*, p. 22.
43   *Id.*
44   *Id*, p. 23.

gradual rise of bilateral investment treaties. The third period ushered in a period of liberalisation and this was further entrenched by institutions such as the World Bank and the International Monetary Fund (IMF) that promoted the traditional standards of investment protection known today.[45] The fourth period saw a scaling back of neo-liberalism where inequality had been on the rise, capitalism unchecked and economic development stagnated in developing countries.[46]

This stagnant economic growth has led developing states to adopt various economic policies and plans with the aim of boosting economic growth. Such policies and plans have sought to protect domestic industries, demanded performance requirements from foreign investors to boost local industries and in some cases led to agrarian reform or changes in monetary policy. Such economic policies have occurred with states carving out a regulatory space for reform despite the presence of investor protection standards in BITs. These developments have led to a spike in ISDS with investors aiming to protect their interests through BITs. Consequently, arbitrators have played a central role in the interpretation of treaties and restricting the scope and impact of domestic regulation of states on the investments of foreign investors. This is occurring at a time when ISDS is facing scrutiny for several deficiencies, which delegitimise the role of ISDS as the accountability mechanism for adherence to the rule of law under international investment law.

While African states have been regarded as rule takers in the field of international law, the tide is changing and international investment law is now increasingly being 'Africanised'. With the aim of increasing African regional economic integration, attracting investment flows and to facilitate intra-African investment, African ministers adopted a resolution in 2008 to develop an investment code for Africa called the Pan-African Investment Code.[47] The decision to adopt a code that applies to all African states was taken partly in acknowledgement of the fragmented approach to investment regulation in Africa through BITs as well as the various regional investment agreements developed by regional economic communities (RECs). There are 14 RECs covering the African continent, though only eight are recognised as the 'building blocks of the African Union'.[48] Consequently, there are 28

45   *Id*, p. 24.
46   *Id*, p. 454.
47   Mbengue M., 2016 'The quest for a Pan-African Investment Code to promote sustainable development', *Bridges Africa*, 5(5), viewed (30 March 2017), from www.ictsd.org/bridges-news/bridges-africa/news/the-quest-for-a-pan-african-investment-code-to-promote-sustainable.
48   www.uneca.org/oria/pages/regional-economic-communities viewed (30 March 2017). The eight preferred African RECs are the Economic Community of West African States (ECOWAS), the Community of Sahel-Saharan States (CEN-SAD), the Economic Community of Central African States (ECCAS), the Common Market for Eastern and Southern Africa (COMESA), the East African Community (EAC), the Inter-Governmental Authority on Development (IGAD), the Southern Africa Development

African countries with dual memberships of various RECs and 20 countries are members of three RECs, with the Democratic Republic of Congo (DRC) belonging to four RECs.[49] Most of these RECs adopted legal instruments concerning the regulation of foreign investment.[50] Consequently, there is a regional instrument governing investment regulation in each African REC.[51] The recently developed regional investment regulations from the twenty-first century onwards are discussed in Chapter 6 of this book.

Due to this fragmented approach to foreign investment flows in Africa, where regional regulations sometimes do not suit the needs of a member state and some of the regional regulations are not binding, BITs including intra-African BITs have gained prominence. This has occurred without much influence on the part of African states in their development, as Chapter 6 of this book demonstrates. Consequently, African states decided to revamp the investment policy framework applicable on the continent in line with the 2005 UNCTAD investment policy framework on sustainable development. The African approach is not to oppose the current system of IIAs, as Latin American countries have done.[52] The Pan-African Investment Code is Africa's attempt 'to shape an international investment treaty according to their own priorities'.[53] This development is an indication that the previously applicable models of investment regulation, which capital-exporting countries are also beginning to oppose, are now seen as detrimental to Africa's developmental interests.

While the Pan-African Investment Code is still in its draft form, it is intended to be a binding treaty subject to ratification by 15 member states.[54] However, recognising the implications of adopting a code that aims to replace existing BITs on expiry or termination, the legal ramifications for states are enormous and it exposes states to the risk of potential claims by investors for reneging on their international law commitments. For example,

Community (SADC) and the Arab Maghreb Union (UMA). The other six RECs are the Economic Community of Great Lakes Countries (ECGLC), West African Economic and Monetary Union (UEMOA), the Mano River Union (MRU), the Indian Ocean Commission (IOC), the Southern African Customs Union (SACU) and the Economic and Monetary Community of Central Africa (CEMAC).

49   Mbengue, *supra* note 47.
50   *Id.*
51   *Id.*
52   Indeed, the recent decision of South Africa not to renew some of its BITs is not intended to move away from the BIT framework in its entirety but for the state to be strategic in deciding which BITs to negotiate in the future; Schlemmer, E.C., 2016 'An overview of South Africa's bilateral investment treaties and investment policy', *ICSID Review*, 31(1), pp. 167–193.
53   Mbengue, *supra* note 47.
54   Art 51, E/ECA/COE/35/18AU/STC/FMEPI/EXP/18(II) Economic Commission for Africa, Committee of Experts, Thirty-fifth meeting, Ninth Joint Annual Meetings of the African Union Specialized Technical Committee on Finance, Monetary Affairs, Economic Planning and Integration and the Economic Commission for Africa Conference of African Ministers of Finance, Planning and Economic Development.

Chapter 6 of this book discusses how the arbitration tribunal in the *Swissborough v. Lesotho* case held Lesotho liable to investors for its vote at the SADC to disband the SADC tribunal.[55] Consequently, given the appetite of some tribunals to apply interpretations that completely erode the sovereign right of states to make policy choices even at regional and international levels, the binding nature of the draft African Investment Code is uncertain and it remains a possibility that the code can simply serve as a model treaty.[56]

However, the African Investment Code is an optimistic perspective of the future of IIAs, which is to be supported. Building on the SADC model BIT, the African Investment Code adopts a human rights based approach to investment regulation. The details of the code are discussed in Chapter 6.

The development of the code is a remarkable development of international investment law and the Africanisation of investment frameworks. This development is consistent with other international initiatives led by the global South to push back against Eurocentric and North American approaches to corporate liability and the duty to respect and protect human rights.

Globally, due to political expediency, the framework for extending obligations to corporations for the protection of human rights has not been extended beyond voluntary mechanisms. The most recent framework is the UN guiding principles on business and human rights, where in its development, there was a missed opportunity to clarify international law to confirm the extension of the binding obligation to protect human rights to private actors. Consequently, it came as no surprise that in 2014, the Human Rights Council passed a resolution sponsored by Ecuador and South Africa where countries agreed 'to establish an intergovernmental working group on a legally binding instrument on transnational corporations and other business enterprises with respect to human rights'.[57]

The resolution was passed due to the majority of votes from the global South bloc, particularly African countries, who believed in the necessity of an international treaty on business and human rights. It is not surprising that both the USA and the EU voted against the resolution since such a treaty will impose obligations on transnational corporations and would limit the ability of these companies to exploit in the absence of strong regulation by weak African governments.[58] The framing of the role of corporations in protecting human rights by the UN Special Rapporteur, John Ruggie, in the development of the UN guiding principles on business and human rights implies that corporations should respect human rights because it is in their interest to do so and not necessarily because they are bound by any

---

55 PCA Case No. 2013-29.
56 Mbengue, *supra* note 47.
57 Human Rights Council, 2014, 'Elaboration of an internationally legally binding instrument on transnational corporations and other business enterprises with respect to human rights', A/HRC/26/L.22/Rev.
58 There were 20 votes in favour of the resolution, 14 votes against and 13 abstentions.

obligation, despite corporations being highly capable of violating human rights obligations.[59]

This lack of accountability for corporations is concerning, yet the feasibility of an international business and human rights treaty is bleak for various reasons, including a weak political mandate due to calls for states to instead implement the voluntary UN guiding principles on business and human rights.[60] However, without an international framework to hold corporations accountable even for the watered down duty to respect human rights, the proposal in the UN guiding principles for access to remedies when violations occur will be subject to the benevolence of corporations.[61]

Extending human rights obligations on corporations is the first step in a long process. The scope and scale of such obligations and access to remedies for the breach of obligations will be harder to achieve. Consequently, in the absence of an international framework and recognising that the feasibility of the adoption of the Pan-African Investment Code and a business and human rights treaty are a long way off, solutions are necessary to use existing frameworks to hold corporations accountable.

As noted by Thomas Walde, investment arbitrators cannot apply a framework outside of the jurisdiction of the investment treaty (especially where only voluntary rules apply and there are no relevant rules of international law to apply), because that would amount to exceeding their jurisdiction.[62]

Given this reality and recognising that there is no global adjudicatory body similar to the International Criminal Court (ICC) to enforce corporate international obligations if they existed and were breached, it is necessary to propose alternative mechanisms to introduce obligations that will be immediately binding and a dispute settlement body that can be tasked to enforce them. IIAs offer this opportunity and this book makes proposals on how to interpret existing BITs with a human rights lens. This book also makes proposals on alternatives to ISDS that will guarantee the consideration and protection of human rights, including investment obligations towards investors.

Emerging trends in investment regulation in Africa

It has been consistently suggested that for African economic development, regional integration must play a pivotal role where there is a joint and

59   Biltchitz D., 2014, 'The Necessity for a Business and Human Rights Treaty', viewed (21 December 2016) from https://papers.ssrn.com/sol3/papers.cfm?abstract_id=2562760, p. 5.

60   John Ruggie articulates some of these reasons in 'Quo Vadis? Unsolicited Advice to Business and Human Rights Treaty Sponsors', viewed (30 March 2017) from www.ihrb.org/other/treaty-on-business-human-rights/quo-vadis-unsolicited-advice-to-business-and-human-rights-treaty-sponsors/

61   Biltchitz, *supra* note 59 at p. 15.

62   Ruggie G.J., 2013, *Just Business: Multinational Corporations and Human Rights*, W.W. Norton & Company, p. 184.

consistent effort between private actors and government.[63] Africa has been fine-tuning and tweaking its integration agenda since the establishment of the defunct Organisation of African Unity (OAU) in 1963. Since then, the OAU has been replaced with the African Union (AU) and several sub-regional economic communities have sprung up.[64] However, RECs are seen as having failed to achieve their purpose of promoting trade and integration despite the proliferation of these communities across Africa.[65] While this may be true of economic integration, integration has happened on other levels, particularly with regard to peace and security, which makes the study of economic integration particularly special.[66]

African economic integration is particularly important because high levels of informal trade in Africa affect the systematic tracking of trade and invest-ment flows within the continent.[67] Furthermore, with an estimated US$50 billion infrastructure funding gap in Africa that affects the productivity of companies in manufacturing goods, accessing markets and increases the cost of production, African state economies need to come together to fund greatly needed infrastructure development.[68] This also extends to making access to finance available. The lack of available access to finance has also hindered integration. It has been reported that only '23 percent of African enterprises have access to loans or lines of credit compared to 46 per cent for non-African developing countries'.[69] The lack of access to finance particularly affects local African companies in being able to extend their footprint across the continent. To achieve integration and advance industrialisation in Africa through infrastructure development investment regulation plays an import-ant role and the AU recognises this.

When the African Union Conference of Ministers of Trade decided it was necessary for IIAs to be examined especially 'the extent to which they may

63   Brenton P. and Hoffman, B. (eds), 2015, 'Political Economy of Regional Integration in Sub-Saharan Africa', World Bank Group, 3, viewed (20 March 2017) from http://documents.worldbank.org/curated/en/601711468010204270/pdf/103324-REVISED-WP-P146857-PUBLIC.pdf

64   The AU was formed in 2001. Though there are several RECs, there are eight considered to be the building blocks of the African economic community. These are the AMU, CEN-SAD, COMESA, EAC, ECCAS, ECOWAS, IGAD and SADC.

65   See in-depth discussion in Brenton P. and Isik G. (eds), 2011, 'De-Fragmenting Africa: Deepening Regional Trade Integration in Goods Services', World Bank, viewed (20 March 2017) from http://siteresources.worldbank.org/INTAFRICA/Resources/Defrag_Afr_English_web_version.pdf

66   The AU has increasingly taken an approach of clamping down against military coups and actively intervening in internal conflicts across the region.

67   Informal trade is said to be the source of income for 43 per cent of Africa's population; Africa J.-G. and Ajumbo G., 2012, 'Informal cross border trade in Africa: Implications and policy recommendations' *Africa Economic Brief*, 3(10).

68   Brenton & Hoffman, *supra* note 63 at p. 10.

69   UNCTAD, 2015, *Strengthening The Private Sector to Boost Continental Trade and Interrogation in Africa*, 2, viewed (21 March 2017) from http://unctad.org/en/PublicationsLibrary/presspb2015d5_en.pdf.

help Africa industrialise and develop',[70] the United Nations Economic Commission for Africa (UNECA) conducted extensive research and produced a report on how investments can be used for economic and social transformation in Africa. In the UNECA report, some of the challenges of investing in Africa identified include 'poor infrastructure, tariff and non-tariff barriers, limited movement of people and capital, high transaction costs, high risk perception, limited access to credit, and rent seeking'.[71]

African RECs have attempted to address these challenges through their various trade and investment regulations. At the beginning of 2012, the AU agreed to establish a continental free trade area (CFTA) by 2017.[72] This will open up the market space in Africa and significantly expand economic growth for African countries.[73] However, while the CFTA does not comprehensively cover issues of management of investor and investment relationships, the new COMESA–EAC–SADC Tripartite Agreement creates a high degree of connectivity in investment regulation involving 45 BITs.[74] The application and relevance of these regional agreements are discussed in Chapter 6 of this book.

One of the ideas behind the development of the Pan-African Investment Code[75] is the development of 'a business climate to stimulate investment at national, regional, and continental levels, and to develop a roadmap and strategy on how African countries can adopt this code to their own contexts'.[76] However, the integration of investment agreements in Africa have been less coordinated, making way for BITs to thrive and for states to conclude agreements with each other that are more in pursuit of national interests than in the pursuit of integration. By the time Egypt and Somalia concluded a BIT in 1982, which was the first time two African countries had concluded a BIT with each other, African countries had already signed 110 BITs with non-African countries.[77] There are currently about 854 BITs in Africa and only 157 of these are intra-African BITs.[78] The majority of BITs by African countries are with countries outside of Africa.[79]

This trend is consistent with the earlier point made about the perception of BITs as attractive for FDI. While the perceived value of BITs has been

70   UNECA, *supra* note 7 at p. viii.
71   *Id*, p. xi.
72   *Id*, p. 5.
73   *Id*.
74   *Id*, p. 20.
75   This came up at the Ninth Meeting of AU-RECs-ECA-AfDB Coordinating Committee, held on 25 January 2012, in Addis Ababa, Ethiopia.
76   UNECA, *supra* note 7 at p. 36.
77   *Id*, p. 21.
78   *Id*, p. 16.
79   Burkina Faso, Comoros, Guinea, Mali and Niger are exceptions where the countries have signed more BITs with African countries than non-African countries.

successfully debunked,[80] the ratification of BITs also comes with great risks. There have been 111 documented investment dispute cases involving African countries since 1972.[81] Sixty-eight of these cases ended up in awards, settlement or were discontinued, while 44 cases are still pending and some cases have been running for over a decade.[82] The International Centre for Settlement of Investment Disputes (ICSID) has been responsible for 107 of the total 111 cases while United Nations Commission on International Trade Law (UNCITRAL) tribunals are handling three cases.[83] Egypt is currently the African state respondent with the highest number of cases with 25 cases followed by the DRC in a distant second with eight cases.[84] It is not surprising that Egypt also has the highest number of BITs in Africa.[85]

The dispute settlement mechanisms in BITS have increasingly generated concerns for some African states that have been at the wrong end of investment disputes with large damages awarded against them. In cases where a dispute spans several years, the costs of losing, damages and accruable interest can be significant for a defendant state. One of the most recent examples of abuse of discretion and questionable use of legal judgment by an ISDS tribunal was in the *Al-Kharafi v. Libya* case, discussed later in this book where the tribunal awarded damages for the loss of a 90-year expected revenue for a resort that was never constructed.[86]

While ISDS has been the default approach to dispute settlement in BITs, on a regional level there has been resistance towards the continued application of the status quo. As a result, there are new trends that reflect calls for reform of ISDS with various approaches proposed including domestic dispute settlement, a permanent international investment court, state–state dispute settlement, more emphasis on political risk insurance and the reform of the current ISDS to include procedural reforms such as transparency and non-disputing party participation. These reform options are discussed in Chapters 3 and 4.

The total number of known treaty-based disputes in January 2016 was 696 and while capital-exporting countries are increasingly becoming the

---

80   See UNECA, *supra* note 7 at pp. 10–11 that shows studies on the effect of BITs on FDI. It largely shows that there is no correlation.

81   *Id*, p. 24.

82   *Id*.

83   *Id*.

84   Algeria has six cases, Guinea has five cases, DRC, Gambia, Zimbabwe, Senegal, Tunisia and Tanzania have four cases, Cameroon, Morocco, Liberia, Ghana, Burundi and Nigeria have three cases, and Central African Republic, Côte d'Ivoire, Gabon, Mali, Seychelles and Uganda have had two cases while Equatorial Guinea, Kenya, Madagascar, Niger, South Africa, Mozambique, South Sudan, Sudan, and Togo have had one case each.

85   Mauritius and South Africa have 21 and 18 BITs with African countries respectively, while Morocco and Tunisia have 15 BITs each with various African countries. Algeria has 11 BITs with African countries.

86   www.italaw.com/sites/default/files/case-documents/italaw1554.pdf (viewed 30 March 2017).

target of investor claims, capital-importing countries still 'bear the brunt of these claims' and most claimants come from advanced economies.[87] According to UNCTAD, of the 70 known new cases initiated in 2015, the majority were brought by investors from advanced economies, which corresponds to the historical trend in which capital-exporting country investors have been responsible for over 80 per cent of all claims.[88] Measures challenged have involved alleged violations of contracts, revocation of licenses, legislative reforms, alleged discrimination against foreign investors, alleged direct expropriation of investments, regulation of exports, bankruptcy proceedings and water tariff regulation.[89]

With the benefit of practice and the trends in investment disputes, some states saw the need to renegotiate their earlier BITs in a bid to clarify the scope of investment obligations, introduce safeguards in investment arbitration proceedings and to ensure investment protections did not come at the expense of the domestic policy space of states.[90] Consequently, in 2013, South Africa announced the non-renewal of some of its BITs with some European countries and adopted a domestic law to regulate investment. One of the reasons cited for this move was concern over the legitimacy of and practice in ISDS.[91] For African governments, the concerns around BITs include the focus on the expansive protection of investors and their investments which exposes states to liabilities with little return for the states.[92]

New investment trends show that investment flows into African countries are coming from emerging economies and not all these countries have treaties with African countries.[93] Consequently, the role of investment treaties in this new economic climate needs to be revisited. With 5 of the 12 fastest growing economies in the world coming from Africa and FDI five times what it was a decade ago, African governments now occupy an influential position that allows them to dictate terms and conditions for the establishment of investments in their respective countries.[94]

African governments have proposed the adoption of a number of approaches to improve international investment rulemaking. Various suggestions have been put forward which include a 'narrow definition of investment, mandatory exhaustion of local remedies, regional approaches to dispute resolution, pre-approval of investment ...' among others.[95] The International

---

87   UNCTAD, *supra* note 1 at p. 104.
88   *Id*, p. 105.
89   UNCTAD, *supra* note at 8 at pp. 112–113.
90   *Id*, p. 124.
91   Vidal-Leon C. 'A new approach to the law of foreign investments: The South African case', in Bjorklund A. (2015) *Yearbook on International Investment Law and Policy 2014–2015*, Oxford University Press. p. 295.
92   These concerns are dealt with in more detail in Chapter 3 of this book.
93   UNCTAD, *supra* note 1 at p. 41.
94   UNECA, *supra* note 7 at p. 42.
95   *Id*, p. 45.

Institute for Sustainable Development (IISD) model BIT and the UNCTAD investment policy framework for sustainable development are seen as good models for alternatives.[96] Some of these approaches also include the development and application of regional agreements for a harmonised approach towards investment.[97] One of the reasons for the suggested regional approach is to allow states to protect their policy space from being encroached by obligations towards investors only and the scope of domestic policies being determined by unaccountable ISDS mechanisms.[98] At the same time, for any policy approach to replace or complement BITs, it should sufficiently protect foreign investors but should not lead to a preferential treatment for foreign investors.[99]

There are several challenges that affect investment in Africa. One of the aims of this book is to identify the role of regulation in addressing these challenges. For investor access to markets and the attraction of foreign investment, it is necessary for the right regulations to be put in place. These regulations must not only protect investors and their investment, but should also impose obligations on investors that safeguard host state interests.

Most investment treaties in Africa, as will be shown in this book, do not impose obligations on investors, which leads to the potential for investments that are unregulated and can violate legitimately expected compliance with national legislative requirements. A correlated issue to this is the lack of transparency and accountability because states do not enforce these principles over foreign investments, which is discussed in depth in this book.

Typical investment agreements by African states cover several standards of protection under BITs such as national treatment, fair and equitable treatment (FET), full protection and security, most favoured nation (MFN) standard of treatment, as well as protection against discrimination and expropriation.

The national treatment standard is a contingent standard that requires equal treatment between nationals and foreign investors and economic considerations are not a justification for discrimination.[100] This protection gives a foreign investor a right of entry and establishment and has consequently become a significant cause of action in investment disputes.[101]

---

96 *Id.*
97 Some of the suggestions being mooted include the use of the African Court of Justice and the CFTA.
98 UNECA, *supra* note 7 at p. 46.
99 *Id.*
100 *Id*, p. 203.
101 *Id*, p. 202. *S D Myers v. Canada*, UNCITRAL, First Partial Award, 13 November 2000, paras 252–253 list two factors to interpret this obligation:
     1. whether the practical effect of the measure is to create a disproportionate benefit for citizens over foreign investors; and
     2. whether the measure appears to favour citizens over foreign investors who are protected by the relevant treaty.

The FET treatment standard has been one of the most controversial protections offered to investors and has been the source of disputes and increased calls for reform under international investment law. Broadly, it connotes the protection of the legitimate expectations of investors.[102]

The MFN standard is another contingent standard that allows investors from a state to benefit from any favourable treatment that may have been accorded to investors from another state by the host state.[103] While the standard on full protection and security can be seen as a duty of avoidance on the part of the state, it has also been interpreted as an affirmative duty on the state to maintain conditions of stability for foreign investment.[104]

The protection against expropriation aims to protect investment assets and secure investors' property from unlawful acquisition by the state without appropriate compensation. Most BITs require the payment of 'prompt, adequate and effective' compensation for expropriation.[105]

All of these protections are enforced through ISDS. With regard to ISDS, it has been suggested that 'African countries have been silent in discussions of the ISDS system and reforms to it, which has led to widespread belief that the system is dormant in Africa, compared with Latin America and Asia and the Pacific'.[106] This is not the case in light of the development of the Pan-African Investment Code, which promotes state–state dispute settlement and given the fact that the COMESA and SADC model agreement propose alternatives to ISDS for member countries to adopt. However, virtually all African BITs have dispute settlement provisions with the majority based on ISDS. ISDS is generally known to restrict the public interest regulation space of states and the concerns around the system as a whole have led to questions around the legitimacy of the system which this book addresses.[107]

---

102   *Id*, p. 204; In *Tecmed v. Mexico*, ICSID Case No ARB (AF)/00/2, para. 154, the court held that 'the foreign investor expects the host State to act in a consistent manner, free from ambiguity and totally transparently in its relations with the foreign investor, so that it may know beforehand any and all rules and regulations that will govern its investments, as well as the goals of the relevant policies and administrative practices or directives, to be able to plan its investment and comply with such regulations … The foreign investor also expects the host State to act consistently, i.e. without arbitrarily revoking any pre-existing decisions or permits issued by the State that were relied upon by the investor to assume its commitments … The investor also expects the State...not to deprive the investor of its investment without the required compensation. In fact, failure by the host State to comply with such pattern of conduct with respect to the foreign investor or its invest-ments affects the investor's ability to measure the treatment and protection awarded by the host State and to determine whether the actions of the host State conform to the fair and equitable treatment principle'.

103   *Id*.

104   Sornarajah, *supra* note 3 at p. 205.

105   *Id*, p. 210.

106   *Id*, p. 23.

107   *Id*, p. 24.

Objectives of this book

Several countries are reviewing their investment regulatory frameworks and are spread across regions, including at least 12 African countries.[108] This book aims to assess regulatory frameworks that would assist developing countries in Africa to establish the appropriate governance mechanisms to attract foreign investment from within and outside Africa. While FDI is important for sustainable development, it cannot entirely replace domestic investment and as a result, one of the central approaches to drive investment should include the development of regulatory and institutional reforms.[109] This book develops and offers alternatives on what these reforms should be.

This book examines the investment law regime with a focus on African experiences and the global trends that are shaping developments in Africa. Several of the current African BITs have been concluded with capital exporting countries. An examination of African BITs shows that a majority of them can be characterised as reflecting the interests and bargaining powers of capital exporting countries, rather than the interests of the capital importing African countries. This book is an attempt to provide a comprehensive analysis of the current regulatory practices within the African region based on a review of BITs concluded by African countries, their domestic regulations and where they stand in comparison to global trends on foreign investment rules. This book will also investigate the trends emerging from the large number of international investment disputes that have involved African states and how they are shaping investment regulation in Africa. What the alternative options to dispute settlement are and how they will affect investor–state relations will be examined in this book. This will aid the understanding of key characteristics of African BITs and will focus on the extent to which African BITs open up market access, promote regional integration and could potentially protect human rights and promote inclusive and sustainable development.

Book overview

Chapter 2 of this book explores the developmental role of investment regulation by examining the various standards of protections offered in African BITs and the relevance of taking into account public interest considerations, which will promote inclusive and sustainable development.

Chapter 3 considers how the current model of ISDS has failed Africa and the emerging public policy concerns. This chapter will also examine some of the different kinds of investment disputes that have arisen in relation to African states, highlighting the possibility of these categories of disputes recurring in the political and economic contexts of some African states.

---

108 UNCTAD, *supra* note 8 at p. 108.
109 *Id*, p. 83.

Chapter 4 focuses on the current objectives and features of ISDS as well as the deficiencies and its intersection with the rule of law. This chapter will identify the different dispute settlement alternatives suggested as a replacement for ISDS and the extent to which these alternatives address the objectives of attracting investment, depolitication of investment disputes, promotion of the rule of law and the provision of remedies.

Chapter 5 explores a suitable paradigm for interpreting investment treaties that ensure the protection of human rights and achieve the realisation of inclusive and sustainable development while effectively protecting investors.

Chapter 6 considers the regulatory developments in sub-regional institutions such as COMESA and SADC and their role in promoting investment flows, the rule of law in the governance of investments, as well as the depoliticisation of investment disputes. Questions are asked about the political economy of regional integration in Africa as a way of promoting economic development, an understanding of the main regional trade agreements in Africa, the role of regional economic communities and the economic benefits of these agreements. In addition, the implications for mega-regionals and the constraints on the domestic policy space of states are examined. This chapter also examines current developments in domestic regulation and explores case studies on domestic approaches taken to investment regulation.

This book concludes by offering policy choices to use IIAs as a vehicle to promote inclusive and sustainable development, as well as protect human rights and the rule of law. It offers well-researched proposals for policy makers to consider in the review of international investment policy and regulation. It also identifies strategies for practitioners and policy makers to take well-informed positions and presents a wealth of knowledge that can push further research.

Conclusion

Ultimately, this book focuses on what ought to be the proper protection of foreign investments in Africa given the unique considerations of balancing economic development and addressing historical and cultural factors that confront African governments. The findings of this book will benefit policy initiatives that focus on inclusive and sustainable development, the rule of law and an understanding of the implications of the policy shifts of African states under international investment law.

2 The public interest role of investment regulation

Introduction

Treaty based international mechanisms were introduced to address developed countries' need to protect foreign investment in developing countries and the desire of developing economies to increase private capital flows, with the promise of increased foreign investment.[1] With treaty based mechanisms in place, the dawn of post-colonialism witnessed the institutionalisation of ISDS, which replaced the traditional state–state dispute settlement mechanisms that prevailed before the wave of independence of states.[2] The ICSID is one of such treaty based institutions. When the ICSID was established at the height of the decolonisation era, it represented an attempt to provide a treaty based international mechanism for settling investment disputes between newly independent developing states and foreign investors.[3] As a result, dispute settlement between investors and states was institutionalised as a depoliticised dispute settlement mechanism.[4] Through treaty based international mechanisms, the foreign investment regime now functions with an ad hoc arbitration body that involves states and investors in its establishment and applies the rules previously agreed to by the parties.

The prevailing investment treaty based rules regime institutionalises neo-liberalism, which argues for a lesser involvement of the state in the market and a reduction in its economic functions.[5] Neo-liberalism has given birth to various economic institutions and rules, which include IIAs.

Despite neo-liberalism's aversion to the role of the state in economic matters, the state is responsible for the public interest and is the highest authority.[6] While states remain important umpires of the law, they now

---

1   Odumosu, I., 2008, 'The law and politics of engaging resistance in investment dispute settlement', *Penn State International Law Review* 26, p. 255.
2   *Id.*
3   *Id.*
4   *Id*, p. 257.
5   See Schneiderman, D., 2008, *Constitutionalizing Economic Globalization: Investment Rules and Democracy's Promise*, Cambridge Studies in Law and Society.
6   Hood in Morgan, B. and Yeung, K., 2007, *An Introduction to Law and Regulation*, Cambridge University Press, p. 4.

operate as agents of multilateral institutions as well who, at a transnational level, influence both international and domestic law. Within international investment law, this benefits private interests and as Sunstein suggests, some government controls regarded as unjustified paternalism can be understood as an effort to facilitate the satisfaction of private desires.[7] This unorthodox role of the state affects the role of law and regulation in social ordering, the effect on society and the significance on the perception of the legitimacy of the rules that are applied. With the emergence of non-state institutions and multiple levels of governance, new insights are needed about the relationship of the state and other actors such as ISDS tribunals and the rules they apply. While a lot of academic debate in international law has focused on the legalistic interpretation of investment rules, I use this interpretation to focus on a different outcome that takes into account the social context in which the law operates.[8] Regulation is generally a response to imperfections including under international investment law. In the case of the public interest regulation theory that is proposed in this book, it is intended to play a facilitative role to create and police the boundaries of the regulatory space of international investment law where public participation thrives and the social context of states is taken into account.[9]

The term 'public interest' is used in this book to include broad and general interests of various stakeholders including non-investment obligations and human rights norms. I acknowledge that public interest and human rights issues are conceptually distinct themes and could be dealt with separately. The broad definition of public interest to include human rights considerations is adopted to deal with the broader questions of ISDS legitimacy. Identifying a single public interest in a state may be impossible but when it comes to a specific investment activity, locating the public interest may not be a problem. While the mandate of dispute settlement regimes is limited to dealing with issues disputed by the parties, ISDS still has the power of interpretation on ancillary issues relevant to the resolution of the primary issues.[10] It is this interpretive power that has led to the consideration of public interest issues in ISDS. This I believe can be achieved broadly by understanding and re-conceptualising the idea of regulation, as well as the relationship between the state and institutions that operate on a transnational level like ISDS tribunals.

The public interest regulation theory applies where the investment obligations of a host state have been allegedly infringed as a result of other competing obligations of the host state and this clash of obligations has significant public implications. This theory seeks to address procedural and

---

7   Sunstein, C., 1993, *After the Rights Revolution: Reconceiving the Regulatory State*, Harvard University Press, p. 51.
8   The work of Morgan & Yeung, *supra* note 6, is very helpful in this regard.
9   *Id*, pp. 5–6, 42 and Chapters 5–6.
10   Odumosu, *supra* note 1 at p. 277.

substantive concerns in ISDS. In the application of this theory, it is important to understand what it means.

Defining the public interest regulation theory

The public interest regulation theory addresses the clash between competing obligations of a state arising under domestic or international law on the one hand and under international investment law, particularly BITs, on the other. This clash of obligations often arises as a result of state action introduced within the regulatory powers of a state but contravenes the duty of states towards the protection of foreign investors.

In applying this theory, it is necessary to introduce safeguards to prevent states from elevating all forms of state regulation to public interest regulation and consequently, use it as a defence when an investment obligation is violated by a state. To determine whether a state regulation has been made in the public interest, various factors should be considered. These factors include:

- the nature and purpose of the state measure;
- the manner in which the measure was introduced and implemented by the state;
- the importance of the public interest that is being protected by the government measure;
- the scope of the measure and the extent to which it violates IIA obligations;
- the suitability and necessity of the state measure to protect the public interest and the alternatives that were considered to avoid the clash of obligations;
- how foreseeable it was for the measure to have been introduced;
- the good faith nature and legitimacy of the measure.

Nature and purpose of the state measure

Virtually all the cases in investment arbitration relate to a breach of obligation by the state as a result of a state measure which affects the treaty protections offered to investors and their investments. These cases cover a number of measures including 'cancellations or alleged violations of contracts or concessions, measures related to taxation and placement of enterprises under external administration, as well as bankruptcy proceedings, … environmental issues, indigenous protected areas, anti-corruption and taxation'.[11] Where a measure is intended to address a public concern such as the impact on public

---

11   UNCTAD, 2016, *World Investment Report 2016*, viewed (31 March 2017) from http://unctad.org/en/PublicationsLibrary/wir2016_en.pdf, p. 106.

health or to address a financial crisis that was unforseeable, a state should be able to introduce a public interest regulation that will serve as a defence to its breach of investment protections.

Manner in which the state measure was introduced

This relates to the conduct of the state in introducing the measure that affects its obligations towards investors. It is important for states to stagger the introduction of measures that potentially violate their obligations under IIAs. Consequently, in cases where extensive consultations are held with affected investors and adequate notice is provided to affected investors to mitigate the impact of an investment, such approaches lend credence to the defence of states when relying on public interest regulation.

The importance of the public interest

The importance of the public interest measure being protected will determine the extent to which other factors such as the scope, suitability, foreseeability and the good faith nature of the state measure would play a role in the remedies offered to investors and the validity of the state defence of public interest regulation.

Scope of the measure and the extent to which a measure violates IIA obligations

State measures should only qualify as in the public interest where the measure is introduced to address a specific problem and there is no policy overreach that could have been avoided to prevent the breach of a state's obligations towards investors. State measures should be introduced based on a standard of justifiable limitation subject to the legal validity of the law imposing the public interest regulation. Where a state measure has a limited impact on the substance of an investment and does not completely erode the value of an investment, there are reasonable grounds for a state to invoke the public interest defence.

This also relates to the impact and consequences of introducing the measure. Where there is no demonstrable evidence of a measure addressing a problem and yet limits the protections for investors, the legitimacy of the measure as a public interest regulation will require increased scrutiny.

Suitability and necessity of a state measure to protect the public interest

Public interest regulation measures should only be introduced where there are no less restrictive measures of ensuring that IIA obligations are not violated. States are expected to take due diligence in complying with IIAs they voluntarily acceded to. To ensure that a measure has indeed been adopted in the public interest, a needs analysis is necessary to assess the extent to which the introduced measure addresses the problem that the state is aiming to resolve. Furthermore, it is expected that this measure should be the most effective or only means to remedy the problem.

The foreseeability of the introduction of the measure

This factor goes to the assessment of risks by an investor. Where investors are entering into politically and economically volatile situations and there are no guarantees of regulatory certainty through stabilisation clauses offered by the host state, then the foreseeability of change in regulation weakens any assertions of treaty violations by states. In cases where a problem such as a public health scare warrants the urgency of introducing a regulatory measure to address the situation, the necessity for states to address the measure becomes heightened and states should not be penalised for the lack of foresight for a problem out of state control.

The good faith nature and legitimacy of the measure

It is not in all cases that a measure introduced by a state will be legally valid in accordance with the laws of a host state. This will especially apply in cases where countries are undergoing transition. Libya and Egypt are examples of countries where measures were introduced in the aftermath of the Arab crisis and took place during the suspension of the rule of law in these countries.[12] In Zimbabwe where illegal land seizures were permitted by the state during a time of economic crisis,[13] as will be discussed in Chapter 3, such measures would not qualify as in the public interest regardless of the claims by the state that they were in pursuit of legitimate economic transformation objectives. Consequently, the good faith nature of a measure always has to be taken into account.

To determine good faith, considerations to be taken into account include how transparent the government was with investors in introducing the measure, the level of public participation in the process of introducing the measure and whether such measure is subject to review.

A case that exemplifies the importance of these factors in determining whether a state measure is valid and in the public interest is the case of *Southern Pacific Properties (SPP) (Middle East) Limited v. Arab Republic of Egypt*.[14] The subject of dispute was a tourism development project. In 1974, the Egyptian government, through its Ministry of Tourism, entered into an agreement with SPP, a company engaged in the development of tourist and

---

12   See ongoing case of *Ampal-American Israel Corporation and Others v. Arab Republic of Egypt* (ICSID Case No. ARB/12/11).
13   *Border Timbers Ltd and others v. Zimbabwe* (ICSID Case No ARB/10/25).
14   ICSID Case No. ARB/84/3.

resort facilities.[15] The project, known as the pyramids oasis project, was to be developed on land to be transferred to a joint venture company. In late 1977, as a result of fears that the construction of the project would affect the possibility of discovering antiquities on the land, the proposed development became a political issue and was subsequently halted by the government in mid-1978.[16] A presidential decree was issued to invalidate the project.[17]

The decision of the government was made in good faith to preserve national artefacts and antiquities. At the time of cancellation of the project, SPP had invested substantial funds and efforts in the project and subsequently instituted arbitration against the government. In 1983, SPP obtained an award of $12.5 million plus interest against Egypt.[18] This award was overturned by a French court, which led SPP to pursue ICSID arbitration and, in 1992, obtained a substantial ICSID award of $27.6 million in its favour.[19] Following the award, Egypt initiated an annulment proceeding through ICSID. However, a settlement agreement was ultimately reached by the parties and the annulment proceeding was discontinued. The claims were based on Egypt's Investment Law and this case was the first ICSID claim brought under a domestic investment law.

Egypt claimed that public officials of the government who authorised the investment did so in contravention of national laws on antiquities.[20] However, the tribunal rejected that defence, stating that even though the actions of the public officials may have been *ultra vires*, Egypt was still to be held liable for them, as the act of public officials' 'acts were cloaked in the mantle of governmental authority'.[21] In assessing the claim of SPP at the initial ICC arbitration, the tribunal ruled that the investment must be assessed in the light of the inherent risks of the project and two types of risk are relevant.

The first relates to the geographic location of the project relating to the discovery of the antiquities.[22] The investors could not have ignored these risks and must have reasonably anticipated that the state could not fully guarantee the implementation of the project. The tribunal here was suggesting that the circumstances of the cancellation were foreseeable. Second, at the time of cancellation of the project, the political and economic climate in Egypt was volatile and the risk of cancellation was higher than in usual circumstances.

In this case, the nature and purpose of the state measure, which related to the protection of cultural antiquities, was driven by a public demand on government. However, given the manner in which the government chose to

---

15   *Id*, para. 42.
16   *Id*, para. 62.
17   *Id*, para. 65.
18   *Id*, para. 68.
19   *Id*, para. 257.
20   *Id*, para. 81.
21   *Id*, para. 82.
22   *Id*, para. 251.

unilaterally terminate the project on a land which the government would have been aware was rich in cultural heritage, this reduced the possibility of asserting that the government's measure was a public interest measure. The aim of protecting cultural antiquities is certainly laudable and it appeared that the government had no other option than to terminate the project on the particular land which inevitably gravely affected the investor's investment. As the tribunal noted, the government's actions were foreseeable which affected the investor's claim. Given the problem was urgent and required a necessary action on the part of the state to halt development, the actions of the Egyptian government turned on the good faith of the government and the legitimacy of the measure. Though the Egyptian government attempted to argue that the decision of its officials to approve the project in the first place was illegal, this was validly rejected by the state since the officials acted within the scope of their duties. Consequently, the viable option available to the state to mitigate its liability was to introduce measures in good faith that would achieve the important objective of safeguarding the cultural antiquities while also compensating the investors. This was ultimately done at a huge financial cost for Egypt when it settled the case out of court several years later.

Implications of the public interest regulation theory

This public interest regulation theory has implications for a three-tier approach of transparency, participation and interpretation of IIAs. For transparency, it means that in addressing any clash of obligations between treaties and domestic law, proceedings must be subject to an open and public process given the public interest angle of investment disputes. Due to the need for the proceedings to be open and public, an implication of this is that a right to participate for non-disputing parties also needs to be taken into account. This right to participate includes the right to submit written and oral submissions, the right to serve not only as non-disputing parties but also as interveners and the right to receive submissions made by the host state and investors. The third implication of this theory is perhaps the most important one which relates to the interpretive approach that should apply in resolving this clash of obligations. The implications here include deference to other applicable body of law, particularly, domestic law of states.

Public interest regulation theory and human rights

The difference between the proposed public interest regulation theory and a strictly human rights based approach is that while the human rights approach is concerned with the application of human rights norms and prioritisation of human rights above any other legal regime, the public interest regulation theory develops a compromise that results in a more equitable outcome that addresses the tensions emerging from the clash between international investment law and human rights. This theory does not seek to prioritise one legal regime over the other but rather focuses on creating a space within the international investment law field to consider the application of these competing interests. What this theory proposes is not for investment arbitration tribunals to make definitive pronouncements in law in terms of human rights obligations but to accommodate them in reaching a more equitable outcome that addresses the legitimacy concerns relating to the manner in which arbitrators currently reach their decisions and interpret treaty obligations.

The public interest regulation theory places as much emphasis on the substantive outcome as on the procedural method of arriving at the outcome. The public participation in the process as well as the transparency of the process is as important as the methods applied in ensuring the consideration of other applicable legal regimes.

Andreas Kulick, who has written on the global public interest law in international investment law, has argued[23] that 'no other international adjudicatory system creates a review and remedy mechanism which is that close in its features to domestic administrative mechanism'.[24] Kulick, in tracing the advent of international investment law, submits that domestic law was considered the primary source of law and international law only played a supplemental and corrective function.[25] With the advent of BITs, the first case under the ICSID considered BIT as the primary source of law while international and domestic law was regarded as supplementary.[26] This position was later reinforced by subsequent tribunals that, relying on Article 42 (1) of ICSID, found international law applicable to the disputes.[27] In a trio of cases against Argentina, the tribunals considered international law as supreme over domestic law, a view which Kulick firmly supports.[28] However, the tribunal in *Wena* did rule that both the international and domestic legal orders had a role to play, which was affirmed by *Enron*.[29] This position is also consistent with trends emerging in recent BITs considered later in this book where domestic law is also increasingly being listed as a choice of law. This is the position that requires taking into account the rule in Article 27 of the 1969 Vienna Convention on Laws of Treaties (VCLT) that a state may not

23   Kulick, A., 2012, *Global Public Interest in International Investment Law*, Cambridge University Press.
24   *Id*, p. 83.
25   *Id*, p. 25.
26   *Asian Agricultural Products Limited v. Sri Lanka* ICSID Case No. ARB/87/3. Award, June 27, 1990; Kulick, *supra* note 23 at p. 31.
27   See *SPP v. Egypt* ICSID Case No. ARB/84/3; *Tradex Hellas v. Albania* ICSID Case No. ARB/94/2; *Wena v. Arab Republic of Egypt*, Decision on Annulment, Feb. 28, 2002.
28   *Id*, p. 11, 39 and 44; *LG&E International v. Argentine Republic* ICSID Case No. ARB/02/1; *Siemens v. Argentine Republic ICSID* Case No. ARB/02/8; *Enron v. Argentine Republic* ICSID Case No./01/3.
29   *Enron v. Argentine Republic* ICSID Case No./01/3, para 207.

invoke the provisions of its internal law as a justification for its failure to perform a treaty.

Relevance of constitutionalism and global administrative law

In analysing the investment rules regime, it has been described as a form of supra-constitutionalism that supersedes domestic constitutional norms.[30] This is based on the idea that investment rules place legal limits on government authority, they isolate economic interests from political power and they assign very powerful protections to investment interests.[31] According to Schill:

> like constitutions, BITs restrict state action and, as part of an international public order, create and safeguard the interests of an international community in the function of the global economic system. Investment treaties comprise constitutional traits by establishing legal principles that serve as a yardstick for the conduct of States vis-à-vis foreign investors.[32]

While the term constitutionalism appears to be strong and places investment rules on a high pedestal, the consideration of investment rules through this perspective shows the need to preserve the sovereign powers of a state to pursue sustainable development goals for the benefit of its citizens.[33]

While there is a view that the current form of foreign investment rules arose from distrust by developing countries about the role of developed countries over a developing country's economic affairs,[34] it is more likely that investment rules were introduced to address the distrust by developed countries of developing states' powers to nationalise foreign investments.[35] Furthermore, the perception of actual or political risk that may affect investments and the lack of faith in domestic systems to offer redress have fuelled the desire for IIAs and ISDS.[36] Chapter 3 discusses the fears and concerns often expressed against domestic systems and the extent to which

---

30 Schneiderman D., 2008, *Constitutionalizing Economic Globalization*, Cambridge University Press, p. 3. See also Petersmann, E.U., 2012, *International Economic Law in the 21st Century*, Hart Publishing. Introducing this new book, Petersmann quoted Allot, P., that the problem of international constitutionalism is the central challenge faced by international philosophers in the twenty-first century; Adeleke, F., 2016, 'Human rights and international investment arbitration', *South African Journal of Human Rights* 32(1) p. 55.
31 *Id*, Schneiderman, pp. 4–5.
32 Schill, S.W., 2009, *The Multilaterilazation of International Investment Law*, Cambridge University Press.
33 Schneiderman, *supra* note 30 at p. 5.
34 *Id*, p. 27.
35 Meyer, G. and Coleman, M., 2009, 'Arbitration in Africa', *Without Prejudice*, p. 46.
36 *Id*.

these concerns are legitimate. ISDS tribunals assume the role of domestic courts with the power to review state action and reconcile it with international investment law.[37] To achieve the process of replacing domestic courts with ISDS tribunals in investment disputes, governments of developing countries have achieved this by being BIT signatories.[38]

However, given the increasing backlash against BITs, while some countries have signed BITs and they have not come into force as a matter of deliberate strategy or policy, other countries in Latin America and South Africa have begun to abandon the supra-national investment rules regime. Despite this growing and subtle resistance to BITs, the number of BITs in force remains high and the preferred choice of law to seek remedies by investors. While BITs appear to be superficially identical, they often vary in the standards of protection that have been set which make the investment rules regime dynamic and evolving.

For a long time, there has been a canvas for a multilateral treaty on foreign investment but it has been unsuccessful. This has largely been due to disagreement on key issues relating to foreign investment.[39] As a result, foreign investment is to a large extent managed by fragmented BITs. While multilateral treaties as proposed for investment law may have many advantages including the establishment of a single framework for consistency and uniformity as well as the reduction of the legal ambiguity surrounding investment related disputes, the current framework regulated by the BIT regime continues to be the preferred rules for investment protection by foreign investors.[40] BITs in particular are favoured for their flexibility to allow states to tailor treaties with other states to meet their specific needs.[41]

The object and purpose of BITs is typically to establish frameworks and favourable conditions for investors in the state that is to benefit from the investment. The definition of an investment is defined in very broad terms and sometimes covers any asset that contributes to economic development.[42]

---

37   Bronckers, M., 2015, 'Is investor–state dispute settlement (ISDS) superior to litigation before domestic courts?: An EU view on bilateral trade agreements', *J Int Economic Law* 18(3), pp. 655–677.

38   It is estimated that there are currently over 750 African BITs and almost 100 ICSID cases have been brought against African countries. See also Gibson, D., 2014, 'Will Africa be lit by "BITS"?', viewed (13 May 2014) from www.gibsondunn.com/publications/Documents/Will-Africa-Be-Lit-By-BITs.pdf, p. 4.

39   See generally Gazzini, T. and De Brabandere E., 2012, 'Bilateral investment treaties', in Gazzini, T. and De Brabandere, E. (eds), *International Investment Law: The Sources of Rights and Obligations*, Martinus Nijhoff Publishers.

40   *Id*, p. 4.

41   *Id*, p. 8.

42   Examples include the BIT between Canada and South Africa provides that 'investment means any kind of asset owned or controlled either directly, or indirectly through an investor of a third state, by an investor of one contracting party in the territory of the other contracting party in accordance with the latter's laws and, in particular, though not exclusively, include movable and immovable property … but does not mean real estate or other property … not acquired in the expectation or used for the purpose of economic

The general standards of protection under BITs are to protect investors and their investment from discrimination, direct or indirect expropriation, ensure fair and equitable treatment and the provision of compensation as well as the resolution of disputes in a selected forum should any of the provisions in the BITs be breached. Increasingly, states are beginning to introduce exceptions to the liability of states in the application of the protections in BITs given the sweeping manner in which BITs tend to limit state sovereignty. For instance, in the protection from the expropriation of foreign investments, good faith expropriations in cases of addressing health, safety or environmental measures are now applicable in new investment agreements.[43]

Schneiderman suggests that because constitutionalism resolves the tension between majoritarian democracy and minority interests, the investment rules regime does the same by treating foreign investors as minority groups and legally constrains government from taking actions that will adversely affect investment interests.[44] According to Petersmann, the regulatory challenges of the twenty-first century require a paradigm shift in international economic law to adopt a more cosmopolitan regulation that more effectively protects human rights, builds democratic support for international economic law by citizens, and constitutional coherence among diverse, national and international legal orders.[45] This is a powerful assertion and considering the binding nature of investment agreements, the difficulty in amending the treaties as well as the enforcement mechanisms, which are also constitution-like, this supports the argument for investment rules to be analysed within a constitutional framework.[46] In addition, Schneiderman states that the prohibition on direct and indirect expropriation as well as the demand for fair and equitable treatment in investment rules represented in a similar way to the rules of civilised justice and limits government capacity in constitution-like ways.[47]

Taking the example of South Africa, in balancing various competing interests, South Africa's constitution recognises expropriations of property for public purpose or in the public interest. Public interest in the context of the right to property in South Africa's constitution is defined as 'the nation's commitment to land reform, and to reforms to bring about equitable access to all South Africa's natural resources'.[48] The rule for compensation in South Africa's constitution is just and equitable to reflect a balance between public

---

benefit'; the BIT between Czech Republic and South Africa provides that 'investment means every kind of asset invested in connection with economic activities by an investor of one Party in the territory of the other Party'; see Schneiderman, *supra* note 30 at p. 31.

43 See also Schneiderman, *supra* note 30 at p. 35, for general discussion including the 2005 Germany-China BIT;

44 Schneiderman, *supra* note 30 at p. 38.

45 Petersmann, *supra* note 30.

46 Schneiderman, supra note 30 at p. 39.

47 Schneiderman, *supra* note 30 at p. 69.

48 The Constitution of the Republic South Africa, 1996, Section 25.

interests and the interests of those affected. This is different from the prompt, adequate and effective compensation usually prescribed in BITs.

Highlighting these distinct features in South Africa's constitution, it is arguable that the constraints on expropriation and nationalisation in the BIT are more onerous than those found in the text of the constitution.[49] The result is that foreign investors get preferential treatment over South African investors. Also, given the fact that BITs generally do not distinguish between deprivations and expropriations and the South African constitution extends expropriation for public interest purposes, BITs arguably represent multiple opportunities to hinder South African public policy objectives.[50]

The investment rules regime have both public and private law dimensions according to Petersmann, which can be viewed either in a positive light as provision of international justice based on progressive multilateralisation of bilaterally agreed standards or negatively 'as power struggles for imposing conflicting interests by avoiding national and international public law courts'.[51] The perception that the investment rules regime is an act of avoidance of national public courts is gaining momentum. It has been suggested that the investment rules regime is intended to protect established investments by imposing the discipline of the rule of law on state regulation of markets which renders domestic legal rules certain and promotes economic liberty, equal treatment or non-discrimination, fair and equitable treatments and prohibits both direct and indirect expropriation.[52] However, a caution is issued against the application of a rules based regime that privileges the market over everything else as this would serve the interests of a privileged few and it would be perilous to embrace a highly defective transnational regime.[53] Therefore, it is important that states retain the right to regulate their markets and develop economic policies that allow the protection of investors as well as other public interest issues. This is the approach that a broad analysis of investment rules in constitutionalism offers with a particular emphasis on the application of administrative law principles.

As a sovereign entity, a state has the power to regulate and protect the interests of the public. International investment rules regime limits government's ability to regulate its own economic affairs in constitution-like ways. Given the inconsistency that sometimes arises between global agreements and domestic laws, it is necessary to develop a mechanism to align investment rules with domestic law. This can be achieved through administrative law to be used as an accountability tool of the investment rules regime. However, the proposition for developing public interest theory through the application of administrative law is not to be taken to suggest that state

49   Schneiderman, *supra* note 30 at pp. 143–144.
50   Schneiderman, *supra* note 30 at p. 147; Adeleke, F., 2016, 'Human rights and international investment arbitration', *South African Journal of Human Rights* 32(1), p. 58.
51   *Id.*
52   Schneiderman, *supra* note 30 at p. 206.
53   Schneiderman, *supra* note 30 at p. 222.

sovereignty can be used as a defence to breach investment obligations. Previously, investment rules regime have been seen within a public international law paradigm but it is about time it is seen from a public adjudication law perspective which protects broader public interests.[54]

Voluntary limitation of state sovereignty through the application of international law occurs when states in the pursuit of goals such as regional and economic integration, sign treaties that limit their sovereignty and make allowances for supra-national and regional bodies to exercise control. Another actor that is increasingly becoming active in the limitation of state sovereignty is the private international corporation through the exercise of rights held by states under BITs. BITs are of course not concluded with private actors. States are the treaty parties with the private investor having enforceable substantive rights bestowed upon them through BITs.[55] With such enforceable rights in place, the private corporation limits state sovereignty when it seeks to assert a particular right in a BIT that clashes with a governmental regulation that protects other non-investment interests. Such limitation can exist for example through stabilisation clauses in BITs which restrict the existing state regulatory regime for the duration of an investment, and also through the restriction on the state regulatory and police powers relating to expropriation. Balancing justifiable governmental regulation that seeks to protect the interests of the public with the enforceable right of an investor has been the subject of wide debate and brings into focus the nature of ISDS mechanisms to resolve these differences.

The public nature of ISDS

The tension between investment protection and human rights largely relates to the ability of a foreign investor to protect an investment in a host state and for the host state to exercise its regulatory powers during the course of the investment in fulfilment of its public interest obligations. The UN Commission on Human Rights in a 2003 report noted that while human rights are fundamental to human dignity, investment rights are instrumental to the achievement of certain policy objectives which are not indispensable for human dignity.[56] The resolution of any tension that arises between the

---

54   Yackee, J., 2012, 'Controlling the International Investment Law Agency', *Harvard International Law Journal* 53, pp. 399–400.

55   'Public interest' is defined in Black *Law's Dictionary* as the 'general welfare of the public that warrants recognition and protection; *something which the public as a whole has a stake* especially as interest that *justifies governmental regulation*'. See also Roberts, A., 2010, 'Power and persuasion in investment treaty interpretation: The dual role of states', *American Journal of International Law* 104, p. 184.

56   Simma, B., 2011, 'Foreign investment arbitration: A place for human rights?', *International & Comparative Law Quarterly* 60, p. 591 quoting the *Report of the High Commissioner for Human Rights, Human Rights, Trade and Investment* (July 2003), para. 24.

two regimes needs to be delicately managed in a forum where both interests can be guaranteed equal treatment. Desierto has argued that:

> the 'public interest' is thus generally concerned with matters of efficiency (the size of the overall endowments available to society) as well as equity (the relative distribution of those endowments to individuals under a fair and just process). It is in this sense that human rights and investment protection are both matters of public interest. Investment hearkens to the efficiency dimension of the public interest by affecting the material conditions contributing to 'inherent dignity of the human person' while human rights protection appeals to the equity dimension of the public interest by guaranteeing and preserving equal and non-discriminatory access of all individuals to social and economic goods. Human rights protection starkly and visibly exemplifies the public interest, it may also be said that generating economic development through welfare-improving and responsible investment practices is also another dimension of the public interest.[57]

Investment and human rights protection are not mutually exclusive. Both aim to contribute to the outcome of improving the welfare of the general public. It is for this reason that when it comes to the resolution of disputes relating to investment protection, the consideration of human rights protection has a huge role to play which can be achieved if ISDS is perceived as a public law adjudication system.

The first BIT was concluded in 1959 between Pakistan and Germany with provisions for arbitration to resolve any dispute that arises. However, the first BIT arbitration did not take place until 27 years later in 1987 and an increase in the number of arbitrations only took an exponential growth in the late 1990s. In a 2007 report, UNCTAD attributed this growth to the increasing number of BITs being negotiated as investment flows increased and the encouragement derived by investors from successful claims initiated in the arbitration system.[58] As BIT awards increase, so does the need to ensure consistency in the interpretations tribunals give to similar provisions in the BITs before them. With almost 3000 BITs in force and with BITs appearing to be similar but occasionally different in the wording, different legal effects will arise in the interpretation of BITs alongside the vastly different factual contexts of BIT disputes. Also, the different forums used for arbitration makes identifying a general trend in the jurisprudence difficult.

57　Desierto, D.A., 2012, 'Calibrating human rights and investment in economic emergencies: Prospects of treaties and valuation decisions', *Manchester Journal of International Economic Law* 9(2), pp. 162–183.

58　UNCTAD, 2007, 'Investor-State Dispute Settlement and Impact on Investment Rule Making', viewed (21 March 2017) from unctad.org>docs>iteiia20073_en.pdf

While arbitration is the preferred method for dispute resolution in BITs, the choice of arbitration depends on a particular treaty. Investors can choose to arbitrate before an ad hoc tribunal formed under various structures including the UNCITRAL Rules, the World Bank's ICSID, the Stockholm Chamber of Commerce, the International Court of Arbitration or the London Court of International Arbitration. Typically, arbitrations are presided over by a panel of three arbitrators with each party selecting its own arbitrator and the presiding arbitrator in the case of ICSID is also chosen by both parties. In instances where they cannot agree, the ICSID will choose the presiding arbitrator.[59] However, for UNCITRAL arbitrations, party-appointed arbitrators agree on the presiding arbitrator.[60]

BITs apply to investments made by investors of a state party in the territory of the other state party. Consequently, to use arbitration, the jurisdiction of the arbitration tribunal will only kick in for instance in cases where ICSID rules[61] are used in disputes arising out of an investment and apply to nationalities and juridical persons of a foreign state where the investment is coming from and not a juristic person from the host state receiving the investment. Despite this, disputes have arisen under this set of rules in identifying what constitutes an investment, the nationality of an investor or whether a juristic person is controlled by foreigners.[62]

---

59   Fry, J.D., 2008, 'International human rights law in investment arbitration: Evidence of international law's unity', *Duke Journal of Comparative & International Law* 18, p. 77.

60   *Id.*

61   Art 25 (1) of the ICSID Convention which provides that:
     The jurisdiction of the Centre shall extend to any legal dispute arising directly out of an investment, between a Contracting State (or any constituent subdivision or agency of a Contracting State designated to the Centre by that State) and a national of another Contracting State, which the parties to the dispute consent in writing to submit to the Centre. When the parties have given their consent, no party may withdraw its consent unilaterally.
     Art 25 (2) of the Convention also provides:
     'National of another Contracting State' means:
     (a)   any natural person who had the nationality of a Contracting State other than the State party to the dispute on the date on which the parties consented to submit such dispute to conciliation or arbitration as well as on the date on which the request was registered pursuant to paragraph (3) of Article 28 or paragraph (3) of Article 36, but does not include any person who on either date also had the nationality of the Contracting State party to the dispute; and
     (b)   any juridical person which had the nationality of a Contracting State other than the State party to the dispute on the date on which the parties consented to submit such dispute to conciliation or arbitration and any juridical person which had the nationality of the Contracting State party to the dispute on that date and which, because of foreign control, the parties have agreed should be treated as a national of another Contracting State for the purposes of this Convention.

62   See *Soufraki v. United Arab Emirates* ICSID Case No ARB/02/7 Award, 7 July 2004; *Klöckner v. Cameroon* ICSID Case No ARB/81/Award, 21 October 1983; *FEDAX N.V. v. Venezuela* ICSID Case No ARB/96/3(1), Decision on Jurisdiction, 11 July 1997.

Because BITs are concluded between sovereign states exercising their sovereign power to conclude agreements with the aim of attracting FDI to the state for the ultimate benefit of the public, looking at BITs simply in that light suggests that BITs should be classified as public law. However, because BITs confer substantive rights on the investor and create a contractual relationship between the host state and the investor, this also brings in the application of contract law. The distinction between public and private adjudication exists in the principle of sovereign immunity, which does not allow a state's authority to be subject to adjudication in another state's courts.[63] Some states however recognise an exception to the general principle of sovereign immunity, which does not apply to commercial acts of the state.[64] Various tests are adopted to distinguish sovereign acts from commercial acts. One of the ways of drawing the distinction is to examine the character and nature of relevant acts of the state rather than the purpose.[65]

Van Harten identifies two types of acts that are carried out by the state in any arbitration involving a claim by an investor against the state. These are the state's act of consent to the compulsory jurisdiction of arbitrators as an alternative to the courts and the state's act that triggers a dispute with the investor bringing the claim.[66] He argues that where both of these acts are uniquely sovereign in nature, the arbitration is best approached as public law.[67]

A state acts in its sovereign capacity when it concludes an investment treaty, which includes resolving investment disputes through arbitration. Though investment arbitrations are private in nature, Van Harten concludes that it is arguable that investment arbitration is nevertheless public law adjudication and the significance of the arbitration system is the delegation of public judicial function to private arbitrators.[68] This means that the private nature of the arbitration hides the fact that the power they wield is, at base, public power. The relevance of the interests of the public in this delegated power can therefore not be over stated.

Aside from private foreign investors, there are also investors controlled by host states. These investors are referred to as sovereign investors.[69] The question that arises is whether sovereign investors are protected as investors under international investment law. Some academics have argued that the

63   Van Harten, G., 2007, 'The public-private distinction in the international arbitration of individual claims against the state', *International & Comparative Law Quarterly* 56, p. 373.
64   *Id.*
65   This distinction was drawn by Lord Wilberforce in an English case in *1 Congreso del Partido* [1983] 1 AC 244, 267 (HL); Van Harten, *supra* note 30 at p. 374.
66   Van Harten, *supra* note 63 at p. 374.
67   *Id.*
68   *Id*, p. 381.
69   See Poulsen, L., 2012, 'Investment treaties and the globalisation of state capitalism: Ppportunities and constraints for host states', in Echandi, R. and Sauve, P. (eds), *Prospects in International Investment Law and Policy*, Cambridge, pp. 73–90.

ICSID does not cover state-to-state disputes and sovereign investors fall into that category, hence, jurisdiction should be denied.[70] It has been suggested that in cases of sovereign investors, disputes should be administered either by diplomatic espousal or only after the consent of both state parties such as in the Australia/US free trade agreement where the states must agree that the investor can arbitrate.[71]

A concern raised about sovereign investors relates to their corporate governance. State entities can have non-commercial motives for their investment activities abroad, and their structure and investment strategies tend to be non-transparent compared to many other foreign investors.[72] To address these concerns, host states have to impose their domestic transparency requirements on the sovereign investors. In order to protect the host state from undue interference from another state through the sovereign investor, regulators may require some disclosure of governance structure and investment plans in order to assess the motives of sovereign investors.[73] Such requirements may conflict with investment treaty obligations. While some tribunals have found that investors have a duty to cooperate and provide information to regulators, others have argued that it cannot be expected as part of investors' good faith obligations to disclose long-term plans with investment projects.[74]

BIT arbitration and public interest

The idea of protecting foreigners' property originated in the early twentieth century before the universal declaration of human rights which expanded beyond rules of state responsibility for injuries to foreigners.[75] Because private actors now have direct access to international remedies without the traditional need for the intervention of their national state, the traditional doctrine of international law changes because only states have international

---

70 Hirsch, M., 1993, *The Arbitration Mechanism of the International Centre for the Settlement of Disputes*, The Hague, Kluwer-Nijhoff Publishers, pp. 64–66.
71 US-Australia Free Trade Agreement (FTA), 2004, Article 11.6, viewed (20 June 2016) from www.ustr.gov/trade-agreements/free-trade-agreements/australian-fta
72 Poulsen, *supra* note 69 at p. 13.
73 *Id.*
74 *Id*, p. 15. The tribunal in *Saluka v. Czech Republic* (UNCITRAL Arbitration Partial Award), 17 March 2006, para. 232 stated that [i]t is both unreasonable and unrealistic to posit an obligation upon an investor to disclose its ultimate objectives in making a particular investment, whether through the purchase of shares or otherwise. Ultimate objectives will … often be highly speculative and not susceptible to precise articulation, and will be subject to change over time.
75 Dupuy, P., 2010, 'Unification rather than fragmentation of international law? The case of international investment law and human rights law', in Dupuy, P. (ed.) *Human Rights in International Investment Law and Arbitration*, Oxford University Press, p. 47.

rights and the internationalisation of the right of access to justice of private actors tends to blur the boundary between the rights of foreign investors and human rights.[76]

Generally, arbitration tribunals lack jurisdiction on human rights issues. The tribunal in *Biloune v. Ghana*[77] confirmed that arbitration tribunals lack jurisdiction to address as an independent cause of action, a claim of violation of human rights. Consent to jurisdiction of tribunals is based on consent of parties. However, though human rights violations may not be treated as independent claims, to the extent that they affect investment, it has been suggested that such violations will become a dispute 'in respect of' the investment and hence become the subject of arbitration.[78]

Human rights provisions are applicable to the extent to which they are included in the parties' choice of law.[79] International law is generally included under choice of law clauses and human rights can be regarded as a component of international law.[80] Looking at the current trend of investment disputes, investors have not alleged violations of human rights perhaps partly because most investors are juristic persons and for host states, they have raised human rights arguments in defence rather than as a breach by the investor. The tribunals themselves have demonstrated a reluctance to consider human rights arguments placed before it by the disputing parties and prefer to dismiss such issues on a procedural basis, lack of sufficiently elaborated arguments, lack of jurisdiction and difference between two branches of international law.[81] Tribunals may also not want their legitimacy impaired by delving into controversial human rights issues. However, there

---

76   Francioni, F., 2010, 'Access to Justice, Denial of Justice, and International Investment Law' in Dupuy, P. (ed.) *Human Rights in International Investment Law and Arbitration*, Oxford University Press, p. 63.

77   UNCITRAL Award on jurisdiction and liability, 27 October 1989. Where a Syrian investor had been deported and property expropriated, the tribunal claimed it lacked jurisdiction on violation of human rights claims as an independent cause of action.

78   Reiner, C. and Schreuer, C., 2010, 'Human rights and international investment arbitration', in Dupuy, P. (ed.) *Human Rights in International Investment Law and Arbitration*, Oxford University Press, p. 84.

79   *Id.*

80   Reiner and Schreuer, *supra* note 78 at p. 85. ICSID Convention in Article 42 makes provision for application of international law and this term, it has been suggested, should be interpreted in the sense of Article 38 of the statute of the International Court of Justice.

81   Hirsch, M., 2010, 'Investment tribunals and human rights: Divergent paths', in Dupuy, P. (ed.) *Human Rights in International Investment Law and Arbitration*, Oxford University Press, p. 97; *Siemens v. Argentina* (ICSID Case No ARB/02/08, 6 February 2007) tribunal addressed arguments on inconsistent investment and human rights obligations. It stated that considerations in determining expropriation are different from considerations for compensation. It also noted the concept of 'margin of appreciation' as developed by the European Convention; *Sempra v. Argentina* (ICSID Case No ARB 02/16, 28 September 2007) tribunal considered argument by Argentina on 'necessity' founded under Argentina's constitutional order. The tribunal found that temporary measures and renegotiation could have accommodated legitimately acquired rights.

are exceptions where the tribunals have cited human rights considerations without being prompted by the parties.[82]

On the one hand, human rights law evolved within the public law sphere and applies to relationships between individuals and the state with different freedoms, rights and obligations imposed. On the other hand, investment law focuses on private law and looks at reciprocal promise based obligations and reliance based obligations.[83] These obligations are protected by umbrella clauses that elevate undertakings to international law obligations, stabilisation clauses that protect investors against regulatory changes and the fair and equitable treatment principle.[84]

According to Devaney,[85] the balancing of host state and investor interests could be considered at the remedies stage where the host state obligation relates to a human right fundamental to the well-being of its population and where it clashes indirectly with the right accorded to the investor.[86] Devaney states:

> the clash between non-investment related host state obligations and obligations towards the investor is indirect and indeed often it is host state regulatory autonomy as opposed to human rights obligations which falls to be balanced against the host state's obligations to the investor as the measure implemented by the state may not be absolutely necessary to promote or protect a particular human right but is regarded by that state as a step towards fulfilling its human rights obligations or, in any event, as being a measure in the public interest. Only in such 'indirect' cases would it seem appropriate to make adjustments at the remedies stage to reflect public interest considerations.[87]

Devaney argues further that balancing public interest with investor interests allows the promotion of good governance taking into account the

---

82   *Tecmed v. Mexico* ICSID Case No ARB (AF)/00/2, 29 May 2003, the tribunal dealt with environmental rights: whether reasonableness and proportionality of state action amounted to expropriation; reliance placed on the European Court of Human Rights (ECHR) jurisprudence and *Mondev v. USA* which applied ECHR, though none of the parties was party to the European convention. The tribunal relied on the jurisprudence of the ECHR to rule that extension of immunity from suits for international torts to a statutory authority breached North American Free Trade Agreement (NAFTA) provisions.

83   Hirsch, *supra* note 81.

84   *Id.*

85   Devaney, M., 2012, 'Leave it to the Valuation Experts?: The Remedies Stage of Investment Treaty Arbitration and the Balancing of Public and Private Interests', Society of International Economic Law, 3rd Biennial Conference, WP No. 2012-06, viewed (31 March 2017) from https://papers.ssrn.com/sol3/papers.cfm?abstract_id=2087777&rec=1&srcabs=2088315&alg=1&pos=4, p. 4.

86   *Id.*

87   Devaney, *supra* note 85 at p.10.

developmental status of a host state; it allows flexibility by balancing interests at the remedies stage because to only consider it at the merits stage leads to an all or nothing approach which ignores the legitimate interest of the investor and the public.[88] It also takes into account host state circumstances such as the stage of economic development, its administrative capabilities and the political situation as well as taking into account the culpability of host states in a violation of a treaty obligation.[89] This is demonstrated in the applicable cases below.

In *Siemens v. Argentina*,[90] Siemens claimed a violation of the expropriation obligation as well as the fair and equitable treatment clauses in the Argentina-Germany BIT following the alteration of a concession contract that was awarded to a subsidiary of Siemens in Argentina. The alteration happened due to the economic crisis in Argentina, which resulted in the introduction of an emergency law that empowered the president to renegotiate all public sector contracts. Argentina argued that 'human rights so incorporated in the Constitution would be disregarded by recognising the property rights asserted by the claimant given the social and economic conditions of Argentina'.[91] The tribunal held that Argentina's arguments were made without sufficient evidence and as a result could not have any relevance to the merits of the case.[92]

In *Azurix v. Argentina*,[93] an American company won a 30 year concession contract to run the water and sewage system of the Buenos Aires province. During the height of Argentina's economic crisis, Azurix alleged that Argentina's failure to apply the agreed tariff regime and its eventual termination of the concession agreement awarded to it, which led to its bankruptcy, violated its BIT obligations of fair and equitable treatment, that it amounted to expropriation and breached the non-discrimination as well as full protection and security clauses.[94] Argentina argued that Azurix failed to comply with the concession agreement and the difficulties encountered by Azurix were of its own making.[95] The tribunal held that while the government had to be vigilant and protect the public health, the government engaged in political interference with the tariff regime and

88   *Id*, pp. 6–7.
89   *Id*, p. 7.
90   ICSID Case No. ARB/O2/8, Award February 6, 2007; see also Vadi, V., 2012, 'Culture Clash: Investor's Rights vs. Cultural Heritage in International Investment Law and Arbitration', Society of International Economic Law (SIEL), 3rd Biennial Global Conference, unpublished paper.
91   *Siemens v. Argentina* (ICSID Case No ARB/02/08, 6 February 2007), para. 75.
92   *Id*, para. 79.
93   ICSID Case No. ARB/01/12.
94   *Id*, para. 43.
95   *Id*, para. 43.

awarded fair market value compensation to Azurix.[96] In the tribunal's analysis, applying the principle of proportionality, the tribunal did not consider the right to water and whether it constituted a significant factor in the award of compensation to Azurix.

These cases establish the relationship between investment obligations and state regulations and also show a diverse line in approach in the jurisprudence emerging from BIT arbitration in the manner in which arbitrators deal with public interest issues when they conflict with BIT obligations. The arbitrators are free to exercise their discretion to select the manner in which they resolve these issues. They often do so by preferring the policy interests underlying BITs to any other interests which are considered secondary. These various competing policy interests fall under public law adjudication and should accordingly be guided by public law principles. The policy interests should be derived from rules that are subject to principles of public participation and a recognition of the accountability of the tribunal to broader public interests which should be balanced and weighed against the interests of the investor.

Policies and interests underlying BITs

Investment treaties create state obligations for the protection and promotion of foreign investments. The purpose of investment treaties is to shield foreign investments and investors from unfavourable state interference and state regulation. Most investment treaties contain four core state obligations. These state obligations are tied to varying policy interests. These policy interests include the kind of protection a state offers to local and foreign investors, the incentives a state introduces to promote investment, the foreign policy of a state that guides the relationship between states and the investment flow as well as a state's policy on ownership of property.

Article 42(1) of the ICSID Convention provides that:

> The Tribunal shall decide a dispute in accordance with such rules of law as may be agreed by the parties. In the absence of such agreement, the Tribunal shall apply the law of the Contracting State party to the dispute (including its rules on the conflict of laws) and such rules of international law as may be applicable.

Other arbitration rules also allow tribunals to choose the law which is applicable to a dispute in the absence of a law chosen by the parties but the ICSID rules are different because of its express mention of international law

---

96   *Id*, para. 376.

as an applicable law.[97] Much discussion has surrounded the meaning of article 42(1) of the ICSID Convention. The interpretations have ranged from a restricted application of international law in a complementary or corrective role to be relied upon only in cases of domestic lacunae or where the law of the contracting state is inconsistent with international law, to a role that calls for the application of international law only to safeguard principles of *jus cogens*.[98] With rules such as the Article 42 provision of the ICSID Convention in place, an opportunity exists for reliance to be placed on both domestic and international human rights law as may be applicable in consideration of possible violations of BIT obligations.

This provision was considered in *Wena Hotels v. Arab Republic of Egypt*,[99] where a dispute arose under the UK-Egypt BIT between a UK company and an Egyptian public company regarding the operation of hotels. The tribunal found that the parties had agreed that the BIT would be the primary source of law but not the only source of law that was applicable. Though the concept of judicial precedents does not apply in BIT arbitration, the tribunal also relied on prior ICSID awards in determining the content of treaty obligations. The tribunal found a violation of fair and equitable treatment and failure to provide full protection and security and in doing so, the tribunal engaged in a robust discussion of the applicability of both domestic and international law. Egypt made a bid to annul this decision before the annulment committee which affirmed the award in the arbitration. Quoting Article 42, the committee held that both Egyptian and international law was applicable.[100] The annulment committee stated that:

> what is clear is that the sense and meaning of the negotiations leading to the second sentence of article 42 (1) allowed for both legal orders to have a role. The law of the host State can indeed be applied in conjunction with international law if this is justified. So too international law can be applied itself if the appropriate rule is found in this other ambit.[101]

---

97   For instance, Article 35 of the UNCITRAL Arbitration Rules provides:

The arbitral tribunal shall apply the law designated by the parties as applicable to the substance of the dispute. Failing such designation by the parties, the arbitral tribunal shall apply the law determined by the conflict of law rules which it considers applicable.

Also, article 17 of the rules of the international court of arbitration provides:

The parties shall be free to agree upon the rules of law to be applied by the arbitral tribunal to the merits of the dispute. In the absence of such an agreement, the arbitral tribunal shall apply the rules of law which it determines to be appropriate.

98   *CMS Gas Transmission Company v. The Argentine Republic* ICSID Case No ARB/01/8, Award of May 12, 2005, para. 115.

99   41 ILM 896 (2002).

100   *Wena Hotels Limited v. Arab Republic of Egypt*, ad hoc Committee Decision on Application for Annulment on February 5, 2002, 41 ILM 933 (2002), paras 38–39.

101   *Id*, para. 40.

It is expected that when treaties are being negotiated, host states will advocate for the selection of its domestic law while investment exporting states will push for the application of international investment law. This is bound to create tensions and while it will be a pragmatic approach on the part of treaty negotiators to create policy spaces when negotiating BITs that will allow the possibility of a choice of law that favours the considerations of public interests, it has rather been left to arbitration tribunals to determine the applicable law. This has devastating effects as the case study on expropriation discussed below shows.

The dilemma of the varying rules of expropriation

In addition to direct expropriations, expropriations can be indirect, wherein state interferences in the use or enjoyment of an investment deprive the investor of all benefits of the property except its legal title.[102] Both direct and indirect expropriations are considered compensable. Customary international law also recognises a third form of property interference known as state regulations. State regulations, enacted as a lawful exercise of governmental powers, may affect foreign investments. These state regulations are not considered to amount to expropriations and are therefore not compensable.[103] The line between indirect expropriations and state regulations which interfere with foreign investments is not clear. The unresolved nature of this issue has the potential to curtail the regulatory powers of a state.

---

102 Choudhury, B., 2009, 'Democratic implications arising from the intersection of investment arbitration and human rights', *Alta L Rev* 46, p. 996.
103 *Id*, p. 57. On the first element, reliance for this is placed on the tribunal's decision in *S.D. Myers*, where in determining the level of interference by government in relation to the export ban it imposed, the tribunal stated that a temporary measure did not result in the transfer of property nor did it directly benefit others, hence, the government's measure was not expropriatory. UNCITRAL, First Partial Award, 13 November 2000, pp. 287–288. The second element dealing with the substantiality of the interference firstly requires the government measure in question to be unreasonable and secondly, that there was a loss of property either through interference or substantial deprivation. On reasonableness, the tribunal in *Feldman v. Mexico* stated that 'governments must be free to act in the broader public interest through the protection of the environment, new or modified tax regimes, the granting or withdrawal of government subsidies, reductions or increases in tariff levels, imposition of zoning restrictions and the like. Reasonable government regulation of this type cannot be achieved if any business that is adversely affected may seek compensation, and it is safe to say that customary international law recognizes this'. ICSID Case No. ARB (AF)/99/1, Award on the Merits, 16 December 2002, p. 103. On the loss of property, the tribunal in *Pope & Talbot v. Government of Canada* referred to a test that has subsequently been used by other arbitrators (UNCTAD, p. 57) that 'while it may sometimes be uncertain whether a particular interference with business activities amounts to an expropriation, the test is whether the interference is sufficiently restrictive to support a conclusion that the property has been "taken" from the owner'. UNCITRAL, Interim Award on the Merits, 26 June 2000,

Jurisprudence on indirect expropriation from arbitration tribunals has produced two doctrines called the 'sole-effect' doctrine and the 'police-powers' doctrine.[104] Under the sole-effect doctrine, 'the crucial factor in determining whether an indirect expropriation has occurred is solely the effect of the governmental measure on the property owner; the purpose of the governmental measure is irrelevant in making that determination'.[105] The police-powers doctrine however does not restrict the analysis to the effects on the investor, but evaluates the broader context that takes into account the governmental interest involved.[106]

According to Montt, the notion of expropriation is a matter of constitutional law because it constitutes a redefinition of the proper relationship between property rights and regulatory powers.[107] He argues further that the notion of constitutional character of no expropriation without compensation must be viewed from the lenses of corrective and distributive justice.[108] The corrective justice principle applies on the basis that where a state appropriates an investment in pursuit of economic objectives, then the state must pay for the investments if public interest requires their appropriation.[109] The corrective justice principle looks at the legality and rationality of a state's behaviour.[110] The distributive justice principle applies on the basis that where the public interest invoked by the state trumps the core of investments, compensation is unnecessary.[111] The distributive justice principle looks at

para. 102. In determining what substantial deprivation means, the *Methanex* tribunal looked to the previous position of the investor before the alleged expropriation by government and the current position afterwards. UNCITRAL, Final Award, 3 August 2005, paras 16–18. The third element dealing with the existence of investment-backed expectations finds support in the *Metalclad v. Mexico* case, where government revoked a licence granted to the investor to build a landfill and declared the land as a state wildlife protected area. The tribunal stated that 'expropriation under NAFTA includes not only open, deliberate and acknowledged takings of property, such as outright seizure or formal or obligatory transfer of title in favour of the host State, but also covert or incidental interference with the use of property which has the effect of depriving the owner, in whole or in significant part, of the use or reasonably-to-be-expected economic benefit of property even if not necessarily to the obvious benefit of the host State'. ICSID Case No. ARB (AF)/97/1, Award on the Merits, 16 December 2002, para. 103.

104   Suda, R., 2005, *The Effect of Bilateral Investment Treaties on Human Rights Enforcement and Realization*, Global Law Working Paper 01/05 Symposium, Transnational Corporations and Human Rights, p. 28.

105   *Id*.

106   *Id*.

107   Montt, S., 2009, 'Investments, indirect expropriations and the regulatory state', in Montt, S., *State Liability in Investment Treaty Arbitration: Global Constitutional and Administrative Law in the BIT Generation*, Hart Publishing, p. 237.

108   *Id*, p. 238.

109   *Id*, p. 239.

110   *Id*.

111   *Id*, p. 241.

equality, fairness and proportionality of the allocation of appropriated investments.[112]

Investment treaties do not adequately provide answers to the doctrinal questions of what constitutes expropriation, how to draw the distinctions, the invocation of public interests and the relevance of the rationality and proportionality of the actions.[113] Hence, there is a push for a renvoi to domestic law of states to deal with these questions. While investment treaties identify what qualifies as an investment, the domestic law of states determines whether an investor possesses the rights and interests qualifying as investments.[114] Questions around the legality and rationality of a state's behaviour, or the equality, fairness and proportionality of actions are more appropriately dealt with through rule of law principles enshrined under administrative law. In cases like South Africa where expropriation is consti-tutionally permitted in section 25 of the constitution, taking into account the history of South Africa where people were dispossessed of their property through racially discriminatory laws, the just and equitable compensation criteria provided in section 25 is closely similar to the distributive justice principle that Montt describes. In international investment arbitration, where compensation is determined based on market value, adopting an exclusively international law approach does not permit an arbitration tribunal to recognise domestic rules like the section 25 rule in South Africa. It also fails to allow the interrogation of the reasons for that rule which in certain instances can be a legitimate justification for a state conduct if expropriation were to take place on this basis and less than market value compensation is offered to the investor.

Regulatory chill and the depoliticisation of law

Odumosu suggests that the depoliticisation of law by ISDS tribunals as a neutral mechanism that ignores the socio-political, economic and cultural background and ramifications makes the applicable legal rules devoid of equitable factors.[115] According to Odumosu, there is a potential to stifle government responses to the genuine concerns of its citizens, preclude states from advancing public interest arguments for fear of being accused of engaging in political acts.[116]

It appears that investment law's answer in resolving conflicting obligations of states is through stabilisation clauses which are found in some BITs and freeze some state actions in favour of other state obligations throughout the

112   *Id*, pp. 243–251.
113   *Id*.
114   *Id*.
115   Odumosu, *supra* note 1 at p. 283.
116   *Id*, p. 285.

period of investment.[117] These clauses aim to protect investors from application of regulatory measures that may affect the interests of investors. Cernic distinguishes three categories of stabilisation clauses: freezing, economic equilibrium and hybrid clauses.[118] Freezing clauses freeze fiscal and non-fiscal legislation in relation to investment for the duration of the project.[119] Economic equilibrium clauses protect against all changes in legislation through compensation or adjustments to the contract to compensate the investor when changes occur.[120] Hybrid clauses protect changes against legislation by requiring compensation or adjustments to the investment contract including exemptions from new laws.[121]

Broad stabilisation clauses may affect the ability of the host state to comply with obligations to respect, protect and fulfil, central tenets of international law in respect of human rights protection and to regulate in the public interest, as any such regulation may give rise to an obligation on the part of the host state to pay compensation.[122] Giving preference to the provisions of investment contracts allow stabilisation clauses to hinder the implementation of the human rights obligations of host states under international and domestic law of host states or the development of domestic regulation to address public concerns about a specific issue.

In most investment disputes, allegations of uncompensated expropriation are often made alongside allegations of breach of the fair and equitable treatment rule because of the nature of the protection this obligation offers. Investment tribunals use the standard of fair and equitable treatment as the standard in measuring the treatment afforded to foreign investors by the exercise of public power by all branches of government of the host state.[123] Fair and equitable treatment has the ability to intrude into host states' regulatory autonomy of all standards of investment protection, given its reach across all areas of domestic law, policy and administration. A number of principles emerge within the fair and equitable treatment obligation. These include the principle of stability which requires host states to maintain a stable regulatory environment in terms of its impact on foreign investors, the obligation of consistency which requires host states to refrain from conduct such as resiling from previous representations made to host states, the emergence of legitimate expectations as a principle of fair and equitable

---

117   Cernic, J.L., 2010, 'Corporate human rights obligations under stabilization clauses', *German Law Journal* 11, p. 212.

118   *Id.*

119   *Id*, p. 213, quoting Shemberg, A., 2008, *Stabilization and Human Rights*, 6-UN Research Project.

120   *Id.*

121   *Id.*

122   *Id.*

123   Henckels, C., 2012, 'Proportionality and Standard of Review in Fair and Equitable treatment Claims: Balancing stability and consistency with the public interest', Society of International Economic Law Conference, unpublished paper, p. 2.

treatment in international investment cases which illustrates the increasing influence of both supranational and domestic administrative law in international investment law.[124]

While host states can regulate and take other measures in the public interest, such measures are expected to be reasonable. However, there are concerns with regard to the sole reliance on the domestic law of a state. For instance, sole reliance on the domestic law of a state creates uncertainty given the possibility of a unilateral change by a state of the laws. Also, the domestic law of a state cannot cover the entire investment law field, hence, the hybrid approach proposed for the application of both domestic law and international investment law as well as in appropriate cases, the consideration of international law and human rights jurisprudence.

To achieve this hybrid approach, proportionality plays a role in controlling the extent to which the exercise of public power by host states in interfering with foreign investments is permissible.[125] Proportionality is linked to the concept of reasonableness because both proportionality and reasonableness suggest a balance of interests and a rational connection between a measure and its objective, and the concept of reasonableness itself may be understood as a search for equilibrium in the context of disagreement.[126]

Conclusion

The evolving trend in BIT awards has highlighted the need for policy makers to apply their minds when negotiating BITs to reduce confusion in the interpretation of very broad provisions and to develop predictability and consistency of decisions in investment disputes. In this chapter, it can be seen that with the increasing number of investment disputes, states are beginning to cite their human rights obligations as a defence to avoid liability under investment treaties. This previously uncharted territory has led to a haphazard determination of public interest considerations by arbitration tribunals. There are two possible solutions. First, in evaluating the conflicting regime of a domestic and international investment regime, the need for the consideration and application of domestic law alongside international law is necessary. Second, in comparing the investment law regime to the international human rights law regime, application of principles of proportionality, reasonableness and deference to other legal regimes, both domestic and international, should occur to balance state and investor interests.

124   *Id*, pp. 2–3.
125   *Id*, p. 6.
126   *Id*, p. 13.

3 The rule of law and depoliticisation of investment disputes

Introduction

ISDS has been the subject of substantial academic debate and research in the last few years. Parts of the debate focus on the substantive policy choices in investment treaties in relation to the protection of investors and their investment, the skills, experience and competence of arbitrators, expansive interpretations adopted by ISDS tribunals and the overall legitimacy of ISDS mechanisms.[1] Consequently, these have led to calls for systemic reform and various proposals have been developed as alternatives to ISDS.

ISDS has not progressively advanced since the boom in arbitration in the 1990s, despite the current developments and global politics that now dominate investor–state relations.[2] When ISDS emerged, it was at a moment of liberalisation where there was a clear divide between capital exporting and capital importing states.[3] In a bid to safeguard investors and their investment, capital exporting states initiated the idea of a neutral and independent forum to protect investors of the capital exporting states.[4] This development arose as a result of the mistrust by investors over the independence and ability of host state courts to provide fair and equal justice to investors and their investment.[5] ISDS gained popularity and became the traditional dispute settlement mechanism in investment treaties because it supposedly provided

1   Dezalay, Y. and Garth, B. G., 1996, *Dealing in Virtue: International commercial arbitration and the construction of a transnational legal order*, University of Chicago Press.
2   In the first ISDS case, *AAPL v. Sri Lanka*, it was stated that states make an offer of arbitration through the conclusion of BITs and investors accepts this offer on behalf of their home states through a request for arbitration.
3   Petersmann, E., 2012, *International Economic Law in the 21st Century: Constitutional Pluralism and Multilevel Governance of Interdependent Public Goods*, Oxford, Hart publishing, p. 116.
4   Miles, K., 2010, 'International investment law: Origins, imperialism and conceptualizing the environment', *Colombian Journal of International Environmental Law & Policy* 21(1), p. 11.
5   UNCTAD, 2010, 'Investor–State Disputes: Prevention and Alternatives to Arbitration', viewed (21 March 2017) from http://unctad.org/en/docs/diaeia200911_en.pdf, p. 14.

a cheaper, faster and more flexible way of resolving disputes.[6] The option for disputing parties to be able to exercise greater control over arbitration by appointing presiding officers preferred by the parties has also led to the rise of ISDS.[7]

However, the initial advantages of ISDS are disappearing as institutional rules and practices change. With increasing costs, prolonged duration of arbitration, treaty interpretations that states dislike, the exclusive focus on payment of damages and the difficulty in managing disputes with varying sources of public law issues, the forum has come under heavy scrutiny. This chapter deals with the nature of ISDS and its flaws, the viability of the various alternatives proposed in terms of improving the current system procedurally through transparency and amicus participation. Finally, this chapter considers the different categories of investment disputes and the effect they have had on African states and their right to regulate.

ISDS: Alternative dispute resolution or privatisation of justice?

The arbitration of investment disputes where public interest issues often arise can in one way be seen as a privatisation of justice which is inimical to the notion of open justice, a principle that most constitutional democracies subscribe to but is subverted by financial interests. However, proponents of ISDS see the system as a form of alternative dispute resolution (ADR), which emphasises the importance of neutrality in ensuring that disputing party interests are not compromised.

Either of these claims raise questions in relation to the confidence placed in the legal system of countries by investors and their home states. Their concerns include whether it is possible to have competent judgments in an efficient and impartial domestic system as well as whether the decision makers, the judges, have the requisite skills and experience to resolve invest-ment disputes. These questions are perhaps one explanation for the settlement of investment disputes through arbitration. Another explanation could be a desire to maximise the recovery of damages, which might be harder to achieve even in cases where a party wins a dispute in a domestic forum.

Historically, ISDS has been regarded as a 'confidential, quick, and cost-efficient method for resolving disputes, which creates an internationally enforceable award'.[8] However, with the increase in the usage of arbitration, the advantages of arbitration can no longer be made in assertive terms owing to the various worrying trends in arbitration. These trends are discussed further below.

---

6   *Id.*
7   *Id.*
8   Franck, S., 2005, 'The role of international arbitrators', *ILSA Journal of International & Comparative Law* 12(1), p. 499.

Confidentiality

First, the new rules of transparency under UNCITRAL and ICSID (the most frequently used rules for investor–state disputes), as well as in newly nego-tiated BITs of states and model BITs, are weakening the claims of confidentiality in ISDS.[9] A 2013 UNCTAD report recognised the need for more transparency in ISDS as a result of the involvement of public service sectors, the possible involvement of broader human rights concerns, the determination of large damages awarded against host states which are funded by public money, the threat of arbitration from an investor having a chilling 'effect on government policy' and the growing appreciation of the impact of procedural matters in investment arbitration.[10] These developing trends forced the need to change the rules of confidentiality in ISDS that has made it so attractive to investors in order to accommodate public and non-disputing parties' interests.

Time and costs

The length of time spent on ISDS has led to increased costs. On the average, it takes about three and a half years for a case to be concluded in interna-tional arbitration, a time period significantly less than what most jurisdictions will take to finalise a case.[11] In a recent study, the average cost of investment arbitration for a claimant is about $4,437,000 while the average respondent pays $4,559,000.[12] Tribunal costs, which include arbitrators' fees/expenses and institutional charges, are $769,000 for ICSID and $853,000 for UNCITRAL[13] and the successful party only recovers some portion of its costs in 44 per cent of cases.[14] These are figures significantly higher than what would be paid for a dispute at a national court, yet, international arbitration remains a preferred option for investors. An explanation for this preference could perhaps be the high amount of damages claimed and awarded. Under the ICSID, publicly reported damages awarded are estimated at

---

9   The ICSID adopted amendments in 2006 dealing with better transparency measures while the UNCITRAL rules underwent a review process in 2013 for improved trans-parency measures. These rules were applicable from April 2014.

10   UNCTAD, 2012, 'Series on Issues in International Investment Agreements II Transparency', United Nations, viewed (31 March 2017) from http://unctad.org/en/PublicationsLibrary/unctaddiaeia2011d6_en.pdf, p. xi.

11   See Sinclair, A., Fischer, L. and Macrory, S., 2009, 'ICSID arbitration: How long does it take?', *Global Arbitration Review* 4.

12   See Hodgson, M., 2014, 'Costs in investment treaty arbitration: The case for reform', *Transnational Dispute Management* 11(1).

13   *Id.*

14   *Id.*

$4.5 billion.[15] The awards in *Occidental v. Ecuador*[16] and *CSOB v. Slovak Republic*[17] cases constitute 59 per cent of this figure.[18] More recently, the tribunal in the *Yukos Universal v. Russia*[19] case awarded $50 billion to an investor in damages and another tribunal awarded $900 million in lost profits including $30 million for moral damages as a result of harm to the professional reputation of an investor who invested $5 million in a tourism development project.[20]

Neutrality

ISDS mechanisms are legally established through IIAs, which allows parties to determine the process of dispute resolution. The parties also pick a specific dispute resolution forum and particular institutional rules, under which arbitrators must exercise their discretion. This raises concerns about the independence of the arbitrators.

Franck asks, given these shifts in arbitration's paradigm, what is left to make arbitration preferable to domestic dispute settlement?[21] She suggests that perhaps it is the neutrality of the process. This includes the neutrality of the forum, which does not unfairly benefit both parties and the neutrality of the decision-making process.[22] If neutrality is highly valued by investors, then the viability of the various alternatives proposed to ISDS and discussed later in the next chapter would depend on whether they offer the same sense of neutrality. However, the claims of neutrality need to be assessed against the contested independence of arbitrators.

Arbitrators' bias and conflict of interest

Judges and arbitrators are said to share certain functional similarities, that is, the adjudicative nature of their decision-making obligations.[23] These similarities include the exercise of their discretion and the management of the dispute process.[24] However, the independence of arbitrator appointments in recent cases has increasingly come under challenge for the perceived biases

15   See Hodgson, M., 2014, 'Counting the costs of investment treaty arbitration', viewed (March 21, 2017) from www.allenovery.com/SiteCollectionDocuments/Counting_the_costs_of_investment_treaty.pdf
16   ICSID Case No. ARB/06/11.
17   Case No. ARB/97/4.
18   Hodgson, *supra* note 15.
19   PCA Case No. AA 227.
20   *Al-Kharafi v. Libya* rendered in Cairo on 22/3/2013.
21   Franck, *supra* note 8.
22   *Id.*
23   *Id*, p. 3.
24   *Id.*

of some of the arbitrators.[25] In a recent study, it was found that arbitrators are more likely to be selected based on their prior experience as arbitrators as well as the established relationship with the parties.[26] As a result, the circle of arbitrators is closed and the exercise of control by parties to select their arbitrators brings up the issue of privatisation of justice. To support the claim that arbitrators are biased and work in their self-interest, an empirical study was conducted recently that suggested that dissenting opinions in awards written by party appointed arbitrators are written in favour of the party who appointed them.[27] This becomes even more concerning where the process of review of the decision of arbitrators are usually limited to procedural review only and not the substantive decision by the arbitrators.[28]

In the work of Dezalay and Garth, their research identified two generations of arbitrators. The first group was called the 'grand old men' because they were males and people who had risen to the top of their national legal professions, but had not specialised in the field of arbitration.[29] The other group was called the technocrats, because they had acquired their credentials through activities in the field of international arbitration, unlike the grand old men who did not necessarily have this technical expertise specifically in arbitration.[30] In a more recent study, a third category of arbitrators was identified. These are the managers.[31] Over and above the mastery of the technicalities of arbitration, parties are now placing more importance on the management abilities of potential arbitrators, which apply to 'the management of the proceedings, the deliberations of the arbitral tribunal, the organisation of work within the tribunal, and the process of producing an award'.[32]

This management role preferred at international forums is perhaps another explanation why arbitration is preferred over other forms of dispute settlement because it allows the disputing parties to guide and agree with the presiding arbitrators on how the proceedings should be managed to reach

---

25   *Burlington Resources v. Ecuador ICSID* Case No. ARB/08/5(2013) – repeated appointments by the counsel of the claimant; *Blue Bank International v. Venezuela* (ICSID Case No. ARB 12/20 2013) – arbitrator is partner of firm that represented claimant in other case; *Caratube v. Kazakhstan* ICSID Case No. ARB/13/13 (2014) – appointment as arbitrator in another case against the same host state.

26   See Puig, S., 2014, 'Social capital in the arbitration market', *The European Journal of International Law* 25(2), p. 387–424.

27   van den Berg, A., 2010, 'Dissenting opinions by party-appointed arbitrators in investment arbitration', in *Looking to the Future: Essays on international law in honor of M. Reisman*, cited in Rogers, C., 2013, 'The politics of international investment arbitrators', *Santa Clara Journal International Law* 12 (223), p. 242.

28   Franck, *supra* note 8 at p. 4.

29   Dezalay and Garth, *supra* note 1.

30   *Id.*

31   Schultz, T. and Kovacs, R., 2012, 'The rise of a third generation of arbitrators? Fifteen years after Dezalay and Garth', *Arbitration International* 28(2).

32   *Id*, p. 162.

the outcome of an award, an opportunity that will not exist through the court system.

Problematic institutional architecture and inconsistencies

ISDS is a central feature of IIAs and it is the most significant institution to promote and protect foreign investment. However, it is increasingly being seen by states as a restraint on their regulatory capacity to undertake reforms and causes regulatory chill to prevent liability to foreign investors.

According to Titi:

> the proliferation and growing importance of these tribunals and exponential recourse to dispute settlement have acted as the catalyst bringing to the fore an uncomfortable tension between investment protection and the states' regulatory interests and by the same token, they have revealed arbitration as part of a problem – the perceived threat to states' regulatory interests.[33]

It was argued further that of particular significance is 'a deepening suspicion that arbitral reasoning has not adequately incorporated host state regulatory interests and that awards tend to be biased in favour of investors at the expense of states' but acknowledges that 'these concerns may appear somewhat exaggerated, since host states are the usual winners in investor-state disputes'.[34] The *CMS* and the *LG&E* tribunal cases illustrate this point where both tribunals dealt with the defence of necessity under customary international law and the annulment committee in both cases reached different conclusions in two cases where the facts were similar. The *CMS* tribunal held that Argentina's crisis 'did not result in total economic and social collapse' and could not preclude wrongfulness,[35] while the *LG&E* tribunal held that the same crisis reached 'catastrophic proportions' that required the defence of necessity advanced by Argentina.[36]

Miles argues against the establishment of ISDS that allows an investor to bring a claim against a state without corresponding mechanisms under international investment law for the hearing of complaints by individuals affected by investor activity.[37] She argues for the adherence to global public law principles where it would be natural for ISDS to consider the 'social, environmental, and developmental needs of the host state in investment

---

33 Titi, A., 2013, *The Right to Regulate in International Investment Law*, Nomos, pp. 67–68.

34 *Id*, p. 69.

35 *CMS Gas Transmission Co. v. Argentine Republic*, ICSID Case No Arb/01/8 para. 355.

36 *LG&E Energy Corp v. Argentine Republic*, ICSID Case No Arb/02/1, decision on Liability, para. 237.

37 Miles, K., 2013, *The Origins of International Investment Law*, Cambridge University Press, p. 337.

disputes'.[38] Miles also argues that 'arbitrators in investor-state disputes comprise an epistemic community responsible for knowledge-creation within international investment law. If the underlying culture of that community requires conservative adherence to private sector commercial values, investor protection will remain at the forefront of arbitrators' concerns'.[39] Given this dilemma of legitimacy and fairness in the resolution of disputes, various alternatives to the ISDS have been proposed and the pros and cons offer interesting insights for the future of international investment law. These are discussed in the next chapter.

International investment law and ISDS have both public and private law dimensions. On the one hand, while it is a 'multilateralisation of bilaterally agreed standards', it also imposes 'conflicting interests by avoiding national and international public law courts'.[40] On the other hand, ISDS is seen as a form of consensual adjudication between an investor and a state, and should rather be viewed as 'a mechanism of adjudicative review in public law because investment arbitration is established by a sovereign act of the state and it is predominantly used to resolve disputes arising from the exercise of sovereign authority'.[41] However, while ISDS mechanisms are established due to sovereign acts of state, these mechanisms significantly subvert the rule of law that was discussed in this book in Chapter 2.

ISDS tribunals are structured like commercial arbitration where a private party initiates the claim and similar procedural rules are used in forming the tribunal and enforcing the award. However, this approach is flawed given the subject matter of regulation and public policy that ISDS deals with. A commercial arbitration perspective of ISDS sees investment arbitration as a private dispute between parties, which would justify confidentiality and an isolation of the issues to only matters brought up by the parties.[42]

Three main fundamental approaches to dispute resolution exist. These include 'gun-boat' diplomacy, a rights approach through adjudication in the courts and the functional approach, which involves the reconciliation of the interests of the parties involved.[43] The functional approach primarily involves ADR techniques, which have not been embraced under current ISDS mechanisms. Where huge damages claims are involved and where challenges are being made against the policy and regulatory choices of states, disputing

38   *Id*, p. 25.
39   *Id*, p. 345.
40   Petersmann, *supra* note 3 at p. 13.
41   Van Harten, G., 2007, *Investment Treaty Arbitration and Public Law*, Oxford University Press, p. 45.
42   Kladermis, D., 'Investment treaty arbitration as global administrative law: What this might mean in practice', in Brown and Miles (eds), 2011, *Evolution in Investment Treaty Law and Arbitration*, Cambridge University Press, p. 149.
43   Echandi, R., 2013, *Prospects in International Investment Law and Policy, Complementing Investor-State Dispute Resolution: A Conceptual Framework for Investor-State Conflict Management*, Cambridge University Press, p. 270.

parties would probably prefer a less adversarial system of resolving their disputes. This is perhaps where the future of investment dispute resolution should lie – the reconciliation of interests of the parties. This idea of mediation or conciliation of disputes is gaining traction in investment law. UNCTAD released a report in 2010 that dealt with the alternatives to ISDS and focused on two categories of alternatives.[44] The first relates to the use of ADR, while the second focuses on dispute prevention to avoid the occurrence of disputes.

ADR approaches are non-binding and usually focus on the resolution of disputes through mediation and conciliation. The objective of a conciliation is an amicable settlement with a degree of formality attached to it particularly in the ICSID.[45] Mediation is a more informal process and unlike conciliation where a set of recommendations can be made by a conciliator with a focus on the substantive issues, mediators are facilitators and the process is led through the active participation of the disputing parties.[46] Like arbitration, both conciliation and mediation require the participation of third parties.

There are several advantages for ADR. It is a flexible process and leaves room for the possibility of parties to make deals at a quick pace while keeping costs low.[47] This also reduces the risk of states being exposed to huge damages in awards. In addition, ADR offers an opportunity to improve good governance and regulatory practices because it allows states to navigate the quagmire of meeting investment obligations while also protecting the domestic policy of states.

However, there are also disadvantages. The decisions in ADR mechanisms are not binding on the parties. In such cases where parties do not commit to the ADR process in good faith, it can lead to a waste of time and money.[48]

ADR mechanisms are also not suitable for all kinds of investment disputes.[49] Where public regulation is involved, it might not be advisable for a state to compromise on policy making with private investors. This exposes the state to political risks and the perception of private power dictating policy making never bodes well for the legitimacy of the process and the state.[50] In addition, because states are expected to operate within the boundaries of the law, it might be difficult for states to justify the legitimacy of any decision taken within an ADR, especially where such decisions would not have the force of law.[51]

44   UNCTAD, 2010, 'Investor–State Disputes: Prevention and Alternatives to Arbitration', viewed (21 March 2017) from http://unctad.org/en/docs/diaeia200911_en.pdf
45   *Id*, p. xiii.
46   *Id*, p. xix.
47   *Id*, p. 32 and 34.
48   *Id*, p. 36.
49   *Id*.
50   *Id*, p. 37.
51   *Id*, p. 37.

ADR processes also face the same criticism that ISDS has been subjected to, which is the lack of transparency and a lack of opportunity for third parties to intervene and represent non-disputing party interests.[52] To address these concerns, three major procedural changes have been suggested for ISDS reform. These are the introduction of transparency rules, non-disputing party participation and the introduction of an investment court.

New transparency rules

The conclusion of IIAs by bureaucrats has traditionally been negotiated behind the scenes without the influence of public opinion or awareness by national law makers. A recent example of this is the negotiation of the Trans-Pacific Partnership (TPP) in secret, which prompted global calls for transparency and the ultimate leakage of the draft agreement.[53] The next frontier of transparency within IIAs relates to the negotiations of the agreements and domestic legal systems have an important role to play in this regard. As a reaction to criticisms against the lack of transparency during the negotiations of the investment chapter of the Trans-Atlantic Trade and Investment Partnership (TTIP), the EU launched a 'public consultation on modalities for investment protection and ISDS in TTIP', thereby opening new perspective for democratic input in this domain.[54] At the ISDS stage, transparency can take different forms.

Transparency can be introduced in two ways. It can be introduced as a requirement in the IIA on which the arbitration is based and it can also be introduced into the arbitration rules. Both mechanisms have been used by states in order to promote transparency in the ISDS process. The former position is preferable to avoid and override many problems that may be encountered in existing arbitration rules. By introducing transparency norms in IIAs, there is a greater opportunity for public participation.

Emerging model BITs have also incorporated rules of access to information that recognise the shift towards transparency norms in the investment legal system. In the SADC model BIT, provision is made for the disclosure of information in three tiers. First, article 12 provides for the disclosure of information by the investor to the host state concerning the investment and recognises the right of the host state to receive timely and

---

52   *Id*, p. 38.
53   Schill, S., 2014, 'Transparency as a Global Norm in International Investment Law', viewed (21 March 2017) from http://kluwerarbitrationblog.com/2014/09/15/transparency-as-a-global-norm-in-international-investment-law
54   *Id*.

accurate information.[55] Second, the provision goes further to recognise the right of the host state to disclose such information to the public in accordance with its domestic law. In the commentary to article 18,[56] which provides that investment contracts and payments must also be made available to the public, it is stated that:

> there is a growing concern for transparency in contract negotiation that many developing countries and international organisations are now responding to. Indeed, many now see this as one of the most important ingredients in the fight against corruption. This article sets out the principle of transparency and an expectation that both investors and governments will act on this expectation.

55   12.1. An Investor shall provide such information to an actual or potential Host State as that State Party may require concerning the Investment in question and the corporate history and practices of the Investor, for purposes of decision making in relation to that Investment or solely for statistical purposes.
12.2. The actual or potential Host State shall have the right to timely and accurate information in this regard. An Investor shall not commit fraud or provide false or misleading information provided in accordance with this Article.
12.3. A material breach of paragraph 12.2 by an Investor or an Investment is deemed to constitute a breach of the domestic law of the Host State concerning the establishment, acquisition, management, operation and disposition of Investments.
12.4. The actual or potential Host State Party may make such information available to the public in the location where the Investment is to be located, subject to other applicable law and the redaction of confidential business information. The State Party shall protect any confidential business information from any disclosure that would prejudice the competitive position of the Investor or the Investment.
12.5. Nothing in this Article shall be construed to prevent a State Party from otherwise obtaining or disclosing information in connection with the equitable and good faith application of its domestic law or in connection with disputes between the Investor and the State regarding the Investment.

56   18.2. Investors or their investments shall make public in a timely manner all payments made to a government related to the establishment or right to operate of an Investment, including all taxes, royalties and similar payments.
18.3. Where feasible, such contracts and payments shall be made available on an Internet website freely accessible by the public.
18.4. The State Party that is the recipient of payments or party to an investment-related contract shall [have the right to] make the payments and contracts available to the public, including through an Internet site freely accessible to the public.
18.5. Confidential business information shall be redacted from contracts made public in accordance with this Article.

Third, the model BIT provides in article 24 that state parties shall make available to an investor, all laws and regulations including policies and administrative guidelines that may affect the investments of investors.[57]

If the approach suggested in this section is followed, it will place state parties in the position to establish the supremacy of their internal access to information laws in these disputes and ensure that no conflict of interest arises when a state is obliged to release information to the public and prevent confidentiality orders by tribunals.

Transparency increases the quality of decision making because in instances where awards are published for public scrutiny, there is a greater pressure on arbitrators to write well-reasoned decisions.[58] The public scrutiny of the arbitration process also decreases the likelihood of corruption by parties. In the *Piero Foresti* case, there was a reported allegation of a demand for bribery by a government representative of South Africa, a fact that would likely have been unknown without the transparency of the process.[59] Access to information is an entrenched principle in most democratic states that allows for the realisation of other rights, as is often theorised.[60] Consequently, transparency within ISDS therefore allows the realisation of other rights, such as access to justice.

The notion of access to justice is conceptualised as the right of everyone to require the state to provide a means of dispute resolution that is equally accessible and socially just.[61] This goes to substance and form, particularly, the right to public participation in ISDS proceedings. Such participation should take into account administrative law standards such as principles of fairness and open hearings, and access to the memorials of the disputing parties. This is closely connected to the protection of interests of the public who are often not aware of their interests within an ISDS dispute and how to protect them. By opening up the ISDS process, there is a likelihood of

---

57   24.1. Each State Party shall promptly publish, or otherwise make publicly available, its laws and regulations of general application as well as international agreements that may affect the Investments of Investors of the other State Party.

24.2. Each State Party shall endeavour to promptly publish, or otherwise make publicly available, its policies and administrative guidelines or procedures that may affect investment under this Agreement.

58   Magraw, D. and Amerasinghe, N., 2008, 'Transparency and public participation in investor-state arbitration', *ILSA J Int & Comparative Law* 15, p. 337.

59   Case No ARB (AF)/07/1 para. 31.

60   Adeleke, F., 2015, 'The Role of Law in Assessing the Value of Transparency and the Disconnect with the Lived Realities under Investor-State Dispute Settlement', Working Paper No. 6, presented at the Law & Society Conference, Seattle May 2015, unpublished paper, p. 18.

61   Cappelletti, M. and Garth, R., 1978, 'Access to justice: The worldwide movement to make rights effective: A general report', in Cappelletti and Garth (eds), *Access to Justice: A World Survey* Vol 1 Milan, Dott. A Guiffre Editore at p. 6 quoted in Adeleke, F., 2012, 'Access to justice and freedom of information: The case of South Africa', *African Journal of Clinical Legal Education and Access to Justice* 1, p. 108.

increasing the consistency and coherence in interpretation of law in similar cases.[62]

Lack of transparency harms the legitimacy and credibility of the dispute resolution bodies, such as limiting scrutiny of government decisions by the public and the cover up of abuse and corruption by investors and government officials.[63] Transparency facilitates the accountability of parties in the ISDS process and as a result, compliance and implementation of ISDS decisions by parties may be more effective.[64]

In 2012, UNCTAD released a report on transparency in IIAs, which sought to address the transparency imperatives from a sustainable development perspective and through a consideration of some of the existing good practices in various investment agreements. It also made recommendations for future investment instruments.[65]

As earlier stated, the report recognised the emergence of transparency in ISDS as a result of the increasing emphasis on the public interest inherent within investor–state disputes which involves public service sectors, the possible involvement of broader human rights concerns, the determination of large damages awarded against host states which are funded by public money, the presence of a state as a party in the arbitration which triggers good governance obligations, the threat of arbitration from an investor having a 'chilling' effect on government policy and the growing appreciation of the impact of procedural matters in investment arbitration.[66]

The UNCTAD report considers transparency from three perspectives. The first is what it called state-centred transparency obligations, which include a binding obligation to make certain information public, a soft obligation to cooperate and consult with the other contracting party, a binding obligation to proactively exchange information with the other contracting party and a binding obligation to respond to information requests.[67] The second deals with investor responsibilities regarding the obligation to comply with laws and regulations, the authority of the host state to collect information from the investor and the duty on the investor to cooperate with the state.[68] The third perspective deals with transparency in the investment arbitration itself in relation to access to information and amicus participation.[69]

---

62 Magraw, D. and Amerasinghe, N., *supra* note 58 at p. 9.
63 *Id.*
64 *Id.*
65 UNCTAD, 2012, *Series on Issues in International Investment Agreements II 'Transparency 2012*, viewed (21 March 2017) from unctad.org/en/PublicationsLibrary/diaeia2013d2_en.pdf
66 *Id*, p. 36.
67 *Id*, p. 25.
68 *Id*, p. 30–35.
69 *Id*, p. 37–42.

The UNCTAD report also recognises the increasing trend in arbitration tribunals to use the preambles of investment agreements in interpretation. The reports states that given the reference to social responsibility practices in the preambles, this point to the expectation of states that foreign investors should be willing to engage in more sustainability reporting which will assist host states in maintaining ongoing investor transparency throughout project implementation.[70]

The transparency approach adopted by the UNCTAD is developed from a perspective where there is an acknowledgement that investment disputes and the issues arising affect the development of states and a more holistic approach is needed to accommodate other competing interests without unfairly prejudicing the parties, particularly, the investors. Consequently, the 2013 UNCITRAL transparency rules were developed, which came into effect in 2014 and apply to IIAs concluded after 1 April 2014. This means that the rules will not retroactively apply to existing UNCITRAL disputes or IIAs concluded prior to this date. The international investment law regime is fluid and is guided by thousands of IIAs, multiple dispute resolution bodies with their own sets of rules guiding the resolution of disputes based on various legal principles which are to a relative extent similar in substance. Therefore, the new UNCITRAL rules still exclude a large number of the investment regimes from the spotlight of transparency.

Despite the portrayal of the lack of transparency within the investment regime, certain areas of the investment regime are publicly accessible, such as the rules of procedure for arbitration and the content of IIAs that are publicly available. However, there are other forms of information that should be available but still kept secret. For example, not all arbitration awards are made public.[71] Information seekers are required to obtain the information from independent researchers who collect information on important areas of the regime relating to issues such as the trends in the interpretation of principles of investment law relating to the similarity or otherwise in arbitration awards. There are other concerning areas of secrecy such as the lack of knowledge on the total number of IIAs in existence or existing disputes.[72] Where disputes are public, not all the relevant information relating to the dispute is publicly disclosed.[73] The UNCITRAL rules are a significant step in addressing some of these information deficits such as the disclosure of the existence of all disputes.

To advance the transparency agenda, various stakeholders have a role to play. Civil society can actively push on the level of negotiating new IIAs or

70   *Id*, p. 55.
71   See Maupin, J.A., 2013, 'Transparency in international investment law: The good, the bad, and the murky', in Bianchi, A. and Peters, A. (eds) *Transparency in International Law*, Cambridge University Press.
72   *Id*.
73   *Id*; Adeleke F., 2016, 'Human rights and international investment arbitration', *South African Journal of Human Rights* 32(1), p. 65.

in the review of existing IIAs for active public participation. They can also access information through domestic access to information laws where possible for information relating to a particular arbitration. The parties themselves benefit from the transparency of certain areas to aid their cases. Where awards are published and interpretation of substantive principles are subject to scrutiny, disputing parties can benefit from ways on how they should approach their particular dispute and anticipate the outcomes of disputes. More importantly however, states should begin to negotiate IIAs that incorporate robust transparency provisions that safeguard the rule of law standards for public participation and representation of important public interests.

Amicus participation

The increase in number of IIAs has led to a corresponding increased interest in the wider social impact of IIAs, especially with regard to arbitration arising under these IIAs.[74] Different arbitration rules have different procedures and the question that has consistently been raised is whether these procedures balance the private nature of arbitration in terms of confidentiality and the interests of the parties with the requirements of promoting transparency and openness where public interest issues are at play.[75]

The primary argument for the participation of *amici* in ISDS is to give more legitimacy and credibility to the ISDS process which allows foreign investors to challenge national laws and regulation through a private and confidential process with a limited possibility of reviewing the decision of the ISDS tribunal.[76] The broad protections afforded under investment treaties to foreign investors, the ambiguity in the scope and application of the treaties and the potential adverse impact of investment protections to wider social concerns are other reasons for advocating for the participation of *amicus curiae* in the ISDS process.

The modern *amicus* perform four identifiable functions. First, an *amicus* provides specialist legal expertise to the court or tribunal, in particular, about matters outside the core competence of the arbitrators.[77] Second, an *amicus* can provide factual information to support the public interest subject matter being put before the court.[78] Third, an *amicus* can provide a measure of due

---

74 Argentina's economic crisis has led to 43 ICSID arbitrations with a potential liability of $8 billion. James Harrison, 2009, 'Human rights arguments in amicus curiae submissions: Promoting social justice?', in Dupuy, P.M., et al. (eds), *Human Rights in International Investment Law and Arbitration*, Oxford University Press, p. 398.

75 *Id*, p. 399.

76 Van Duzer, A., 2007, 'Enhancing the procedural legitimacy of investor-state arbitration through transparency and amicus participation', *McGill Law Journal* 52(681), p. 686.

77 Bartholomeusz, L., 2005, 'The *amicus curiae* before international courts and tribunals', *Non-St Actors & International Law* 5(209), p. 278.

78 *Id*.

process to interested parties who cannot be parties to arbitration proceedings but whose interests may be affected by the decision.[79] Finally, an *amicus* can represent public interest considerations.[80]

While local and community organisations are not expected to provide legal expertise to ISDS tribunals, factual information that support the consideration of a relevant public interest matter that should affect the outcome of a dispute are often within the direct knowledge of the community organisations. An example of this is the case of *Tecmed v. Mexico*, where protests by the local communities influenced the government to relocate a landfill elsewhere.[81] The tribunal focused on the legality of the resolution by the Mexican government and found no principle that excludes state regulation or administrative actions from the scope of BITs.[82] The tribunal downplayed the significance of the protests as a factor that should validate the state measure and was of the opinion that the protests needed to be 'massive' and thus introduced a quantitative criterion for a social crisis to be given any significant weight in determining the justifiability of a state action.[83]

Odumosu argues that it is difficult to quantify peoples' suffering, the strength of their opposition and the impact of their voices.[84] While non-governmental organisations (NGOs) can in some cases represent the interests of local communities, these NGOs do not always adequately represent the local interests, hence, the need to give an additional platform for these local concerns to be voiced and given due consideration.[85] The approach taken in the *Tecmed* case for instance is the strict separation of law from politics. Odumosu argues that the depoliticisation of law by stripping it of its socio-economic, political and cultural backgrounds is partly responsible for the inability to effectively allow consideration of mass participation and resistance in decision making.[86] She argues that when a government's action is measured against the provisions of investment treaties, it involves investigations into the rationale for adopting the domestic regulation to aid the interpretation of an action in light of an applicable law.[87] These are political inquiries, which result in adopting some regulatory measures being valued over others.[88]

---

79   *Id*, p. 279.
80   *Id*.
81   *Tenicas Medioambientales Tecmed S.A. v. United Mexican States*, 43 I.L.M. 133 (2004).
82   *Id*, para. 121.
83   *Id*, para. 144.
84   Odumosu, I., 2008, 'The law and politics of engaging resistance in investment dispute settlement', *Penn St International Law Review* 26(251), p. 282.
85   *Id*.
86   *Id*, p. 271.
87   *Id*, p. 272.
88   *Id*.

The decision by the tribunal in *Pezold/Border Timbers v. Zimbabwe* illustrates this point. The tribunal took a restrictive interpretation of rule 37(2) of the ICSID rules[89] after a German-based NGO, the European Center for Constitutional and Human Rights (ECCHR) and four indigenous communities from Zimbabwe sought *amicus* participation in two joined proceedings against Zimbabwe.[90] The ECCHR and indigenous chiefs from Zimbabwe attempted to bring the attention of the tribunal to the claim that the properties in dispute were located on the ancestral territories of indigenous people.[91] The tribunal stated that the first requirement of *amicus* participation, in terms of Article 37(2) of the ICSID Arbitration Rules, is the independence of the applicants. The tribunal stated that this was not present with the *amicus* applicants in this case because the claims of the indigenous communities were in conflict with the claimant's position and the applicants were assisted by an NGO whose director favoured the government policy.[92]

The two petitioners sought to present submissions on the interdependence of investment treaties and international human rights law, and to argue that human rights law was directly applicable in the dispute.[93] Both the foreign investors and Zimbabwe, according to the petitioners, held shared responsibility towards the indigenous communities, who traditionally lived on the land at issue in the ICSID proceedings.[94]

In particular, the petitioners sought to highlight the importance of the 2007 UN Declaration on the Rights of Indigenous Peoples, under which states have certain obligations to protect traditional lands.[95] The petitioners also pointed to principles developed by the Organisation for Economic Co-operation and Development (OECD) and the World Bank, which were allegedly applicable to the claimants.[96] However, the tribunal observed that

89   According to the amended ICSID rule 37(2).
After consulting both parties, the tribunal may allow a person or entity that is not a party to the dispute … to file a written submission with the Tribunal regarding a matter within the scope of the dispute. In determining whether to allow such a filing, the Tribunal shall consider, among other things, the extent to which:
(a) the non-disputing party submission would assist the Tribunal in the determination of a factual or legal issue related to the proceeding by bringing a perspective, particular knowledge or insight that is different from that of the disputing parties;
(b) the non-disputing party submission would address a matter within the scope of the dispute;
(c) the non-disputing party has a significant interest in the proceeding.
The tribunal shall ensure that non-disputing party submission does not disrupt proceeding or unduly burden or unfairly prejudice either party, and that both parties are given an opportunity to present their observations on the non-disputing party submission.
90   ICSID ARB/10/15 and ARB/10/25, Procedural Order No. 2, 26 June 2012.
91   *Id*, para. 21.
92   *Id*, paras 51–56.
93   *Id*, para. 26.
94   *Id*, para. 25.
95   *Id*, para. 27.
96   *Id*, para. 28.

because the indigenous communities sought to occupy parts of the property in dispute, this suggested that the communities were not independent but in fact pitted against the claimants.[97] According to the tribunal, neither party had pleaded the relevance of international law on human rights or indigenous peoples' rights in the ICSID proceedings.[98] The tribunal also noted that the ECCHR lacked significant interest in the case since the organisation's mission related to corporate responsibilities for human rights abuses, which was not alleged in this case.[99] The tribunal failed to expand on the meaning of the apparent lack of independence in excluding the *amicus* petitioners.[100] It also contradicted itself in ruling that the *amicus* applicants were required to be independent while also demonstrating significant interest in the case.[101]

The decision of the tribunal was absurd and further affirms the necessity of a forum that recognises the importance of contextual determination of disputes taking into account competing considerations and historical injustices that states have to grapple with. While these historical complexities should not be regarded as a justification for violations of the rule of law and for the state to act with impunity, dispute resolution bodies have a heightened need in high profile disputes to reach decisions taking into account the full dimension of issues.

The approach taken by the tribunal is inexplicable. The decision suggests that *amicus* representation cannot favour a particular position even in cases where the applicants in this case argued that both parties to the dispute should recognise their claimed rights. The tribunal's construction of independence is a difficult hurdle to cross. It cannot be expected that an *amicus* submission can be completely neutral without favouring a position taken by one of the parties. The stringent independence requirement also ignores the condition that *amicus* applicants should have a significant interest in the proceedings. This suggests that the mere existence of a right, which an *amicus* applicant seeks to enforce, is enough to compromise the independence of an amicus and to deny participation. The tribunal also held that reference to general international law does not include the application of human rights law and for human rights law to apply; there must be a specific reference to human rights treaties in BITs or the pleadings of the parties.[102] The tribunal's ruling suggests that *amicus* applicants cannot submit human rights related arguments where there is no specific reference to human rights law or the parties have not raised it. This is problematic where there is a

97   *Id*, para. 51.
98   *Id*, para. 57.
99   *Id*, para. 61.
100 *Id*, para. 56.
101 See generally Bastin, L., 2013, 'Amici curiae in investor-state arbitrations: Two recent decisions', *Australian International Law Journal*, viewed (31 March 2017) from www.austlii.edu.au/au/journals/AUIntLawJl/2013/7.pdf.
102 *Id*, para. 57.

deliberate choice by the parties to ignore human rights considerations. It also reduces the public interest element of disputes. The tribunal's interpretation, which limits the choice of law interpretation under international law not to include international human rights law and to isolate a body of law from international law, is arcane under a well-reasoned legal interpretation.

The tribunal also ruled against allowing amicus participation because it would unfairly prejudice the claimants and fail to meet the criteria in rule 37.[103] The tribunal suggested that consent of the parties in terms of article 44 is not necessary where the criteria in rule 37 are satisfied.[104] The tribunal had initially suggested that *amicus* participation would not be allowed where it adversely affected the interest of any of the disputing parties and later on that regardless of the views of a disputing party on whether an *amicus* application would adversely affect its interests, the decision on adverse effect solely rested with the tribunal and it could discard the requirement of consent of the parties.[105] This clearly contradicts the explicit ICSID consent requirement. While the specific interpretation taken by the tribunal in this case to the consent requirement favours the advocacy for a liberal approach towards *amicus* participation, the tribunal's clear misinterpretation of the law lays down the case for why alternatives to ISDS are necessary for reasoned decision making.

To safeguard the acceptance of amicus participation in investment arbitration and to alleviate the concerns of disputing parties, the role of an *amicus* should be clarified to recognise the *amicus curiae* as an entity whose role and function is to render assistance to the court in reaching a judicious outcome that not only protects the rights and interests of disputing parties but also recognises the public interests at play that need to be addressed. Arbitrators have a crucial role to play in ensuring that *amicus* parties are accepted into ISDS proceedings and should develop their understanding of *amicus* beyond NGOs to include other stakeholders such as communities and regional institutions.

Recurring investment disputes in Africa and the implications for state regulation

Julie Maupin has identified six categories of disputes that are always recurrent and politically problematic.[106] Applying this rubric, the extent to which the various categories of disputes have featured against African states are considered in this section.

103   *Id*, para. 62.
104   *Id*, para. 6.
105   *Id*.
106   Maupin, J., 2015, 'Recurring Problems in Investor-State Disputes & How South Africa Might Respond to Them', Max-Planck Institute, viewed (31 March 2017) from www.saiia.org.za/doc_download/699-2015-02-10-investor-state-disputes-pres-by-julie-maupin

Ordinary regulatory disputes

The first type are ordinary regulatory disputes where the host state enacts a new law which in some way reduces either the actual value or expected profitability of the investment.[107] This is the most prevalent type of dispute for African countries where enacted host state measures are challenged for their effect on investor protections.

This was the case with the *Piero Foresti v. South Africa* case where investors argued that the enactment of a new law on mineral and petroleum resources extinguished their mining rights and also required compulsory divestiture requirements because foreign investors were required to sell 26 per cent of their shares to South Africans over a ten year period.[108] Investor challenges are not limited to change in regulation but also extend to state measures and policies that are implemented in the absence of regulation, which curbs the investor interests.[109] Also, these challenges are no longer strictly within the ambit of BITs but also extend to investor–state contracts.[110]

Extraordinary crisis disputes

The second category of disputes are extraordinary crisis disputes where a big event occurs within a host state that reduces either the value or expected profitability of a large number of investments and given the sometimes volatile situations developing countries find themselves in, the potential for such events occur which exposes the liability of states.[111]

In the case of *Bernhard von Pezold and others v. Republic of Zimbabwe*,[112] the claims arose out of the government's expropriation without compensation of three estates owned by the claimants, including forestry and

107   *Id.*
108   Case No ARB (AF).07/1 paras 54–56.
109   In the case of *African Petroleum Gambia Ltd. v. Gambia* ICSID Case No ARB/14/6, the investor, a British coproration had its licence revoked under a general policy issued by the government against speculation in the oil industry. Despite the government's attempts to introduce the policy with the aim of fast-tracking investment in its natural resource sector, the government had to withdraw the policy after reaching a settlement in which it reinstated the licences and extended the initial exploration period.
110   In an ongoing case, *Vanoil Ltd. v. Kenya*, Vanoil, a Canadian oil company, initiated arbitration against Kenya after failure to secure extension of a pair of production sharing contracts for onshore oil exploration in Kenya. Rights to onshore blocks in the Anza basin region in Kenya were acquired by the company in October of 2007 and commenced arbitration against the Kenyan government under concession agreements, seeking $150 million in compensation. See Mohamadieh, K. and Uribe, D., 2016, 'The rise of investor-state dispute settlement in the extractive sectors: challenges and considerations for African countries', Research paper 65, viewed (31 March 2017) from www.southcentre.int/wp-content/uploads/2016/02/RP65_Rise-of-investor-state-dispute-settlement-in-extrative-sectors_EN.pdf, p. 6.
111   Maupin, *supra* note 106.
112   ICSID Case No ARB/10/15.

agricultural businesses, in the context of Zimbabwe's land reform programme.[113]

Bernhard von Pezold and his family, who are dual Swiss and German nationals, bought three large estates in Zimbabwe starting in 1988. Their estates were heavily invaded, with settlers occupying the farmland, which was a response to political events including the slow pace of land reform.[114] The invasions were accompanied by a racial rhetoric that was anti-white and the invasions occurred with logistical support from organs of government.[115] In 2005, when the constitution was amended, the Zimbabwean state acquired title to most of the claimants' properties and revoked their right to challenge the acquisition.[116] The claimants continued to occupy the land but argued they were reduced to 'mere licensees at the will of the respondent'.[117]

The new constitution enacted in 2013 provided full compensation for land seized from indigenous Zimbabweans, but reaffirmed that foreign nationals will be protected by a BIT whose agricultural land had been acquired and are entitled to full compensation under the BITs.[118]

In its award, the tribunal found the following treaty breaches: direct expropriation, fair and equitable treatment, minimum standard of treatment including denial of justice claims, full protection and security, transfer of funds as well as arbitrary, unreasonable and/or discriminatory measures. The expropriation was without compensation and thus unlawful, according to the tribunal.[119] Furthermore, the government's action was also held to be racially discriminatory because the vast majority of the farms expropriated were white-owned, and the few black owners affected were compensated for the land seized.[120] Finally, the tribunal found the expropriating acts had no legitimate public purpose because the properties had not actually been redistributed, and the claimants were still in possession though government had acquired title.[121] The arbitral tribunal awarded $65 million to investors in compensation. It also ordered Zimbabwe to return farms it seized in 2005.[122]

Relying partly on case law of the ECHR, Zimbabwe argued that its conduct was a proportionate response to quell serious protests peacefully,

---

113 This is the second ICSID case to see European claimants pursue BIT arbitration over Zimbabwe's land policies. The earlier case, *Funnekotter and others v. Zimbabwe*, ICSID Case No. ARB/05/6, resulted in an award in favour of the Dutch claimants, although the claimants have since struggled to collect their award.
114 *Id*, para. 112.
115 *Id*.
116 *Id*, para. 141
117 *Id*, para. 159
118 *Id*, para. 162
119 *Id*, para. 503
120 *Id*, paras 648–657.
121 *Id*, para. 502.
122 *Id*, para. 453.

without resorting to potentially deadly military action.[123] According to the government, its land reform project was applied in good faith, which deserved a wide margin of appreciation from the tribunal.[124] Meanwhile, the claimants contested the applicability of any human rights inspired notions of margin of appreciation or proportionality in investment arbitration, noting that tribunals had generally not accepted proportionality arguments. The claimants also emphasised that racially discriminatory measures could not be considered proportionate, since they were domestically unlawful and also constituted a breach of the peremptory norms under international law.[125]

The tribunal ruled that 'due caution' should be exercised in importing concepts from human rights law, and stated that the concept of margin of appreciation had little support in international investment law.[126] In any case, the tribunal considered that neither proportionality nor the margin of appreciation could justify breaches of *erga omnes* obligations such as the prohibition on racial discrimination.[127] The tribunal added that for the proportionality defence of the government to apply, the state's measures would need to be a response to a serious emergency and to social or political pressures caused by the investor's own conduct which had not occurred and was rejected by the tribunal.[128]

Zimbabwe invoked the customary international law defense of necessity, as expressed in the International Law Commission's (ILC) Articles on State Responsibility.[129] According to the government, during the time of the land seizures, its economy had entered a crisis and 'a grave danger to the existence of the State itself, to its political and economic survival which constitutes conditions of necessity under international law and suggests that the "ongoingness" of the State was threatened through the uprisings in 2000'.[130]

The tribunal disagreed and saw Zimbabwe's crisis as related more to the political survival of the president's government, rather than any essential interest of Zimbabwe.[131] Second, the tribunal found no 'grave and imminent peril' to Zimbabwe justifying the expropriations.[132] The initial incursions onto the properties were not a threat to Zimbabwe's survival, the tribunal held, and could have been controlled by police.[133] According to the tribunal, the economic crisis and alleged peril only arose after the land policies were

123   *Id*, para. 591.
124   *Id*, para. 451.
125   *Id*, para. 622.
126   *Id*, para. 465.
127   *Id*, para. 467.
128   *Id*, paras 455–457.
129   *Id*, para. 613.
130   *Id*, para. 614.
131   *Id*, para. 631.
132   *Id*, para. 637.
133   *Id*, para. 644.

implemented, and the peril was not imminent before the measures were taken.[134]

While the government of Zimbabwe erred in its conduct, it is incongruous that the tribunal rejected the authority of the ECHR case law presented by the state, noting the need for caution in importing human rights norms into arbitration and denied *amicus* participation of the ECCHR and Zimbabwean communities. Yet, the tribunal relied on the ILC Articles and the *Barcelona Traction* International Court of Justice (ICJ) case in order to support the holding that racial non-discrimination was an obligation *erga omnes* on the state.[135]

The tribunal missed an opportunity to be progressive in the application of the rules of interpretation of BITs, which requires the consideration of relevant rules of international law. How this can be achieved and has been done in the past is considered in Chapter 5. The tribunal erred not to consider the margin of appreciation doctrine because its origins are not from international investment law. Such narrow constructions of applicable law are myopic and the tribunal failed to consider that legal systems only develop through comparative analysis of other legal frameworks.

Transition disputes

The third category of disputes are transition disputes, which often happen in developing states where there is a change in the host state's government form that makes it 'politically difficult and/or ethically problematic for a new regime to honour the old regime's commitments to foreign investors even though legally required to do so'.[136] The aftermath of the Arab crisis affecting Libya and Egypt are examples of this where a change in government from a dictatorship and transition to democracy makes it politically difficult for the new governments to honour the commitments of the previous governments. However, in the very unique case of Sudan and South Sudan, this has also occurred.

In *Sudapet Company Ltd v. Republic of South Sudan*, the claimant, Sudapet Company Limited, is a state-owned oil company based in the Republic of Sudan.[137] The company has been embroiled in a publicised dispute with South Sudan following the seizure of the company's stake in South Sudanese oilfields shortly after South Sudan ceded from Sudan.

South Sudan defended its decision to assume control of the shares held by Sudan's state-owned petroleum company in southern oil fields, calling it a 'legitimate act of sovereignty'. South Sudan's oil ministry stated that the two governments of Sudan and South Sudan agreed during pre-secession negotiations that the shares would be transferred to southern ownership along with

134 *Id*, para. 636.
135 *Id*, para. 320.
136 Maupin, *supra* note 106.
137 ICSID Case No ARB/12/26.

the oil fields upon independence.[138] In January 2012, the government of South Sudan decided to halt shipments to northern Sudan and begin constructing an alternate pipeline route to the Kenyan coast.[139] The president of Sudan had initially indicated Sudan would not seek international arbitration over South Sudan's takeover of oil assets when it won independence in 2011, however, this public commitment was not followed through and the arbitration was finalised in 2016.[140]

Despite mediation by the AU, both states could not agree on how much South Sudan should pay Sudan in compensation for taking over oil facilities once owned by state firm Sudapet.[141] The outcome of the award was not published but this case highlights the interconnectedness of regional integration in investment regulation and the need for the development of homegrown African dispute resolution systems to resolve disputes between states.

Tax disputes

The fourth category of disputes relates to tax where 'a change in a host state's tax regime alters the financial framework in a manner that reduces profitability of the investment'.[142]

In the ongoing case of *Total E&P Uganda v Republic of Uganda*,[143] the subject of dispute is the production of oil and the claims arise out of an alleged unlawful tax levied by the government. Total acquired four oil exploration blocks in the Lake Albert region and challenges the imposition of stamp duty by the Uganda Revenue Authority on the acquisition of Total's interest in Uganda's Lake Albert Rift basin. Total has not disclosed how much tax is at the heart of the dispute or why it objects to the tax levy but it has been widely reported that Total's production sharing agreement with the government includes a tax waiver.[144]

The claim by Total is one of many by foreign investors in Uganda's oil sector, often arising out of taxation related issues. Total had purchased its Ugandan interests from Tullow Oil and had also initiated arbitration against Uganda in relation to the capital gains taxes assessed on the sales transactions.[145]

138   *Id.*
139   *Id*; Reeves, E., 2012, 'Oil revenues controversy – country's obstructionism threatens war', viewed (31 March 2017) from http://allafrica.com/stories/201201250523.html.
140   *Id*; 'Sudan Drops Demand for Compensation for Confiscated Oil Assets', viewed (31 March 2017) from www.sudantribune.com/spip.php?article45301.
141   *Id.*
142   Maupin, *supra* note 106.
143   Trevino C., 2015, 'Uganda faces investment treaty arbitration by Total oil company', *IA Reporter*, viewed (29 November 2016), from www.iareporter.com/articles/uganda-faces-investment-treaty-arbitration-by-total-oil-company/
144   Mohamadieh, K. and Uribe, D., *supra* note 110.
145   *Id.*

Culturally sensitive disputes

Additionally, the fifth category of disputes are known as culturally sensitive disputes that might force a state to adopt measures which might affect the interests of an investor.[146] The *Southern Pacific Properties (SPP) (Middle East) Limited v. Arab Republic of Egypt*[147] case is a classic example of this.

The government cancelled a tourism project as a result of fears that the construction of the project would affect the possibility of discovering antiquities on the land.[148] A presidential decree was issued to invalidate the project[149] but the decision of the government had been out of a genuine concern to preserve national artefacts and antiquities.

In African countries where culture and customary law often clash with the exploration of natural resources, taking measures to balance the objectives of resource extraction while safeguarding investor rights and their investment can be challenging for governments. Consequently, it is important to introduce corporate governance obligations such as the development of a framework for consultations and public participation, transparency, obtaining prior agreement from affected communities to guarantee community beneficiation and to secure a company's social license to operate.

Financially disproportionate disputes

Finally, there is the category of financially disproportionate disputes where 'the financial implications of the claim are so large relative to the host state's available resources, that it is financially or politically unfeasible for the government to compensate the investor in full, even if legally obliged to do so'.[150] A timely example of this case in Africa is the *Al Kharafi v. Libya* decision.

In *Al Kharafi v. Libya*, the claimant and investor, Al Kharafi, is a large Kuwaiti conglomerate.[151] The subject of dispute is a lease agreement for the establishment of a tourism project. The claims arise out of the issuance of a decision by the Libyan minister of industry to annul a licence previously granted to the investor for the establishment of an investment project on tourism in Tripoli, Libya.[152]

In 2006, Libya's tourism development authority contracted Al Kharafi to transform 24 hectares plot of land in Tajura, a suburb of Tripoli into a tourist destination.[153] The investment project was authorised to operate over a

---

146 Maupin, *supra* note 106.
147 ICSID Case No. ARB/84/3.
148 *Id*, para. 62.
149 *Id*, para. 65.
150 Maupin, *supra* note 106.
151 Final award rendered under the Unified Agreement for the investment of Arab Capital in the Arab States March 22, 2013, viewed (31 March 2017).
152 *Id*, pp. 4–6.
153 *Id*, p. 21.

period of 90 years, with the first seven and a half years to be devoted to construction and development of the facility.[154] However, construction of the facility was delayed due to the inability of the investor to take control of the land. For several years after signing its contract, the investor would complain repeatedly to authorities that it was hindered and obstructed by various third parties who were using parts of the designated land for recreational and commercial activities and representatives of the claimant were physically assaulted on certain occasions.[155] It also emerged that another local entity, a Libyan bank, had been granted overlapping rights of usufruct to the same land plot.[156] In January of 2009, tourism officials proposed that the investor accept an alternative land, which the investor rejected as impractical.[157] After a further period of inactivity, the Ministry of Industry issued a decree in 2010 annulling the earlier approval of the investor's project.[158] The investor initiated arbitration against the Libyan government in March 2011 and was awarded $935 million by the tribunal. It is the second largest monetary award in the history of treaty based ISDS.

The tribunal had initially dismissed a jurisdictional objection by Libya that the investors had not transferred any capital into Libya, particularly, the 10 per cent fee of the projected costs of $130 million for the project and thus had failed to make any investment that should enjoy coverage under the Unified Agreement on the Investment of Arab Capital into the Arab States.[159] The tribunal found that the investor transferred 0.1 per cent of the project investment value – amounting to $130,000 – to the account of Libya's Tourism Development Authority.[160] The tribunal held that Libya's domestic investment laws prohibit the freezing of projects and the 2010 annulment of the contract was an arbitrary move amounting to a seizure or confiscation of the investment under a false pretext that the claimant had failed to perform its contractual obligations.[161]

In its final award, the tribunal ruled that the investors were entitled to future lost profits of $900 million due to the projected period of operation of 83 years after the seven year development of the project.[162] The tribunal's decision implied that the investors were guaranteed a 'zero risk' return on investment. The tribunal ignored a good faith offer of alternative land by the Libyan government to the investors. Other tribunals have in the past

154   *Id*, p. 4.
155   *Id*.
156   *Id*, p. 27.
157   *Id*, p. 5
158   *Id*.
159   *Id*, p. 50 and 81.
160   *Id*, p. 24 and 81.
161   *Id*, p. 171.
162   *Id*, p. 382.

declined to compensate for future lost profits and the decision of the tribunal in the Libya case is confounding.[163]

The tribunal also awarded the investor $30 million as compensation for moral damages incurred as a result of the damage caused to its reputation, stock and business market around the world.[164]

While the Libyan government certainly erred in its conduct and treatment of the investors, the decision of the tribunal to award a highly disproportionate compensation in favour of the investor shows the importance of carefully weighing the balance of interests between disputing parties, especially where a disputing party is a state. The decision of the tribunal affects a number of issues in this case. The $2 million cost of the arbitration, which progressively increased as the claimant increased the damages, raises some of the concerns around ISDS tribunals and their legitimacy. The tribunal provided a decision that ignored the political reality faced by the Libyan government, which would affect its ability to comply with the award. The tribunal also failed to apply an interpretive approach to the investment contract that would have limited the claim for future lost profits by the investor. On the part of the state, the arbitrariness of the decision of the state in annulling the investment contract, the failure to successfully resolve the dispute out of arbitration in order to mitigate its liability and the inefficiency of the state in concluding a contract that posed unmanageable risks in the eventuality of breach highlights the need for African states to reconsider their approach to concluding IIAs in general.

IIAs have the potential to limit the ability of states to attract investment flows that can support sustainable development. The worrying trend relating to the prohibition of performance requirements is a cause for concern. It has been noted by UNCTAD and other research that 'performance requirements are indispensable in obtaining benefits from foreign investment'.[165] Performance requirements usually cover foreign markets and increase in export capacities, value addition at the national level, technology transfer, research and development, employment generation and spill over in management skills. For host states to benefit from these, their policies need to specify a need for this contribution.[166]

---

163   *PSEG v. Turkey* ICSID Case No ARB/02/5, *Siag v. Egypt* ICSID Case No ARB/05/15 and *Al-Bahloul v. Tajikistan* SCC Case No. V (064/2008).
164   *Al Kharafi v. Libya, supra* note 151 at p. 385.
165   Mohamadieh, K. and Uribe, D., *supra* note 110 at p. 16
166   *Id.*

Conclusion

The essence of the argument being made in this chapter is that concerns around ISDS are more related to substantive outcomes which procedural changes cannot resolve and the focus should rather be on changing international investment law itself. Indeed, arbitration does not exist in a legal vacuum and as a result, the viability of arbitration is dependent on investment protection agreements and criticism should be directed not so much on arbitral interpretation but at the indeterminacy of some of the rules under interpretation.[167] Changing the focus of investment arbitration in favour of a policy choice that is more favourable to states is simply replacing one bias with another, rather than creating a neutral forum. What then are suitable alternatives to current models of ISDS?

Rogers challenges the proposal by Gus Van Harten for the establishment of an international investment court, which rests on the argument that arbitrators are not suitable for the resolution of public law issues that are increasingly arising in international investment arbitration.[168] For Van Harten, the lack of permanency in ISDS affects the independence and impartiality required for judicial adjudication.[169]

Rogers argues that Van Harten's proposal is premised on the idea of a restricted scope of review of state actions, which might be possible in a court structure as opposed to the current system where arbitrators often take an approach that extends the jurisdiction and scope of interpretation of treaties.[170] In support of Van Harten's argument for an investment court, Gathi and Odumosu also propose the establishment of an international court 'to address investor-state disputes that implicate matters that are constitutional in nature and extend beyond purely commercial issues'.[171] However, opponents of the investment court proposal argue that should an investment court be established, the judges would come from the same crop of current arbitrators who take a maximalist approach to ISDS and the system will not improve.[172] Furthermore, the suggestion has been made that the lack of control by developing states over the appointment of arbitrators is the reason why state interests are not being represented adequately in

---

167   Titi, *supra* note 33 at p. 71.
168   Rogers, C., 2013, 'The politics of international investment arbitrators', *Santa Clara Journal. International Law* 12 (223), p. 248.
169   Van Harten, G., 2007, *Investment Treaty Arbitration and Public Law*, Oxford University Press, p. 20.
170   Rogers, *supra* note 168 at p. 269.
171   See Gathi, J. T. and Odumosu, I., 2009, 'International economic law in the third world', *International Commercial Law Review* 11, p. 349.
172   Rogers, *supra* note 96 at p. 251.

ISDS and this anomaly is unlikely to be remedied through the creation of a permanent court.[173]

The political feasibility of an international investment court is weak. There is already a backlash towards the establishment of an international business and human rights treaty and consequently, a global adjudicatory body to enforce such treaty. Consequently, the next chapter proposes four primary alternatives that currently exist and could be utilised to replace ISDS.

173   *Id*, p. 253.

4 Developing alternatives to investor–state dispute settlement

Introduction

There are four main objectives for ISDS. The first is increasing investment flows by providing potential investors with additional security and protections.[1] The second objective is the depoliticisation of investment disputes through ISDS where states are expected to play a lesser role in the resolution of disputes.[2] The third objective is the promotion of the rule of law and the fourth is the provision of remedies.[3] However, the value of ISDS is increasingly being challenged because of its failure to achieve some of these main objectives.[4] The lack of statistical evidence to demonstrate increase in investment flows as a result of BITs and ISDS, the continued presence of state diplomatic pressure to resolve investment disputes and the weakening of the rule of law of domestic systems due to the existence of ISDS are some of the reasons why support for ISDS is eroding. As explained in Chapter 3 of this book, the creation of a parallel legal system through ISDS without the democratic features of participation and transparency among others has been concerning.[5]

As a result, four main alternatives to ISDS are proposed. These are strengthening domestic legal systems, offering political risk insurance to lessen the need for arbitration on investment disputes, using human rights mechanisms for dispute settlement or through state–state dispute settlement mechanisms.[6] These alternatives are assessed with the objective of showing how they complement each other and the value in adopting a combination of options as alternatives to ISDS.

---

1   Johnson, L. and Sachs, L., 2010, 'The outsized costs of investor-state dispute settlement', *Academy of Business Insights* 16(1), p. 10, viewed (25 March 2017) from http://ccsi.columbia.edu/files/2016/02/AIB-Insights-Vol.-16-Issue-1-The-outsized-costs-of-ISDS-Johnson-Sachs-Feb-2016.pdf
2   *Id.*
3   *Id.*
4   *Id*, p. 11.
5   *Id*, pp. 10–11.
6   *Id*, pp. 12–13.

Strengthening domestic legal systems

Emerging BITs of some states have moved towards the application of domestic remedies and the exhaustion of such remedies before any form of ISDS can apply.[7] According to Sornarajah, the legality of an investment is a matter of domestic law and what the local courts have to say about the issue should be given great weight.[8] This is consistent with the view that investments are established in accordance with host state laws and as a result, should be governed by the domestic law of establishment.[9]

Role of domestic legal systems in meeting objectives of ISDS

Investment flows

UNCTAD's research over a period of 15 years suggest that foreign investment flows are determined by a variety of factors including a country's economic attractiveness, policy framework and investment promotion efforts.[10] BITs have been portrayed as one of the many policy instruments available to host countries, which seek to attract foreign investors. It is often assumed that BITs encourage investments by mitigating political risk, liberalising investment flows and, more generally, signal a welcoming business climate to foreign corporations. However, these assumptions are increasingly being challenged as this chapter attempts to demonstrate.

Foreign investment determinants must be used in conjunction with each other to be effective and no individual factor could attract investment flows by itself. In this context, it is difficult to establish the importance of one particular factor. A number of authors have tried to determine the relevance of BIT in attracting foreign investments.[11] One of the first studies looking at the relationship between BITs and investment flows, which was carried out by UNCTAD in 1998, showed that BITs played a minor role in attracting

---

7   Miles, K., 2013, *The Origins of International Investment Law: Empire, Environment and the Safeguarding of the Capital*, Cambridge University Press, p. 379.

8   Sornarajah, M., 2015, *Resistance and Change in International Law on Foreign Investment*, Cambridge University Press, p. 164.

9   *Id*, p. 165.

10   UNCTAD, 2014, IIA Issues Note: The Impact of International Investment Agreements on Foreign Direct Investment: An Overview of Empirical Studies 1998–2014. Working draft, viewed (25 March 2017), from http://investmentpolicyhub.unctad.org/Upload/Documents/unctad-web-diae-pcb-2014-Sep%2016.pdf

11   Sachs, L. and Sauvant, K., 2009, 'BITs, DTTs, and FDI flows'. In Sachs, L. and Sauvant, K., (eds.) *The Effect of Treaties on Foreign Direct Investment: Bilateral Investment Treaties, Double Taxation Treaties and investment Flows*, Oxford, p. xxvii.

investments.[12] Similarly, Hallward-Driemeier looked at the investment flows of 20 developed countries towards 31 other countries between 1980 and 2000, and found an insignificant correlation between BITs and investment flows.[13] Overall, the studies have concluded that if BITs did attract foreign investment, their role was at best enabling and economic factors such as market size and growth, skills, resources and costs proved far more important when making the decision to invest.[14]

Depoliticisation of disputes

Domestic courts can offer an appealing alternative to ISDS. Under this option, the litigation would not be handled by ISDS tribunals but by local courts, which would render definitive and binding decisions. This system would be particularly effective in cases where well-functioning legal systems based on good governance and competent local courts are already in place.[15] Where this is not the case, investment disputes help with strengthening the rule of law in countries with deficient domestic systems. Local judges would be able to develop their expertise in this field thereby enhancing the efficiency and stability of the system in the longer term. However, departing from ISDS would indeed be easier for states that are able to rely on strong pre-existing capabilities within the judicial system, as these would have the potential of constituting a credible alternative. By channelling efforts towards the development of national institutions through domestic judicial reform, states can address some of the deficiencies that burden the current international investment regime.[16]

In states with weaker institutions in particular, there are concerns that courts might lack independence and neutrality and that the executive might interfere with the judicial process through pressure on judges. In terms of applicable procedure, investors might also be concerned that procedures might be delayed and decisions will remain unenforced. However, all these are inherent risks that foreign investors face when investing abroad and should not be used as reasons against the domestic system in flouting respect

---

12   UNCTAD, *supra* note 10; Sachs, L. and Sauvant, K., 2009, 'The impact on foreign direct investments of BITs'. In Sachs, L. and Sauvant, K., (eds) *The Effect of Treaties on Foreign Direct Investment: Bilateral Investment Treaties, Double Taxation Treaties and investment Flows*, Oxford University Press, p. 324.

13   Hallward-Driermeier, M., 2009, 'Do bilateral investment treaties attract FDI? Only a bit … and they could bite', in Sachs, L. and Sauvant, K., (eds.) *The Effect of Treaties on Foreign Direct Investment: Bilateral Investment Treaties, Double Taxation Treaties and Investment Flows*, Oxford University Press, p. 350.

14   UNCTAD, *supra* note 10 at p. at liii.

15   UNCTAD, 2015, *World Investment Report 2015 Reforming International Investment Governance*, viewed (21 March 2017) from http://unctad.org/en/Publications Library/wir2015_en.pdf

16   *Id*, p. 154.

for domestic institutions. Substantive and procedural rules of law such as 'rules of standing, statutes of limitation, requirements of exhaustion, doctrines of abstention, limits on judicial review, limits on available remedies, and rules regarding discovery, privilege, and evidence' have been developed over time to safeguard the integrity of domestic legal systems.[17]

Rule of law

A majority of domestic legal systems are built on the doctrine of separation of powers and checks and balances. In advanced legal systems, well-established processes constitute a safeguard against inconsistency and unpredictability. In addition, administrative or constitutional courts are used to regulate the interactions of governments with private parties.[18] This leads to the establishment of specialised courts in some cases. Consequently, the creation of a domestic court in national jurisdictions entirely dedicated to the treatment of investment disputes is feasible. In the context of the negotiations about the TTIP, the EU's recent proposal to establish an 'investment court system' goes in this direction.[19] Also, some countries such as South Africa, rely on the regime set forth in their constitution to protect foreign investors.[20] These instruments equally support the development of the rule of law by ensuring that regulations are clear, publicised and predictable.

Arbitration at a domestic level is often exclusively accessible by an elite group, which have specific interests in local institutions supporting arbitration.[21] Consequently, when trying to empower domestic legal systems, it is in the interest of the host state that reliance on domestic arbitration should be limited considering the fact that domestic arbitration will also face the same challenges that ISDS faces and might slow down the development of the courts.

---

17 Johnson and Sachs, *supra* note 1.
18 Hindelang, S., 2014 'Part II: Study on Investor-State Dispute Settlement ('ISDS') and Alternatives of Dispute Resolution in International Investment Law Study of Investor-State Dispute Settlement ('ISDS') and Alternatives of Dispute Resolution in International Investment Law', European Parliament, EXPO/B/INTA/2014/08-09-10, p. 76, viewed (21 March 2017) from www.europarl.europa.eu/RegData/etudes/STUD/2014/534979/EXPO_STU(2014)534979(ANN01)_EN.pdf
19 European Union, 2015, *Proposal of the European Union for Investment Protection and Resolution of Investment Disputes, Chapter II – Investment*, European Union, viewed (21 March 2017) from http://trade.ec.europa.eu/doclib/docs/2015/november/tradoc_153955.pdf
20 Section 25, Constitution of the Republic of South Africa, 1996.
21 Rogers, C. A., 2015, 'International arbitration, judicial education, and legal elites', *Journal of Dispute Resolution* 2015, p. 72.

Remedies for investors

BITs provide various legal remedies available to foreign investors such as market compensation for expropriation. Investors sometimes fear that such remedies would not be available should national courts adjudicate investment disputes. An example of this is South Africa where compensation for expropriation follows the constitution's compensation rule of just and equitable compensation. States generally have the right to regulate foreign investments with limited exceptions such as the application of an international treaty such as BITs.[22] However, the interpretation of these agreements in courts will lead to interpretation of BITs against the whole spectrum of domestic law including applicable remedies.

Although the names and categorisations can differ depending on the legal tradition of the host state, local law remedies available to foreign investors can take the form of judicial review or pecuniary remedies.[23] In most judicial systems, non-pecuniary remedies are the primary sources of relief offered to investors in their dispute against the state. However, for claims other than expropriation, pecuniary remedies might be more difficult to obtain before national courts.[24]

Notable features of the domestic legal system

Transparency

Domestic legal systems often employ the principle of open justice to ensure that dispute hearings and the documents of disputing parties are accessible by the public. The publication of judgments also aids the development of the system and gives investors much coveted regulatory certainty. In response to the demands of civil society in terms of accountability of the public and private sectors, governments are taking an increasing number of transparency measures. For example, initiatives such as the Open Government Partnership have attracted 70 member states that develop various commitments including openness within the judiciary as a branch of government.[25] This initiative aims to make states 'more transparent, more accountable, and more responsive to their citizens, with the ultimate goal of improving the quality

---

22   Sornarajah, M., 2010, *The International Law on Foreign Investment*, 3rd edn., Cambridge University Press, p. 88.
23   Gaukrodger, D. and Gordon, K., 2012, *Investor-State Dispute Settlement: A Scoping Paper for the Investment Policy Community*, OECD Working Papers on International Investment, No. 2012/03, 79 (2012) viewed (21 March 2017) from http://dx.doi.org/10.1787/5k46b1r85j6f-en
24   *Id*, p. 80.
25   Marchessault, L. and Jarvis, M., 2013, 'The trend towards open contracting: Applicability and implications for international investment agreements', in Bjorklund, A. (ed.) *Yearbook on International Investment Law Policy*, Oxford University Press, p. 553.

of governance, as well as the quality of services that citizens receive'.[26] An increasing number of countries particularly within developing regions are also adopting freedom of information laws in order to allow citizens to access documents produced by governments.[27] Such laws often provide for narrow exceptions to confidentiality in agreements, which are in direct conflict with confidentiality provisions in traditional BITs. These developments, alongside other initiatives such as the implementation of open contracting principles, are increasingly allowing domestic courts to require the disclosure of BIT awards and details of contracts or concessions awarded by states to foreign investors. These various initiatives play an important role in signalling a country's respect for the rule of law and that traditional investor concerns relating to arbitrary conduct of states that may jeopardise investments can be corrected.[28]

Non-disputing party participation

Domestic legal systems allow third parties to make oral and written submissions to allow judicial officers to take into account broader interests of the public that may have an impact on the outcome of a dispute. However, in civil law jurisdictions, third party submissions are not part of the tradition and courts have not accepted them, although this trend is slowly changing.[29] This trend is also true in investment disputes as more and more rules, including the UNCITRAL Transparency Rules[30] or the ICSID Arbitration Rules,[31] now allow for *amici curiae* submissions.

Correctness

The lack of an appeals procedure, which makes awards final and binding, is mostly considered as one of the advantages of ISDS. However, one of the consequences is that governments only have limited procedural issues that they can rely on to challenge awards. For instance, Article 5 of the New York Convention only provides seven grounds that domestic courts can rely on to

---

26 Open Government Partnership, *Mission and Strategy*, viewed (1 September 2016) from www.opengovpartnership.org/about/mission-and-strategy

27 The website freedominfo.org lists 113 countries that had adopted freedom of information regimes as of 31 June 2016. See *Chronological and Alphabetical lists of countries with FOI regimes*, viewed (3 October 2016) from www.freedominfo.org/?p=18223.

28 Drabek, Z. and Payne, W., 2001, *The Impact of Transparency of Foreign Direct Investment*, World Trade Organization, ERAD-99-02, 7 viewed (25 March 2017) from www.wto.org/english/res_e/reser_e/erad-99-02.doc

29 Kochevar, S., 2013, 'Amici curiae in civil law jurisdictions', *Yale Law Journal* 122, p. 1653

30 UNCITRAL Transparency Rules, Article 4.

31 ICSID Arbitration Rules, Article 37(2).

refuse the recognition or enforcement of an award and these do not include errors of law or facts made by an ISDS tribunal.[32] The lack of a review mechanism has led to inconsistencies in the interpretation of key standards such as fair and equitable treatment or the most favoured nation clause.[33]

In contrast, domestic legal systems often involve multiple layers of appeals. Consequently, the odds of reaching the right result are therefore increased as erroneous decisions in lower courts will have the opportunity to be corrected by higher courts.[34] In common law jurisdictions, the fact that precedents bind lower courts decided by higher courts also support a more stable and predictable system.

Cost

Although the costs of litigation can vary substantially depending on the country and the legal system, they are generally lower that those incurred in arbitration.[35] Furthermore, claims only constitute a portion of the final costs of the arbitration as parties also need to pay the costs related to the administration of the dispute by arbitration institutions such as the ICSID, the fees and expenses of arbitrators and their respective counsels. Some investors have also used costs as a threat against states in the context of business negotiations.[36]

This is structurally different in domestic systems where disputing parties do not have to pay the salaries of judges. Most countries follow the rule of the loser pays with respect to the costs of the proceedings and legal expenses, but few countries have adopted an approach according to which every party has to bear its own costs.[37] In most cases, where a claim is dismissed at the domestic level, the claimant does not have to pay the legal expenses of the government.[38]

32 Bernasconi-Osterwalder, N. and Rossert, D., 2014, *Investment Treaty Arbitration: Opportunities to Reform Arbitral Rules and Processes*, IISD, viewed (25 March 2017) from www.iisd.org/pdf/2014/investment_treaty_arbitration.pdf, p. 15.
33 *Id*, p. 32.
34 Johnson and Sachs, *supra* note 1 at p. 76.
35 Rossert, D., 2014, *The Stakes Are High: A Review of the Financial Costs of Investment Treaty Arbitration*, IISD, viewed (25 March 2017), from www.iisd.org/sites/default/files/publications/stakes-are-high-review-financial-costs-investment-treaty-arbitration.pdf
36 Gallagher, K. and Shrestha, E., 2011, 'Investment treaty arbitration and developing countries: A re-appraisal', *Global Development and Environmental Institute*, Working Paper No. 11-01.5 viewed (25 March 2017) from http://ase.tufts.edu/gdae/Pubs/wp/11-01TreatyArbitrationReappraisal.pdf.
37 Schill, S., 2006, 'Arbitration risk and effective compliance: Cost shifting in investment treaty arbitration', *Journal of World Investment & Trade* 7, pp. 654–655.
38 *Id*.

Impartiality

Domestic legal systems through decades of practice 'have evolved to protect investors' rights and interests from improper treatment and undue interference by government'.[39] Various legal remedies are available to corporations in contract, tort, administrative and constitutional law. The democratic process of appointing judicial officers reduces the likelihood of bias that has confronted arbitrators in some ISDS cases. Though it has been suggested that all countries engage in some form of discrimination or preferential treatment and it is often one of the main fears of foreign investors,[40] there have only been eight known cases out of 600 where allegations of violations of the national treatment obligation have been successfully raised and none of the tribunals in those cases found the violation intentional.[41] Furthermore, investing in a foreign country is intrinsically a risky enterprise as suggested by the arbitral tribunal in *Salini*, which held that investments by definition involve 'an element of risk'.[42] Therefore, the role of host states is not to prevent any kind of financial losses but rather, they are to be treated fairly. Investors have the option of minimising their risk through political risk insurance, which is one of the alternatives discussed in this chapter.[43]

Efficiency

Not all domestic legal systems resolve disputes in a timely manner but procedural rules such as statutes of limitation and the limits on judicial review ensure that the average time for dispute resolution is less than the three and a half year average in ISDS.[44] Another element to take into account in support of the efficiency of the process before local courts is the experience of the judges. Many domestic courts have to refer to public international law as part of the consideration of the whole spectrum of applicable law in domestic legal systems.[45] Furthermore, the knowledge, understanding and expertise of domestic courts on the local legal

---

39   Johnson, L., Sachs, L. and Sachs, J., 2015, 'Investor-State Dispute Settlement, Public Interest and US Domestic Law', viewed (31 March 2017) from http://ccsi. columbia.edu/files/2015/05/Investor-State-Dispute-Settlement-Public-Interest-and-U.S.-Domestic-Law-FINAL-May-19-8.pdf, p. 4.

40   Stiglitz, J.E., 2008, 'Regulating multinational corporations: Towards principles of cross-border legal frameworks in a globalized world balancing rights with responsibilities', *American University International Law Review* 23, p. 451 and 548.

41   Johnson, Sachs and Sachs, *supra* note 39 at p. 12.

42   *Salini et al v. Morocco*, ICSID Case No. ARB/00/4, Decision on Jurisdiction, 152 (Jul. 23, 2001), 42 I.L.M. 609 (2003).

43   Gordon, K., 2008, 'Investment guarantees and political risk insurance: Institutions, incentives and development', *OECD Investment Policy Perspectives*, pp. 92–122, viewed (31 March 2017) from www.oecd.org/finance/insurance/44230805.pdf

44   Johnson, Sachs and Sachs, *supra* note 39 at p. 11.

45   Johnson and Sachs, *supra* note 1 at p. 89.

environment increases the likelihood of courts rendering a decision that is coherent with the relevant legal regime as opposed to ISDS awards that are created in isolation from local regimes.[46]

Accessibility

Domestic rules of access to justice give equal treatment to domestic and foreign investors to approach the courts for dispute resolution. The laws in different countries have evolved to accommodate different forms of dispute settlement including conciliation, mediation, arbitration and the courts, which are all available to investors. Furthermore, the current costs associated with ISDS might preclude small and medium companies from using this system.[47] Resorting to a less costly domestic legal system might therefore enhance access to a fair adjudication of investment disputes.

Deficiencies of the domestic legal system

Domestic courts offer a number of advantages addressing some of the common critiques against ISDS. However, domestic courts will only constitute a viable alternative to ISDS if it is a well-functioning and advanced legal system. Indeed, in a number of cases, there might be perceptions that domestic courts are susceptible to local pressures and favour the state over foreign investors.[48] In other situations, they might also not have the sufficient technical knowledge to adjudicate ISDS disputes in a timely and effective manner.[49]

Nonetheless, no known ISDS case has supported this deficiency claim, which suggests that this deficiency is more fictional than real. Furthermore, foreign investors sometimes see domestic systems as incompetent due to the inability of the judges to appreciate the notion of 'special rights' for investors which investment treaties protect. However, the notion of special rights is the antithesis of the rule of law where all should be treated equally and fairly under the law.

Intersection with the rule of law

The appeals systems in domestic legal regimes ensure that judges and their judgments are reviewed by a higher authority and potentially corrected. The publication of the judgments and the opportunities to appeal also ensure consistency and predictability. Most domestic law systems allow both disputing and non-disputing parties to attend the hearing or make third

46   *Id*, p. 76.
47   UNCTAD, *supra* note 15, at p. 149.
48   Johnson and Sachs, *supra* note 1 at p. 77.
49   *Id*.

party submissions. Domestic systems provide the same substantive protections to states and investors while allowing both parties to initiate proceedings. All these features preserve the judiciary from pressures from the executive and allow for an oversight of executive commitments that may be advantageous to foreign investors. The publicity of the procedures and of the decisions as well as the representation of various interests before democratically appointed judges will ensure shorter time periods for disputes than in ISDS, the outcome of which will be more predictable, ultimately making this option more favourable to investors.

The advantages of resorting to domestic courts may vary significantly based on the unequal levels of development across different legal systems.[50] The corollary of this diverse situation is that it is difficult to establish a blanket solution suitable to every case. BITs could introduce a requirement to litigate a dispute before domestic courts before taking it to arbitration.[51] Another option would be to require ISDS only in cases where local courts fail to meet international standards.[52] In cases where domestic legal systems fail to address some of the investor's concerns, the purpose of BITs should be to use 'cooperative institutional mechanisms' to try to address these weaknesses rather than bypass the domestic process entirely.[53] In doing so, BITs will contribute to strengthening those legal systems so that they can constitute credible alternatives to ISDS, in the interests of both states and investors.

State–state dispute settlement

The idea of state–state arbitration comes across as a retreat to gunboat diplomacy where disputes are politicised. In the SADC Model BIT and in South Africa's recently passed domestic law that aims to protect foreign investors, a preference for state–state arbitration has been expressed.[54] This involves both the host and home states of an investor lodging a dispute in a World Trade Organization (WTO) style approach and the states represent the investors. While the WTO model of dispute settlement has been quite successful, it has been successful as a result of the existence of a multilateral agreement on trade and a permanent structure to resolve disputes. In the absence of a multilateral agreement or convention, the dispute settlement procedure for state–state arbitration will be ad-hoc and remain decentralised. As a result, state parties will be confronted with the current problems facing ISDS in relation to arbitrator bias and procedural mechanisms that might be less favourable to third party participation.

50   *Id*, p. 89.
51   UNCTAD, *supra* note 15 at p. 149.
52   Johnson and Sachs, *supra* note 1 at p. 90.
53   Johnson, Sachs and Sachs, *supra* note 39 at p. 16.
54   Southern African Development Community, 2012, *Southern African Development Community Model BIT*, Article 28.

State–state dispute clauses already exist in many IIAs, but have rarely been activated since ISDS has been the prevailing means of resolving investment disputes.[55] State–state dispute settlement includes dispute resolution through international organisations and tribunals[56] or through an ad hoc quasi-judicial mechanism.[57] Some early IIAs also allowed for judicial remedy at the ICJ or a regional court, such as the COMESA Court of Justice.[58]

Historically, the state played a key role in investment disputes.[59] The criteria for recognising a state–state dispute were through the recognition of (1) a dispute between treaty parties, (2) concerning interpretation and or application of a treaty, (3) remaining after exhaustion of consultative and diplomatic remedies, and (4) pertaining to an issue capable of settlement in accordance with applicable rules of international law.[60] These criteria have been tested in a few state–state arbitrations, but there is still little guidance on how to apply them systematically.

The remedies sought through state–state dispute settlement have taken several forms. At first, it was primarily seen as a way to advance the diplomatic protection claims of individual investors or host states. It has also been used to address questions of interpretation that focus on the meaning and scope of treaty obligations. And finally, it may be used to obtain declaratory judgments about the proper application or interpretation of a treaty.

Partly due to the backlash against ISDS, several countries have started developing investment treaties, such as the Brazilian Cooperation and Investment Facilitation Agreements (CIFAs) that explicitly reject ISDS in favour of state–state dispute settlement.[61] Some scholars have argued that we are now entering a third phase of investment dispute resolution which

55   Only four known state–state arbitrations have been brought under a bilateral investment treaty. See Bernasconi-Osterwalder, N., 2014, 'State-State Dispute Settlement in Investment Treaties', International Institute for Sustainable Development, viewed (31 March 2017) from www.iisd.org/sites/default/files/publications/best-practices-state–state-dispute-settlement-investment-treaties.pdf, p. 1.

56   ASEAN Economic Community, 2004, *ASEAN Protocol on Enhanced Dispute Settlement Mechanism*, Appendix I (Covered Agreements).

57   Bernasconi-Osterwalder, *supra* note 55 at p. 2.

58   Investment Agreement for the COMESA Common Investment Area, Annex A, Article 6.

59   Alschner, W., 2014, 'The return of the home state and the rise of "embedded" investor-state arbitration'. In Lalani, S. and Lazo, R.P. (eds) *The Role of the State in Investor-State Arbitration: Nihoff International Investment Law Series* 3, Koninklijke Brill, pp. 293–333; Trevino, C. J., 2014, 'State-to-state investment treaty arbitration and the interplay with investor-state arbitration under the same treaty', *Journal of International Dispute Settlement* 5(1), pp. 199–233.

60   *Id.*

61   Singh, S. and Sharma, S., 2013, 'Investor-state dispute settlement mechanism: The quest for a workable roadmap', *Merkourious: Utrecht Journal of International Law and European Law* 29(76), pp. 88–101.

combines the initial state focused and the current investor focused approach to create a hybrid that includes both types of mechanisms.[62]

Investment flows

Given the paucity of successful state–state dispute settlements under BITs, it is impossible to definitively state what impact this mechanism may have on investment flows. However, this lack of empirical evidence applies equally to ISDS, and the two mechanisms may both contribute to investment flows as part of a larger infrastructure for international economic activity.[63]

Theoretically, state–state dispute settlement may contribute to investment flows in three ways: encouraging activities among states that strengthens the rule of law, increasing diplomatic negotiations among states and improving domestic state policy.[64]

First, state–state dispute settlement can help bring consistency to the interpretation of investment law by creating a consistently applied process, introducing the potential for appeal and enabling more proactive responses to emerging disputes.[65] For example, WTO jurisprudence, given its consistency and quasi-jurisprudential approach, has demonstrated a high deterrent value and encouraged compliance with free trade agreements.[66] Increasing the use of state–state dispute settlement could have a similar effect for BITs, encouraging investor confidence in treaty application and the rule of law more generally.

Second, by encouraging states to take a more active role in investment treaty implementation, the states themselves will be encouraged to negotiate and articulate clear and mutually beneficial trade agreements. For example, in negotiating its CIFAs with several countries, Brazil has included provisions to facilitate information sharing between parties outside of the dispute resolution process.[67]

---

62   See Roberts, A., 2014, 'State-to-state investment treaty arbitration: A hybrid theory of interdependent rights and shared interpretive authority', *Harvard International Law Journal* 55(1), pp. 1–70.

63   See Franck, S.D., 2007, 'Foreign direct investment, investment treaty arbitration, and the rule of law', *Global Business and Development Law Journal* 19, pp. 337–373.

64   Bernasconi-Osterwalder, *supra* note 55, at p. 2.

65   Alschner, *supra* note 59, at p.194–195.

66   Davis, C., 2008, 'The Effectiveness of WTO Dispute Settlement: An Evaluation of Negotiation Versus Adjudication Strategies', *Annual Meeting of the American Political Science Association*, p. 37.

67   See Bernasconi-Osterwalder, N. and Dietrich-Brauch, M., 2015, 'Comparative Commentary to Brazil's Cooperation and Investment Facilitation Agreements (CIFAs) with Mozambique, Angola, Mexico, and Malawi', *International Institute for Sustainable Development*, viewed (31st March 2017) from www.iisd.org/sites/default/files/publications/commentary-brazil-cifas-acfis-mozambique-angola-mexico-malawi.pdf, p. 7.

Finally, state involvement in investment disputes will help policy makers to better understand the needs and concerns of investors. States will be able to ensure that their intentions, as enshrined in a treaty are advanced, and also to align treaty implementation with wider goals of inclusive development and human rights. This is especially true given the changing nature of both FDI and international economic activity, as new types of entities enter the global marketplace and investment flows deviate from the traditional North–South paradigm. A state–state dispute settlement model ensures that different types of investors, who may be locked out of the ISDS model due to resources or influence, will have the opportunity to advance grievances through their home state.

Depoliticisation of investment disputes

One driver towards ISDS was the legitimate anxiety that state–state dispute settlement is prone to politicisation. For example, the majority of trade disputes at the WTO arise when there is domestic political pressure to adjudicate or when respondent states prove resistant to diplomatic pressure.[68] Home states often try to protect the rights of their own investors, while host states are influenced by their own political reality and unique state of affairs. States are also repeat players, and may have incentives to collude with other states to further their interests rather than those of individual investors.[69]

However, no matter who participates in the dispute settlement process, most investment disputes have a political character; their transnational nature and the sectors that disputes often arise in – mining, oil, gas – are highly politicised arenas.[70] This inevitability means that allowing state involvement may not actually create further politicisation, but rather ensures that interested parties are able to efficiently advance their own interests and ensure an efficient outcome.

This danger can also be mitigated through procedural agreements and rules. State–state dispute settlement can draw on the leadership of a standing body to drive reform and ensure fairness, similar to the role of the WTO secretariat.[71] State–state disputes can also be depoliticised through proactive establishment of neutral bodies with cooperative decision making powers. For example, the Brazilian CIFAs establish both a joint committee, with representatives from both state parties, and two independent ombudspersons, who

---

68   Davis, *supra* note 66 at pp. 35–36.
69   Alschner, *supra* note 59 at p. 193.
70   See Lubambo, M., 2016, 'Is state-state investment arbitration an old option for Latin America?', *Conflict Resolution Quarterly* 1.
71   Smith, J., 2004, 'Inequality in international trade? Developing countries and institutional change in WTO dispute settlement', *Review of International Political Economy* 11, p. 542 and 544.

provide information or assistance to solve issues before they escalate.[72] Such mechanisms can help to diffuse tensions between states caught up in diplomatic wrangling.

Rule of law

Unlike ISDS, some state–state dispute mechanisms require exhaustion of domestic remedies, which can help strengthen domestic legal systems by adding an additional layer of review. Using tools such as declaratory relief may also provide more clarity for domestic legal systems on accepted interpretations of treaty provisions.[73]

However, state–state mechanisms can also compromise domestic rule of law. By giving effect to administrative decisions or interpretations that have not been subject to democratic review, the process weakens domestic institutions. Similar to ISDS, state–state dispute settlement may also compromise rule of law by giving international investors preferential treatment over domestic investors, due to the additional layer of review/appeal that is available to foreign investors after the exhaustion of domestic remedies.[74] Decisions that advance the rule of law for all investors may be comparatively harmful when established through state–state dispute settlement since they are outside of a *stare decisis* legal framework.[75]

Making state–state dispute settlement a more open and transparent process mitigates this danger to some extent. Another way to mitigate is to ensure that the scope of state–state dispute settlement is confined to very narrow grounds of treaty interpretation or application. In this regard, only the most significant or contentious cases could rise to the level of state–state dispute settlement, with investors expected to utilise domestic systems for most disputes.

At an international level, ISDS has serious collateral implications on the rules of state responsibility.[76] Conversely, state–state dispute settlement has proven more willing to apply and align with principles of customary international law.[77] For example, the WTO has gradually recognised that trade disputes often have human rights implications, and WTO provisions should align with international human rights law where possible; an example is the

---

72   See Bernasconi-Osterwalder, N. and Dietrich-Brauch, M., 2015, 'Brazil's Innovative Approach to International Investment Law', International Institute for Sustainable Development, viewed (31 March 2017) from www.iisd.org/blog/brazils-innovative-approach-international-investment-law

73   *Id*, p. 14.

74   Franck, *supra* note 63 at p. 365.

75   *Id*.

76   Paparinskis, M., 2013, 'Investment treaty arbitration and the (new) law of state responsibility', *European J. Int'l L.* 24(2), p. 24.

77   Pauwelyn, J., 2001, 'The role of public international law in the WTO: How far can we go?', *Am J. Int'l L.* 95, p. 535 and 540.

Doha Declaration on Trade-Related Aspects of Intellectual Property Rights (TRIPS) and Public Health, which established standards of public health within the WTO system.[78] The CIFAs in Brazil also include voluntary principles of responsible business conduct that align with both domestic and international legal norms.[79]

This embrace of international legal norms is not without limit, and a shortcoming of state–state dispute settlement may be that the mechanism will not be empowered to interpret or apply international legal norms outside of the IIA itself. The WTO has struggled with this problem because they are limited to interpreting and applying legal norms within the narrow confine of the WTO legal framework. This will limit state–state dispute settlement in a similar way to ISDS because collateral issues such as human rights and state responsibility may be outside the scope of the state–state dispute settlement jurisdiction. One means of addressing this would be to resolve claims through a standing international tribunal, such as the ICJ or a specially created international investment court, similar to the proposal advanced by the EU. Such a court could be empowered, with the consent of the parties, to apply state obligations beyond the confines of the IIA in dispute.

Additionally, utilising state–state dispute settlement may actually complement the existing ISDS framework.[80] Investors and states have very different interests when it comes to investment treaties, and allowing a complementary process will ensure that there is more equitable distribution of power within the dispute settlement process.[81] Furthermore, state–state dispute settlement may also help capital importing countries to obtain more influence by encouraging capital exporting countries to agree to definitive interpretations.[82]

For ISDS and state–state dispute settlement to work together, Roberts argues that it should be based on the idea of states and investors sharing interdependent rights in any dispute.[83] Therefore, any arbitral decision should have precedential influence over any subsequent disputes, either through a theory of *res judicata, lis pendens* or *collateral estoppel*; in this

78   World Trade Organization, 2003, Introduction to the WTO dispute settlement system, pp. 53–54 viewed (25 March 2017) from www.wto.org/english/tratop_e/dispu_e/disp_settlement_cbt_e/intro1_e.htm; Marceau, G., 2002, 'WTO dispute settlement and human rights', *European J. Int'l L.* 13, p, 753 and 756.
79   Bernasconi-Osterwalder and Dietrich-Brauch, *supra* note 72.
80   For a discussion of potential alignment of ISDS and state–state dispute settlement, see Trevino, C.J. *supra* note 59.
81   Roberts, *supra* note 62.
82   *Id*; Alschner, *supra* note 59 at p. 216.
83   Roberts, *supra* note 62 at p. 37.

paradigm, the home state and its investors share the same claim and the same rights over that claim, but only one can advance the disputes.[84] Roberts suggests that investment disputes would be the domain of investor–state disputes, while states could advance interpretative, diplomatic protection, or declaratory judgments that would create binding precedent for any subsequent investor–state disputes.[85]

Remedies

State–state dispute settlement can expand potential remedies for investors by considering a broad range of obligations, which ISDS is not capable of enforcing.[86] State–state dispute settlement has typically addressed three types of claims: diplomatic protection cases, interpretive questions or a request for declaratory relief due to breach.

Claims for diplomatic protection seek reparation for internationally wrongful acts against an individual investor. These claims require exhaustion of local remedies, and are often pursued at the discretion of the state.[87]

While standing courts like the ICJ often act in an advisory capacity, state–state dispute settlement has not been used to determine abstract interpretative questions.[88] However, it has the capability to do so such as in the case of *Mexico v. the United States*, where a claim was not brought on behalf of a specific investor.[89] Using state–state dispute settlement to solve interpretive problems may help improve efficiency by curtailing costly and complex disputes early. For example, the Joint Committees in Brazil's CIFAs provide a mechanism for state parties to discuss 'questions of interest to an investor' before there is a formal dispute.[90] The interpretative powers can also facilitate decisions in parallel investor–state arbitration, as it did in the cases of *Peru v. Chile* and *Ecuador v. United States*.[91]

State–state dispute resolution may also be able to provide declaratory relief by determining that a specific act or initiative has violated a treaty. Obtaining restitution or pecuniary compensation has traditionally been difficult through state–state dispute settlement. New models, however, such as the Brazilian CIFAs allow for payment of monetary compensation.[92]

84   *Id*, p. 43.
85   *Id*.
86   Lubambo, *supra* note 70 at p. 18.
87   Trevino, *supra* note 59 at p. 8.
88   *Id*, pp. 6–7, especially the discussion of *Ecuador v. United States*.
89   Bernasconi-Osterwalder, *supra* note 10 at p. 1.
90   Bernasconi-Osterwalder AND Dietrich-Brauch, *supra* note 72.
91   *Id*. at p. 1.
92   Lubambo, *supra* note 70 at p. 16.

Notable features of state–state dispute settlement

Transparency

Transparency remains an issue in state–state dispute settlement. While the WTO has improved transparency mechanisms,[93] resolution of state–state disputes is still a closed process. Only member states have direct access to the dispute settlement system, and non-disputing parties do not have direct access to ongoing disputes.[94] The submissions of the complainant, respondent and third party states are only released with the parties consent.[95]

Non-disputing party participation

Under the WTO state–state dispute settlement, panels and appellate bodies have the discretion to accept or reject *amicus* submissions, but are not obliged to consider them; the panels have, however, allowed submissions from civil society actors on human rights issues.[96] However, *amici* have no access to the submissions of the parties. Other international fora, such as NAFTA, have much clearer rules for *amicus curiae* participation.[97]

Correctness

One concern among states has also been the substantial inconsistency in the decisions of ISDS, since it means that states have little control over how the treaties that they are signatories to are interpreted and applied.[98] State–state dispute settlement would mitigate this by allowing states to represent their own views on interpretation.[99]

The legitimacy of international fora for state–state dispute settlement can also contribute to perceptions of correctness. For example, the WTO is a highly regarded system that ostensibly correctly interprets and applies multilateral rules; the priority of the WTO is to settle a dispute and not pass judgment.[100] Furthermore, many state–state dispute settlements have the

93   Marceau, G. and Mikella, H., 2012, 'Transparency and public participation: A report card on WTO transparency mechanisms', *Trade, Law and Development* 4, pp. 42–43.

94   WTO, *supra* note 78.

95   *Id.*

96   *See* Marceau and Hurley, *supra* note 93 at pp. 30–31.

97   *Id*, p. 35.

98   See OECD, 2012, 'Government perspectives on Investor-State Dispute Settlement: A progress report' viewed (25th March 2017) from www.oecd.org/daf/inv/investment-policy/ISDSprogressreport.pdf

99   *Id.*

100   World Trade Organization, Introduction to the WTO dispute settlement system (2003), viewed (25th March 2017) from www.wto.org/english/tratop_e/dispu_e/disp_settlement_cbt_e/intro1_e.htm

benefit of a built-in appeals process that allow parties to seek second opinions, such as the WTO Appellate Body. An appellate structure would, however, implicate many questions about standard of review, choice of law and domestic remedies.[101]

Costs

State–state dispute settlement is not markedly different from ISDS in terms of total cost. State–state dispute settlement generally has an equitable cost structure, and states equally share the costs of proceedings. Costs of arbitrations will vary based on the mechanism established. A WTO dispute that goes through the panel proceedings may cost an average of $1.5 million and can easily exceed this for complex and lengthy disputes. However, the cost burden can be shifted and help ensure that less wealthy investors, such as small and medium sized enterprises (SMEs), will not be shut out of the system. State–state dispute settlement may also reduce costs by seeking declaratory or interpretative pronouncements that will preclude or prevent further investor-state disputes.

Impartiality

State–state dispute settlement can politicise investment disputes by maintaining the involvement of states. However, state–state dispute settlement at the ICJ or the WTO demonstrates that state politics do not necessarily hinder equitable and binding outcomes. The impartiality of arbitrators at the WTO has garnered some criticism, as arbitrators are selected by the parties and represent a similar "multiple hats" problem as seen in ISDS.[102]

There are, however, other models of arbitrator appointment for state–state dispute settlement. NAFTA establishes a five member panel, with each party selecting two panellists who are citizens of the other disputing party, and the disputing parties selecting the chair of the panel.[103] The COMESA process stipulates that the COMESA secretary-general will select all panels or arbitrators.[104] The proposed EU multilateral investment court would replace arbitrators altogether in favour of sitting judges at a permanent court.[105]

---

101 Sachet Singh and Sooraj Sharma, *supra* note 61.
102 Bernasconi-Osterwalder, *supra* note 1 at p. 3.
103 North American Free Trade Agreement (NAFTA), art. 2011(3) (1994).
104 Investment Agreement for the COMESA Common Investment Area, Annex A, Article 6.
105 European Commission, 2016, 'Establishment of a Multilateral Investment Court for investment dispute resolution', viewed (25 March 2017) from http://ec. europa.eu/smart-regulation/roadmaps/docs/2016_trade_024_court_on_investment_ en.pdf

State–state dispute settlement could be integrated into proposals for an international investment court with jurisdiction over state–state disputes and standing judges. Not only would this improve consistency in decision making, it would also ensure that individual parties are not able to cherry pick favourable arbitrators.

Efficiency

State–state dispute resolution protects the rights of the sovereign to regulate in the public interest and to pursue their own strategic interests. Not only does this ensure that foreign investors are not empowered to unduly influence host governments, but it also allows states to negotiate in the best interests of both the states and the investors. Most state–state dispute settlements will also need to demonstrate that disputes could not be resolved through consultations or other diplomatic channels, by requiring negotiation or mediation attempts before bringing the court into an adversarial system.[106] This prevents unnecessary cases that will need to be arbitrated.

However, most attempts at preliminary consultation and mediation are ad hoc. At the WTO, these consultations are confidential and are not required to produce any documentation, but the claims and facts laid out during the consultation phase have significant bearing on the shape of subsequent panel and appellate decisions.[107] Under the still amorphous CIFA system in Brazil, the initial consultation in the Joint Committee must collectively produce a report that details their respective positions and efforts to resolve the dispute, which will be used to determine the initial recommendations.[108] While all of the documents and meetings of the proceedings are confidential, the summary report will be publicly available.[109]

A limitation to the efficiency of state–state dispute settlement is that it can be a time consuming process, with the target for WTO dispute resolution set at one year and three months, which includes a consultation period, a panel process and an appeal; the actual time period is often longer.[110]

Accessibility

State–state dispute settlement would foreclose direct access by investors, whose interests would need to be represented by their home state. State–state dispute settlement will also not be open to domestic investors in their

106 Trevino, *supra* note 59 at p. 13.
107 Horlick, G.N. and Butteron, G.R., 2000, 'A problem of process in WTO jurisprudence: Identifying disputed issues in panels and consultations', *Law & Policy in International Law* 31, pp. 573 and 574–579.
108 Bernasconi-Osterwalder and Dietrich-Brauch, *supra* note 72 at p. 14.
109 *Id.*
110 WTO, *supra* note 100.

own state, which may lead to inequitable outcomes between foreign and domestic investors. There are, however, ways of ensuring that the process is less discretionary. For example, there could be established rules about when states should or should not pursue claims of one of its investors. Some suggestions that have been made to improve the regularity of claims include having a formal, administrative procedure for advancing claims, insulating the division making decisions from more politicised decisions, or the creation of a special court of international claims or a commission.[111] Additionally, in the USA, the State Department provides informal support to claimants even if espousal is not possible, and is able to link potential claims to other diplomatic tools, like sanctions, which encourages timely and efficient decisions on the merits of each claim.[112]

Additionally, most forms of state–state dispute settlement are open to third party participation and transparency, which would allow investors to be involved. While the Brazilian model precludes initiation of disputes, the investor is allowed to participate in the proceedings.[113] Investors' representatives can submit briefings to the joint committees and can participate in the meetings of the Joint Committee.[114] Furthermore, the parties agree to make reasonable efforts to be transparent to relevant stakeholders.[115]

Deficiencies of state–state dispute settlement

State–state dispute settlement may share many of the same deficiencies as ISDS. It is often an ad hoc and secretive process utilising the same body of arbitrators, it may have deleterious effects on domestic rule of law, and the links to increased investment flows are tenuous. It is a slow and laborious process that would require significant resources from both states. Furthermore, it presents the risk of further politicising investment disputes. However, unlike ISDS, many of the deficiencies for state–state dispute settlement can be mitigated through procedural consistency and through leveraging the diplomatic standing of states to find alternative solutions.

Intersection with the rule of law

State–state dispute settlement allows for a procedurally fair and consistent process that gives interested state parties access to several tiers of legal review. It expands the scope of remedies available to parties by virtue of increased

---

111   Christenson, G.A., 1962, 'International claims procedure before the Department of State', *Syracuse Law Review* 13, pp. 527 and 531–532.
112   *Id*, pp. 539–540.
113   Bernasconi-Osterwalder and Dietrich Brauch, *supra* note 72.
114   Brazil-Mozambique Cooperation and Investment Facilitation Agreement, 2015, Article 15.
115   *Id*, Article 13.

state involvement, and often allows for involvement of third parties to a dispute to make submissions. State–state dispute settlement systems differ in their level of transparency and their protections for investors, but strong procedural rules could overcome these shortcomings.

State–state dispute settlement is, however, not without flaws. Any legal mechanism that may give legal effect to an administrative official's actions without legislative sanction can compromise the domestic rule of law. This 'undermines the role of domestic institutions and courts in their core responsibilities of developing, interpreting, and applying the law'.[116] Therefore, the exhaustion of domestic remedies is crucial for aligning state–state dispute settlement with the rule of law.

Improving transparency, developing coherent participation rules for interested parties and guidelines for the selection of arbitrators or judges, and clarifying the intersection of state–state dispute settlement mechanisms with other domestic and international legal fora would improve the current system of state–state dispute settlement. State–state dispute mechanisms should consider non-disputing party submissions and allow access to the proceedings. This means clarifying third party participation, improving transparency of submissions and also being more proactive in integrating stakeholders into the system.[117] State–state dispute settlement should also draw from an expanded pool of panellists who can bring diverse viewpoints and expertise to the proceedings.[118]

In order to ensure that state–state dispute settlement does not seriously compromise the rule of law, BITs should ensure that domestic remedies have been exhausted before recourse to an international body.[119] Several scholars have also recognised the potential value of an interdependent system of state–state and investor–state settlement.[120] However, in order for this system to function, it is necessary to clarify boundaries between systems.

Political risk insurance

Political risk insurance (PRI) is rapidly emerging as an alternative and complement to existing mechanisms for resolving clashes between foreign investors and host states. PRI '[c]overs political events, including the direct

116   Johnson and Sachs, *supra* note 1.
117   Bernasconi-Osterwalder and Dietrich Brauch, *supra* note 72.
118   Sacerdoti G., 2016, 'Panelists, arbitrators, judges: A response to Joost Pauwelyn', *AJIL Unbound* 19, pp. 283 and 286.
119   Bernasconi-Osterwalder, *supra* note 10, at p. 20.
120   Roberts *supra* note 62; see also Wong, J., 2014, 'The subversion of state-to-state investment treaty arbitration', *Columbia Journal for Transnational Law* 53, viewed (25 March 2017) from http://jtl.columbia.edu/wp-content/uploads/sites/4/2015/01/Wong-Article-53-CJTL-6.pdf, p. 7.

and indirect actions of host governments'.[121] Events that are traditionally covered by various types of PRI include: expropriation, currency inconvertibility, transfers restriction, political violence (war, terrorism and civil disturbance), breach of contract and arbitration award default.[122] Over the past few decades, three major forms of PRI have emerged: national public PRI, multilateral public PRI and private PRI. All these forms are discussed systemically below.

Investment flows

Economic trends show that FDI has been steadily increasing since the 1980s.[123] However, the proportion of FDI that is covered by PRI has actually been decreasing.[124] PRI can increase investment flows because insurers peg the premiums charged to investors based on the political risk of a state which disciplines states into avoiding political events that might deter FDI if a state is rated as highly risky by an insurer. However, if a host country knows that an investor has insurance against a disruptive legal reform, the host country might be more likely to engage in that behaviour than it would otherwise. Likewise, an insured company might engage in less oversight and due diligence in its dealings with a host country if it has insurance. This moral hazard could make companies more willing to invest because the costs of oversight and diligence are lowered, or might repel investment out of fear that these moral hazards will result in a less cooperative host country.

Depoliticisation of disputes

The degree to which PRI can ameliorate politicisation depends on the type of PRI. In the case of public PRI, which is funded by government, agencies must operate within the confines of legislative mandates and executive oversight. This ensures public insurance providers are pressured democratically into including human rights requirements in their threshold conditions for providing coverage. However, this could also lead to either direct or indirect pressure on the insurance agency to provide coverage, refuse to pay out a claim or go after a host country in a politically biased way.[125]

---

121 Multilateral Investment Guarantee Agency (MIGA), *World Investment and Political Risk 09*, p. 47 viewed (25 March 2017) from www.miga.org/documents/WIPR13.pdf
122 *Id.*
123 *Id*, p. 46.
124 *Id.*
125 The Overseas Private Investment Corporation (OPIC) is congressionally mandated to foster private initiatives in less developed countries and to be responsive to their developmental needs. OPIC is controlled, in some respects by the political climate in Congress (Khachaturian, A., 2005, 'Are we in good hands: The adequacy of American and multilateral political risk insurance programs in fostering international development', *Connecticut Law Review* 38, p. 1041).

Governments have inside, non-public information that can be priced into policies[126] and can use their diplomatic clout to avert triggering events before they occur.[127] This is valuable for public insurers because they have to pay out less often, and can also protect an investor's stake in overseas projects. Furthermore, even if a claim is paid out, if the public insurer gains subrogation rights, national governments can obtain compensation from foreign governments reducing the final cost of the pay out.[128]

In the case of multilateral PRI, dynamics inherent to organisations such as the World Bank's Multilateral Investment Guarantee Agency (MIGA) are political. From a global perspective, there are 53 African countries that are part of MIGA and can offer political risk insurance to foreign investors. MIGA is composed of multiple countries – both capital exporting and capital importing countries – that collectively control its decision making with regard to coverage and subrogation.[129] This means that the ways in which MIGA goes after claims after an investor claim has been subrogated are less related to a single nation's political agenda and more likely the result of international consensus.[130]

Rule of law

The strength of a host country's rule of law may determine whether an investor wants PRI. For example, in the case of currency inconvertibility, the US Overseas Private Investment Corporation (OPIC) is more likely to successfully compensate for investor loss than an ISDS tribunal.[131] In addition to being influenced by the ambient strength of a nation's rule of law, PRI can itself support the rule of international law. PRI providers, especially public providers such as OPIC, can specifically require compliance with certain international human rights norms before an investor can gain coverage. For example, OPIC imposes a set of requirements or restrictions on a potential investor – the proposed project must '(i) apply consistent and sound environmental standards; (ii) apply consistent and sound workers' rights standards; (iii) observe and respect human rights; (iv) have no negative impact on the US economy; and (v) encourage positive host State development effects'.[132]

126   DeLeonardo, J.M., 2004, 'Are public and private political risk insurance two of a kind? Suggestions for a new direction for government coverage', *Virginia. Journal of International Law* 45, p. 769 (discussing the application of George Ackerlof's *Market for Lemons* in the context of PRI).
127   *Id.*
128   Bekker, P. and Ogawa, A., 2013, 'The impact of bilateral investment treaty (BIT) proliferation on demand for investment insurance: Reassessing political risk insurance after the "BIT Bang"', *ICSID Rev.* 28(2), p. 339.
129   *Id.*
130   *Id*, pp. 17–18.
131   Bekker and Ogawa, *supra* note 128 at p. 346.
132   *Id*, pp. 341–342.

These provisions put public PRI insurers in stark contrast to ISDS, where governments rarely incorporate 'environment, labor, anti-corruption or human rights' into their BITs.[133]

Remedies

The remedy available under PRI is simply the pay-off associated with the triggering political event. In some cases, PRI such as MIGA require an exhaustion of local remedies before a claim will be paid out. Therefore, the failure to gain a remedy under local court systems (or failure to successfully enforce an arbitral win against a host country) is required before a PRI remedy can be claimed.

Notable features of PRI

Transparency

Public (and multilateral) insurers are typically more transparent about their insurance decisions, and the entities they cover, than private actors. State sponsored insurance is more likely to be made publically available whereas private insurers are more likely to keep contract information confidential.[134] However, public PRIs only publish aggregate financial information[135] and as Gordon notes, 'there is no standard disclosure practice by publicly-sponsored investment guarantee programs and there is little publicly-available information about some programs'.[136]

Correctness

The determination of PRI claims is made not by courts but rather by insurers themselves. Therefore, while investors can arbitrate or mediate with insurers over contested claims, there is no public, judicial precedent or appellate review. Lack of precedent and review allows individual and political biases to creep into insurer decisions. Multilateral insurance organisations, like MIGA, have higher levels of correctness compared to single state PRI providers because MIGA relies on coordinated governance and consensus of a majority of countries. Therefore there are less likely to be political or

---

133 Gordon K., 2008, 'Investment Guarantees and Political Risk Insurance: Institutions, Incentives and Development', *OECD Investment Policy Perspectives*, viewed (25 March 2017) from www.oecd.org/finance/insurance/44230805.pdf, p. 107.

134 Bekker and Ogawa, *supra* note 128 at p. 323. Note that this may be true in name only, public PRI releases information in batches that might not allow political risk attributable to human rights violations to be readily discerned.

135 Gordon, *supra* note 133 at p. 98.

136 *Id.*

diplomatic biases that drive particular decisions or outcomes. Since political risks can occur over a period of time, there is uncertainty as to when an insurance claim is triggered.

Cost

Structurally, insurance and arbitration have different constraints and outcomes. For example, a PRI claim cannot exceed the amount insured, while an ISDS settlement has no upper limit.[137] This is consistent with the claim that the net costs of PRI are higher than those of ISDS. In addition, because disputes over claims can arise between the insurer and the investor, the transaction costs of arbitration or mediation in a claims dispute need to be added to the insurance premium costs. Though not a direct cost to investors, the transaction costs of arbitration in the case of subrogation also weigh against the net social utility of PRI as compared to ISDS.

Efficiency

ISDS claims average three years and seven months, while insurance claims from OPIC, for example, are processed in less than five months.[138] However, efficiency is not a guaranteed attribute of PRI because some insurers, like MIGA, require investors to 'first exhaust domestic remedies before seeking insurance compensation'.[139] In that case, PRI can be as long as domestic legal systems or ISDS.

Accessibility

PRIs are not designed to offer every type of coverage.[140] For example, MIGA does not cover '[m]easures normally taken by governments to regulate their economic activities such as taxation, environmental and labor legislation as well as normal measures for the maintenance of public safety'.[141] Similarly, while OPIC has coverage gaps related to expropriation, OPIC does not compensate investors for 'partial expropriations, actions provoked by the investor, lawful regulation or taxation by host states, or actions taken by the host acting in its commercial capacity'.[142]

---

137   See generally Bekaert, G. et al., 2014, 'Political risk spreads', *Journal of International Business Studies* 45(4), p. 326.
138   Bekker and Ogawa, *supra* note 128 at p. 327.
139   Khachaturian, *supra* note 25 at p. 1041.
140   *Id.*
141   *Id.*
142   *Id.*

Deficiencies of PRI

Due to PRI coverage, host countries engaged in a PRI covered project have 'reduced market incentives' to make reforms and take advantage of learning opportunities.[143] If host countries know that investors are insured, they are less likely to take other steps to signal that their environment is safe for investment.[144] This also means that host countries are less encouraged to strengthen their rule of law.[145]

Intersection with the rule of law

In so far as public PRI is backed by the home government, the agency will be accountable to the legislature and the executive – therefore the government has more direct responsibility for the activities of insured investors. Private insurers are less accountable and they are governed by industry regulations applicable to all insurers. Multilateral insurance bodies such as MIGA are accountable to the various governments of the international system as a whole and must abide by the consensus of the majority of the international community. It is advisable that PRI agencies develop disclosure practices in order to allow consistency, uniformity and transparency for investors and the PRI claims covered by the various entities. PRI providers can also provide procedural safeguards against moral hazards built into coverage such as excluding coverage that an investor could have reasonably avoided.[146]

Regional human rights courts

There are three major regional human rights courts currently in operation: the European Court of Human Rights (ECHR), Inter-American Court of Human Rights (IACHR), and the African Court on Human and People's Rights (ACHPR). There are procedural practices in the ECHR and IACHR that would improve the utility of the ACHPR as an investment dispute resolution forum.

Investment flows

The existence of human rights mechanisms may have a positive signalling effect for potential investors, since it suggests adherence to the rule of law.[147] Regional human rights mechanisms may also promote investment flows

143   Gordon, *supra* note 133 at p. 94.
144   *Id.*
145   *Id.*
146   *Id.*
147   The relation between economic growth and democracies has been explored by a vast literature, with conflicting findings. *See* UNDP, *Human Development Report, 2002,* viewed (31 March 2017) from http://hdr.undp.org/sites/default/files/reports/263/hdr_2002_en_complete.pdf. Furthermore, there is a strong claim that democratic

because they can directly protect investors against state abuse. Nevertheless, this ability is conditioned by jurisdiction, which is limited to claims framed as human rights violations. In the Inter-American and African systems, rules of jurisdiction prevent companies from directly accessing the system, since the courts only analyse claims related to the rights of natural persons.

Depoliticisation of investment disputes

Regional human rights courts are international institutions. As a result, they are shielded from domestic politics and are regarded as impartial dispute settlement mechanisms. There is a robust appointment process, which ensures the appointment of independent and impartial judges.[148] States nominate candidates, which are then subject to an election by state parties to the relevant treaty.[149] In order to ensure that such procedure does not hinder judicial independence, judicial guarantees are established similar to those of domestic courts, as well as measures specific to the international system, including analysis by an independent committee (ECHR), the prohibition to participate in decisions related to one's country of nationality (IACHR)[150] and diplomatic immunities and privileges (African Court).[151]

The possibility of deferment to the domestic law, courts and policies of states may raise concerns about the effectiveness of regional human rights mechanisms. In the ECHR, the court uses the doctrine of margin of appreciation as a methodology to decide whether or not to defer to the expertise of domestic courts. Such doctrine grants states broad discretion in relation

practices associated to civil and political rights contribute to stability because they prevent social and economic shocks. See also Vizaed, P., 2006, *Poverty and Human Rights: Sen's 'Capability Perspective' Explored*, Oxford University Press, p. 117. Among other reasons, this is because they provide institutional forms of managing and overcoming conflict. See UNDP, *Human Development Report, 2002*, p. 57.

148   In all three systems, lack of transparency and accountability has led to questions about states' reasons to appoint an individual, as well as about judges' freedom from undue influence. *See* Lambach, J. et al., 2003, *Judicial Independence: Law and Practice of Appointments to the European Court of Human Rights*, Interights, viewed (6 May 2017) from www.lhr.md/images/appointment.pdf; Ruiz-Chiriboga, O., 2012, 'The independence of the Inter-American judge', *The Law and of International Courts and Tribunals* 11(1), pp. 111–135; Viljoen, F., 2012, *International Human Rights Law in Africa*, 2nd edn, Oxford University Press, p. 11.

149   Organization of American States, American Convention on Human Rights art. 21, Nov. 22, 1969, O.A.S.T.S. No. 36, 1144 U.N.T.S. 123 [American Convention] at art. 53; Convention for the Protection of Human Rights and Fundamental Freedoms art. 34, Nov. 4, 1950, 213 U.N.T.S. 221 [European Convention] at art. 22; Organization of African Unity, Protocol to the African Charter on Human and People's Rights on the Establishment of an African Court on Human and People's Rights, [African Protocol] at art. 11–22.

150   Art. 55, The American Convention on Human Rights, Advisory Opinion OC-20/09, Inter-Am. Ct. H.R. (ser. A) No. 20.

151   Art. 11–22, *African Protocol, supra* note 149.

to protection of property rights.[152] In particular, the determination of which circumstances justify public interest interferences falls within the states' margin of appreciation, meaning the court only steps in to prevent arbitrary interferences.[153] Nevertheless, such possibility of deferment does not necessarily amount to politicisation of disputes – it merely recognises that the institutional features of domestic courts' as well as knowledge and expertise on the entire spectrum of domestic law make them more capable of reaching a decision that considers the relevance and application of domestic law.

In the Inter-American and African systems, the smaller number of precedents related to investment law hampers generalisations. However, deferment to states is unusual, and therefore a theory of consistent deferment to domestic authorities has not been developed.[154]

Rule of law

Human rights mechanisms are the ultimate upholders of the rule of law because they apply multilateral human rights treaties that safeguard universally agreed human rights for all. Their involvement in the resolution of investment disputes gives much needed legitimacy to investor–state dispute resolution.

Aside from adding legitimacy to particular investment settlements, the oversight of state–investor relations by human rights courts might strengthen the rule of law in a broader sense. The consistent application of universal human rights standards to investments might clarify how international human rights law will be applied in relation to investment claims, benefiting not only investors but also individuals and communities affected by their activities. In order to avoid future claims, states might replicate those standards in national policies, effectively spreading the implementation of human rights and strengthening the rule of law.

In the Inter-American and the African courts, states may directly ask the regional human rights court for clarification of provisions in treaties by submitting a request for an advisory opinion. Once the opinion is issued, states could use the advisory opinion to strengthen their defences in ISDS

---

152 Contreras, P., 2012, 'National discretion and international deference in the restriction of human rights: A comparison between the jurisprudence of the European and the Inter-American Court of Human Rights', *Northwestern Journal of International Human Rights* 11, p. 28.

153 See de Sena, P., 2009, 'Economic and non-economic values in the case law of the European Court of Human Rights', in Dupuy, P. et al., (eds) *Human Rights in International Investment Law and Arbitration*, Oxford University Press.

154 Contreras, *supra* note 152.

cases, producing evidence of obligations under international law and fostering human rights awareness within investment disputes.[155]

However, because of the requirement to exhaust domestic remedies, the decision of regional human rights courts and the subsequent implementation of the judgment might have a negative result in unsettling the applicable domestic law of states.[156] The authority of the court may be questioned, leading to an overall decrease in legal certainty.[157] However, in practice, it is unlikely that decisions of a regional human rights court can strike down a law that is consistent with applicable international human rights principles.

Under international human rights regimes, the possibility of review is narrowly tailored to the protection of human rights within the scope of such norms. Most importantly, states specifically consent that their actions – including judgments from their highest courts – be subject to international scrutiny. International human rights frameworks, which were designed by states through the exercise of their sovereignty, operate under the premise that their regional courts' decisions prevail whenever there is a conflict with previous domestic rulings.

Remedies

Breaches of international law must be remedied through adequate, effective and prompt reparation.[158] Remedies may include restitution, monetary compensation, rehabilitation (in the form of medical, psychological, social or legal services), satisfaction (relates directly to the nature of each violation, but may include measures directed at stopping violations, truth seeking, official apologies and public recognition of the violations) and non-repetition (directed at preventing future violations).[159]

The IACHR systematically determines wide ranging remedies, which combine some or all of the above mentioned measures.[160] If applied to

155   For an exposition about the possible use of advisory opinions in relation to investment; see Cordes K.E., et al., 2016, 'Land deal dilemmas: Grievances', *Human Rights, and Investor Protections*, Columbia Center on Sustainable Investment, viewed (6 May 2017) from http://ccsi.columbia.edu/files/2016/03/CCSI_Land-deal-dilemmas.pdf, p. 34.

156   For example, *Gomes Lund et al. ("Guerrilha do Araguaia") v. Brazil*, Preliminary Objections, Merits, Reparations, and Costs, Judgment, Inter-Am. Ct. H.R. (ser. C) No. 219 (Nov. 24, 2010).

157   For example, *Indigenous Communities of the Xingu River Basin, Pará v. Brazil*, PM 382/2010, Inter-Am. Comm'n H.R. (2011), viewed (October 31 2016) from www.oas.org/en/iachr/decisions/precautionary.asp

158   Basic Principles and Guidelines on the Right to a Remedy and Reparation for Victims of Gross Violations of International Human Rights Law and Serious Violations of International Humanitarian G.A. Res. 60/147 Law, viewed (31 March 2017) from http://legal.un.org/avl/pdf/ha/ga_60-147/ga_60-147_ph_e.pdf, art. 18–23.

159   *Id.*

160   Pasqualucci, J.M., 2013, *The Practice and Procedure of the Inter-American Court of Human Right*, 2nd edn, Cambridge University Press.

investment related issues, such a broad range of measures could foster the consolidation of a friendly environment for investors, with decreased risk of arbitrary interferences. However, with the exception of monetary compensation measures,[161] compliance rates with IACHR rulings are relatively low. In addition, monetary awards tend to be significantly lower than those established by ISDS, and the determination of specific values might be deferred to national authorities.[162]

In the ECHR, although other types of measures are possible, remedies are usually in the form of monetary payments.[163] While ISDS applies market value for expropriation compensation, the ECHR takes different circumstances into account and balances competing interests.[164]

Notable features of regional human rights courts

Transparency

All three regional human rights systems have publicity rules which apply to decisions, hearings and documents related to the proceedings.[165] Although requests for confidentiality may be permissible, they must be grounded on compelling reasons and are subject to approval by the court.[166]

---

161 Dulitzky, A., 2011, 'The Inter-American human rights system fifty years later: Time for changes', *Quebec Journal of International Law*, special edn.

162 Nikken, P., 2009, 'Balancing of human rights and investment law in the Inter-American system of human rights', in Dupuy, P. et al. (eds), *Human Rights in International Investment Law and Arbitration*, Oxford University Press.

163 Eur. Ct. H.R., Rules of Court, 2016, viewed (25 March 2017) from www.echr.coe.int/ Documents/Rules_Court_ENG.pdf.

164 Reiner, C. and Schreuer, C., 2009, 'Human rights and international investment arbitration', in Dupuy, P. et al. (eds), *Human Rights in International Investment Law and Arbitration*, Oxford University Press; Kriebaum, U., 2009, 'Is the European Court of Human Rights an alternative to investor-state arbitration?', in Dupuy, P. et al. (eds), *Human Rights in International Investment Law and Arbitration*, Oxford University Press. These applicable standards are: Unlawful interferences must be fully compensated:
   (i) Lawful interferences are subject to scrutiny by the Court, which may result in compensation awards amounting to less than market value.
      (i) In cases of expropriation, compensation is subject to a nuanced analysis, in light of the specific circumstances of the case, such as the purpose of the interference and the proportionality of adopted measures.
      (ii) In cases of regulations of use or other lawful interferences, states enjoy a wide margin of appreciation.

165 Eur. Ct.H.R., Rules of Court, *supra* note 163, at arts. 33, 63, 78; Organization of African Unity, Protocol to the African Charter on Human and People's Rights on the Establishment of an African Court on Human and People's Rights, 1998, viewed (31 March 2017) fromvb www.refworld.org/docid/3f4b19c14.html. [*African Protocol*], art. 10; Inter-Am. Ct. H.R., Rules of Procedure art. 32, viewed (31 March 2017) from www.cidh.oas.org/Basicos/English/Basic20.Rules%20of%20Procedure%20of%20the%2 0Court.htm

166 Eur. Ct.H.R., Rules of Court, *supra* note 163.

The three courts also foster transparency within states subject to their jurisdiction. For example, in a case related to environmental damage, the Inter-American Court held that freedom of speech entails not only the right to impart information, but also to receive and access information.[167]

Nevertheless, there are concerns about transparency of the human rights systems themselves. There have been concerns on the lack of information about the initial phases of proceedings,[168] budget management and institutional arrangement.[169] Overtime, this double standard, which requires states to comply with certain transparency parameters but does not enforce them within the institution itself, might erode a court's legitimacy and credibility. It might also decrease predictability (in terms of duration of proceedings, standards applied to initial stages, among others), therefore increasing uncertainty and associated costs.

Non-disputing party participation

Although proceedings vary, all three regional human rights systems allow non-disputing parties to make representations that address other interests beyond those of the complainants and the defendants.[170]

Correctness

Exhaustion of domestic remedies gives regional human rights courts the advantage of examining disputes after they have gone through the whole spectrum of domestic law. Therefore, they are in a position to reach an equitable decision. However, only the ECHR offers the possibility of appeals[171] – in the African and Inter-American systems, the judgment of the court is final.[172] In the African Court, a party may apply for a review of a

---

167   *Claude Reyes et al. v. Chile*, Merits, Reparations, and Costs, Judgment, Inter-Am. Ct. H.R. (ser. E), No 151 (Sep. 19, 2006).

168   For example, in accordance with the Rules of Procedure of the Inter-American Commission on Human Rights, the Commission only makes cases public after it reaches a decision on their admissibility. Cases that are not opened for processing are never made public.

169   Jimenez, M.P., et al., 2016, 'Towards a model of transparency and access to information in the Inter-American human rights system', in Reynolds, K.A. (ed.), *The Inter-American Human Rights System Changing Times, Ongoing Challenges*, Due Process of Law Foundation, pp. 95–128.

170   *Id*; Inter-Am. Ct. H.R., Rules of Procedure, art. 44; European Convention, *supra* note 149 at art. 36; Eur. Ct.H.R., Rules of Court, art. 44; African Court on Human and Peoples' Rights, Rules of Procedure, art. 70, viewed (25 March, 2017) from http://en.african-court.org/images/Protocol-Host%20Agrtmt/Final_Rules_of_Court_for_Publication_after_Harmonization_-_Final__English_7_sept_1_.pdf

171   European Convention, *supra* note 149 at art. 44.

172   American Convention, *supra* note 149 at art. 67; African Court on Human and Peoples' Rights, Rules of Court, *supra* note 170 at art. 61.

previous judgment due to the discovery of new evidence.[173] At the IACHR, the court might issue clarifications about how prior judgments should be interpreted, but there is no possibility of substantial review.[174]

Costs

Costs of litigating before a regional human rights court are substantially lower than those of ISDS.[175] In addition, human rights mechanisms have introduced cost mitigation rules to aid applicants approaching them. For instance, at the ECHR, the court is allowed to reimburse applicants the costs and expenses incurred at the domestic level. These costs include legal assistance, court registration fees, travel and subsistence expenses for attendance at a hearing of the court. Although in a less comprehensive manner, the IACHR and the African Court also provide financial assistance for victims lacking resources for litigation. These provisions increase access to justice, especially for individuals who may have limited budget available for legal costs.

However, pursuing a claim before regional human rights courts might be a lengthy endeavour due to the exhaustion of domestic remedies, and investors may see this delay as a cost. In addition, although the ECHR proceedings last an average of three years,[176] in the other systems, cases are longer. Both at the IACHR and at the African Court, cases need to pass a regional human rights commission before reaching the court. At the IACHR, considering both the commission and the court phases, the total duration of the proceeding has been estimated to last ten years.[177]

Impartiality

Appointments of the judges are through nomination and election processes by member states. The members of the court are often esteemed legal experts in their countries of origin and are tasked to interpret multilateral treaties agreed to by states and not the domestic law of states. As a result, the systems are designed to be impartial to any country's rules, and judges must act in an independent capacity, not as representatives of the interests of the state which appointed them.

173 African Court on Human and Peoples' Rights, Rules of Court, *supra* note 170 at art. 67.
174 American Convention, *supra* note 149 at art. 67.
175 Kriebaum, *supra* note 164.
176 Eur. Ct. H.R., European Court of Human Rights: The ECHR in 50 questions, 2014, viewed (25 March 2017) from www.echr.coe.int/Documents/50Questions_ENG.pdf
177 Sanchez, N.C. and Ceron, L.L., 2016, 'The elephant in the room: The procedural delay in the individual petitions system of the Inter-American system', in Reynolds, K.A. (ed.), *The Inter-American Human Rights System: Changing Times, Ongoing Challenge*, Due Process of Law Foundation, pp. 207–248.

Efficiency

If determined in terms of costs, duration and outcomes (understood as compliance to rulings), then the measurement of efficiency is dependent on the institutional capacities of each system. The ECHR has the most solid institutional arrangement and provides a relatively low cost proceeding and high compliance rates. However, the institutional vulnerabilities of the other systems result in long proceedings, limited access to financial legal assistance, unpredictable delays and low compliance rates.

Accessibility

Access to human rights mechanisms only takes place after domestic remedies have been exhausted. Once this requirement is met, the ability of human rights mechanisms to directly protect investors depends on two factors: jurisdiction *ratione personae* that enables investors and companies to present their claims; and jurisdiction *ratione materiae* that allows courts to analyse the relevant rights and issues. For a human rights court to have *ratione materiae*, investors must frame their claims within the scope of rights protected by the applicable human rights treaties. In general, their interests are mainly protected through the protection of property rights and protections against discrimination. Most regional human rights courts have their own rules on jurisdiction. However, unlike ISDS, in all regional human rights courts, nationality is not relevant to the determination of jurisdiction.[178]

The ECHR protects property rights through the concept of possession,[179] which encompasses legitimate expectations of gains.[180] Protection of property rights is comprehensive under the ECHR and the court considers claims related to expropriation, as well as regulations of use and other state interferences.[181] The European Convention, which is the applicable law under consideration in the ECHR, extends these rights and protections to legal entities.[182] Accordingly, companies may present a petition in relation to its own rights. The standing of shareholders is independent to the company's standing, which means they may present independent claims if the company (or its liquidators) cannot do so.[183] Nevertheless, the court does not have jurisdiction to analyse shareholders' claims related to indirect damages.[184]

178   Kriebaum, *supra* note 164.
179   European Protocol, *supra* note 149 at art. 1.
180   *Pine Valley Developments Ltd et al. v. Ireland*, 1991-XIV Eur. Ct. H.R. (ser. A) 319.
181   Kriebaum, *supra* note 164.
182   European Convention, *supra* note 149 at art. 34.
183   *Agrotexim v. Greece*, 1995-XXI Eur. Ct. H.R. (ser. A) 250.
184   Kriebaum, *supra* note 164.

The American Convention on Human Rights also protects the right to property.[185] However, the rights established by the American Convention apply exclusively to natural persons.[186] Therefore, although legal entities may present a petition to the Inter-American system, it must refer to the rights of an individual.[187] However, the American Convention offers some protection to companies, since the IACHR has jurisdiction to analyse rights of natural persons exercised through legal entities.[188] In such circumstances, in order to establish jurisdiction, the applicant must demonstrate that damages to the company affected shareholder's property.[189] The same logic applies to other Convention rights relating to non-discrimination where the court requires demonstration of a clear link between the legal entity and the rights of a natural person.[190]

Similarly, companies do not have independent standing before ACHPR,[191] but the African Convention expressly protects the right to property.[192] In that regard, the African Commission on Human and People's Rights has ruled that the Convention grants 'protection from arbitrary deprivation of the enjoyment of property rights, adequate compensation for public acquisition, nationalisation or expropriation, peaceful enjoyment of property and protection from arbitrary eviction'.[193] However, the African Court – which is the most recent of the regional courts – is yet to develop any jurisprudence on this right.

---

185 American Convention, *supra* note 149 at art. 21.
186 *Id*, art. 1.2; *Banco de Lima v. Peru*, Case 10.169, Inter-Am. Comm'n H.R., Report No. 10/91, OEA/Ser.L/V/II.79. doc. 12, rev.1 (1991); Entitlement of Legal Entities to Hold Rights Under the Inter-American Human Rights System, Advisory Opinion OC-22/16, Inter-Am. Ct. H.R.(ser. A) No. 22 (Feb. 26, 2016) [*Entitlement of Legal Entities*].
187 American Convention, *supra* note 149 at art. 44.
188 *Cantos v. Argentina*, Merits, Reparations, and Costs, Judgment, Inter-Am. Ct. H.R. (ser. C) No. 97 (Nov. 28, 2002); Granier et al. (Radio Caracas Television) v. Venezuela, Preliminary Objections, Merits, Reparations, and Costs, Judgment, Inter-Am. Ct. H.R. (ser. C) No. 293 (Jun. 22, 2015); *Entitlement of Legal Entities*.
189 *Perozo et al. v. Venezuela*, Preliminary Objections, Merits, Reparations, and Costs, Judgment, Inter-Am. Ct. H.R, (ser. C) No. 19 (Jan. 28, 2009); *Granier et al. (Radio Caracas Television) v. Venezuela*, Preliminary Objections, Merits, Reparations, and Costs, Judgment, Inter-Am. Ct. H.R. (ser. C) No. 293 (Jun. 22, 2015); *Entitlement of Legal Entities*, *supra* note 186.
190 *Entitlement of Legal Entities*, *supra* note 186.
191 African Protocol, *supra* note 149.
192 American Convention, *supra* note 149 at art. 14.
193 *Dino Noca v. Democratic Republic of the Congo*, Communication 286/04, Afr. Commission H.P.R. (Oct. 12, 2013), viewed (25 March 2017) from www.achpr.org/files/sessions/52nd/comunications/286.04/achpr52_286_04_eng.pdf

Besides property protections, the three regional frameworks protect individuals against arbitrary interference with other rights including non-discrimination, legality and due process of law.[194] In particular, the principle of non-discrimination is a central feature of international human right regimes, which has been considered a norm of *jus cogens*.[195] This means it is hierarchically superior to other international legal obligations. Likewise, one of the cornerstones of ISDS is to protect foreign investors against discriminatory treatment, both in relation to nationals (materialised in the requirement to provide national treatment) and to other foreign investors (embodied in the concept of most favoured nation treatment).[196] In principle, foreign investors claims related to either of these situations can be framed within international human rights norms protecting against discrimination.[197]

Deficiencies of regional human rights courts

Some of the deficiencies of regional human rights courts to effectively serve as alternatives to ISDS include limits to jurisdiction *rationa personae*. Although jurisdiction might be established indirectly in the case of the African Court and IACHR, all damages must be demonstrated in direct relation to a natural person, significantly limiting the scope of analysis. There are also limits to jurisdiction *rationa materiae* as well because all claims must be framed as human rights claims. Although human rights treaties protect property and other associated rights, jurisdictional limits might hinder analysis of issues specific to investment law.

Furthermore, the standards of jurisdiction *rationa materiae*, particularly, in relation to the African Court and IACHR, which have not yet developed a robust jurisprudence on investment related claims, are unclear. However, even in the ECHR, there are issues, which remain open, such as the possibility of granting special protections to foreign investors in cases of lawful expropriation.

The length of proceedings and associated costs, mainly as a result of the requirement to exhaust domestic remedies, the fragile institutional capacity of the courts and the low values of monetary compensation are additional concerns.

---

194   For a comprehensive rights-based approach to business development, *see* FRA, 'Freedom to conduct a business: Exploring the dimensions of a fundamental right', 2015, viewed (25 March 2017) from http://fra.europa.eu/sites/default/files/fra_uploads/fra-2015-freedom-conduct-business_en.pdf

195   Juridical Condition and Rights of Undocumented Migrants, Advisory Opinion OC-18/03, Inter-Am. Ct. H.R. (ser. A) No. 18, 101 (Sep. 17, 2003).

196   Diebold, N.F., 2011, 'Standards of non-discrimination in international economic law', *Int'l & Comp. L. Q.* 60, pp. 831 and 866.

197   de Sena, *supra* note 153.

Intersection with the rule of law

Like domestic legal systems, human rights mechanisms offer a transparent process and representation for non-disputing parties. The mechanisms operate after the exhaustion of domestic remedies, and the courts consistently apply multilateral treaties to disputes. These procedures offer an institutional framework that ensures the outcomes of the disputes are fair and legitimate. Human rights courts also allow the publication of judicial opinions and ensure equal rights of disputing parties to access judicial remedies.

In addition to these features, regional human rights systems offer a substantial advantage in relation to ISDS. They are not limited to the provisions of a specific IIA, allowing courts to take into consideration other obligations that the parties may have under international law. This possibility, combined with the courts' human rights expertise, enables more comprehensive assessments of complex scenarios. In addition, people adversely affected by investment activities may also assess regional human rights courts, both through third party intervention and by directly filing petitions. These factors offer significant advantages from a rule of law perspective such as striking a fair balance between the rights and obligations of states, investors and affected communities.

Conclusion

All the alternative proposals to ISDS have some level of credibility and advantages but they also have flaws. The adoption of alternatives to ISDS requires a combination of the various approaches discussed in this chapter. There is no perfect system to replace ISDS and ultimately, perhaps our collective energy and focus should be directed towards dispute prevention. Roberto Echandi has led the charge for states to focus on dispute prevention. The proposal is supported by UNCTAD and involves the development of various state 'institutional mechanisms to prevent disputes from emerging and to avoid the breach of contracts and treaties on the part of government agencies'.[198] This also takes into account obligations under investment agreements when developing domestic policies.[199]

198   UNCTAD, *supra* note 10 at p. xiv.
199   *Id.*

5 Promoting sustainable development and human rights through investment treaties

Introduction

As discussed in Chapter 2 of this book, one of the reasons for a backlash against ISDS is the broad scope of interpretation adopted by tribunals, which extends beyond the scope of investor protections to the public policy space of states. This chapter aims to understand how investment agreements can be drafted and interpreted to ensure that public policy interests to promote sustainable development and to hold foreign investors accountable for human rights are taken into account in investment rule making. This chapter focuses on how tribunals can apply rules of treaty interpretation to consider relevant rules of international law, including human rights law. It also considers how states can raise defences that allow the use of other international obligations of a state as a justifiable infringement on the limitation of investor and investment protections.

Applicable rules for treaty interpretation

The ILC codified the customary rules on the interpretation of treaties in the Vienna Convention in article 31. Central to the text of article 31 are several tenets of interpretation for international treaties. The concept of 'good faith' in interpretation, 'ordinary meaning', 'context', 'object and purpose of the treaty', 'the text of the treaty including its preamble', 'agreement or instrument made in connection with the treaty', 'subsequent agreement or practice between the parties', 'relevant rules of international law' and the 'intention of the parties' are some of the relevant considerations arising from article 31 and are important for developing a human rights friendly IIA.

Good faith

The ICJ in the *Nuclear Tests* case stated that 'one of the basic principles governing the creation and performance of legal obligations, whatever their source, is the principle of good faith'.[1] This was further developed in the *Pulp Mills* case where it was held 'that "every treaty in force is binding upon the parties to it and must be performed by them in good faith."

That applies to all obligations established by a treaty, including procedural obligations which are essential to co-operation between states'.[2] According to Bjørge, 'there is a connection between the obligation upon states to, on the one hand, create and perform their legal obligations and, on the other hand, to interpret the same legal obligations ... and just as interpretation depends upon creation, performance depends upon interpretation'.[3] Therefore, the connecting thread between the creation, performance and interpretation of investment obligations is the good faith of both parties in entering an investment relationship based on the intention of the parties.

Good faith interpretation means dispute settlement tribunals are not bound by any preferred interpretation of the disputing parties. According to Kingsbury and Schill, 'a good faith reading of the text of the applicable treaty in context and in light of the object and purpose of the treaty may well indicate that interpretation calls for a balance to be struck between investor protection and state regulatory powers'.[4] Tribunals are to engage in an objective review of the language of treaties and determine what the treaty parties intended. Such good faith interpretation requires tribunals to consider the ordinary meaning, text, object and purpose of the treaty.

Ordinary meaning

This is the starting point of any textual interpretation. Determination of ordinary meaning is not a grammatical analysis of the treaty language only. It also involves looking for the understanding of the meaning of a text in the

---

1   'It is well recognised that declarations made by way of unilateral acts, concerning legal or factual situations, may have the effect of creating legal obligations. Nothing in the nature of a quid pro quo, nor any subsequent acceptance, nor even any reaction from other States is required for such declaration to take effect. Neither is the question of form decisive. The intention of being bound is to be ascertained by an interpretation of the act. The binding character of the undertaking results from the terms of the act and is based on good faith; interested States are entitled to require that the obligation be respected' (Summaries of Judgments, Advisory Opinions and Orders of the International Court of Justice, *Nuclear Tests (Australia v. France) (New Zealand v. France)* ICJ Rep 1974).

2   *Pulp Mills on the River Uruguay (Argentina v. Uruguay)*, Judgment ICJ Rep 2010, para. 145.

3   Bjørge, E., 2012, 'Evolutionary Interpretation and the Intention of the Parties', University of Oslo Faculty of Law Research Paper No. 2012–33, (October 2012) SSRN 6.

4   Kingsbury, B. and Schill, S., 2009, 'Investor-state arbitration as governance: Fair and equitable treatment, proportionality and emerging global administrative law', Public Law and Legal Theory Paper Series, Working Paper No. 09–46, Sept. 2009, p. 23 quoted in Kulick, A., 2012, *Global Public Interest in International Investment Law*, Cambridge University Press, p. 170.

treaty through reference to other provisions in the treaty such as the preamble, which will give a consistent meaning to what the parties intended throughout the treaty. An example of this is how to treat an exceptions clause as either self-judging or non-judging. Where the exception in a treaty can be constructed to be non-judging but every other text in the treaty including the preamble shows that the intention of the parties was for the exception to be a self-judging clause, then a good faith review of a tribunal in applying the ordinary meaning of a text should reflect the true intention of the parties. This highlights the importance of treaty drafters defining treaty provisions more clearly, ensuring that they utilise a number of interpretive frameworks such as country statements, the preamble, and interpretive notes to clarify the language of treaties and ensure that there is no room for ambiguity.

Context

The context in which a treaty was concluded also assists tribunals in qualifying the ordinary meaning of the terms of a treaty. It prevents sole reliance on literal interpretation and aids the determination of the true intention of the parties if more than one meaning exists. The context of the terms of a treaty includes a consideration of the stated aims and objectives of a treaty which will be reflected in the preamble to the treaty, the title of the section in which a provision has been placed for such as an exemption, a state obligation or investor protection, and other factors such as whether the treaty being considered is a translated version of a treaty concluded in a different language. Article 32 of the Vienna Convention provides that:

> Recourse may be had to supplementary means of interpretation, including the preparatory work of the treaty and the circumstances of its conclusion, in order to confirm the meaning resulting from the application of article 31, or to determine the meaning when the interpretation according to article 31:
> (a)   leaves the meaning ambiguous or obscure; or
> (b)   leads to a result, which is manifestly absurd or unreasonable.

This rule is a subsidiary to article 31 and remains an exception to the rule that the ordinary meaning of a treaty prevails. There is a strict separation from article 31 to discourage resort to article 32 where article 31 applies. However, it allows for the consideration of the circumstances of the conclusion of a treaty and confirms the meaning of a provision.

Object and purpose

The object and purpose of a treaty are two separate elements, however, they are one unitary concept and are subordinate to the consideration of ordinary meaning of the text of a treaty. The starting point is finding the purpose from the preamble of the treaty. The preamble sheds light on the object and purpose of a treaty. In the *LG&E Energy Company et al v. The Argentine Republic* case, the tribunal referred to the preamble of the treaty in defining the scope of the fair and equitable treatment protection for investors. The tribunal held that:

> In considering the context within which Argentina and the United States included the fair and equitable treatment standard, and its object and purpose, the Tribunal observes in the Preamble of the Treaty that the two countries agreed that "fair and equitable treatment of investment is desirable in order to maintain a stable framework for investment and maximum effective use of economic resources." In entering the Bilateral Treaty as a whole, the parties desired to "promote greater economic cooperation" and "stimulate the flow of private capital and the economic development of the parties". In light of these stated objectives, this Tribunal must conclude that stability of the legal and business framework is an essential element of fair and equitable treatment in this case, provided that they do not pose any danger for the existence of the host State itself.[5]

Spears argue that in the interpretation of investment agreements, the preamble of the agreements which sets out the objectives of the parties in concluding the agreement must be considered.[6] As a result, new IIAs should contain statements that relate to principles of sustainable development, that the policy objectives are self-standing objectives of the agreement and parties do not intend to relinquish their right to regulate in the public interest.[7]

---

5   ICSID case no ARB/02/1(Decision on Liability) 3 October 2006, para. 122–124; see also *Saluka Investments BV (The Netherlands) v. The Czech Republic* (Partial Award) 17 March 2006, para. 298 where the tribunal held 'the immediate "context" in which the "fair and equitable" language of Article 3.1 is used relates to the level of treatment to be accorded by each of the Contracting Parties to the investments of investors of the other Contracting Party. The broader "context" in which the terms of Article 3.1 must be seen includes the other provisions of the Treaty. In the preamble of the Treaty, "the Contracting Parties recognised that agreement upon the treatment to be accorded to such investments will stimulate the flow of capital and technology and the economic development of the Contracting Parties and that fair and equitable treatment is desirable." The preamble thus links the "fair and equitable treatment" standard directly to the stimulation of foreign investments and to the economic development of both Contracting Parties'.
6   Spears, S., 2011, 'Making way for the public interest in international investment aagreements' in Brown, C. and Miles, K. (eds), *Evolution in Investment Treaty Law and Arbitration*, Cambridge University Press, p. 292.
7   India-Singapore Agreement, Canada-Colombia Agreement and ASEAN-China Investment Agreement.

Subsequent agreement and practice of the parties

Aside from the object and purpose of a treaty, the agreement or instrument in connection with the conclusion of a treaty is also relevant.[8] Parties to a treaty have the freedom to vary treaty terms after the conclusion of a treaty. The agreement of all the parties will be required and subsequent practice of the parties will constitute objective evidence of the understanding of the parties regarding the meaning of the treaty. Evidence of subsequent agreement includes joint publications of investment guides and interpretive statements. For subsequent practice, an example of objective evidence will include subsequent agreements concluded by parties with other states or arguments made by parties in other dispute settlement proceedings in relation to the meaning of a treaty text.

Due to the way investment treaty obligations have been interpreted broadly, states can develop the approach of including interpretive language in their investment agreements that require a balancing exercise to determine whether a government's actions in response to legitimate regulatory concerns have violated investors' rights.[9]

Legitimate expectations are often used by investors in making the case against states in breach of treaty violations. Consequently, state practice and conduct are becoming increasingly central to the interpretation of treaty obligations. All the proposals discussed here are interlinked and favour an integration of various rules for a coherent approach to interpretation.[10]

Integrating socio-economic development and human rights in BITs

The rise of investment treaties, investment disputes and the scope of some interpretations of investors' rights by some arbitration tribunals have fuelled a considerable amount of literature suggesting that international investment law may be in a crisis of legitimacy.[11] The recent activities by some states not to renew BITs or to develop model BITs that restrict investor protections and denounce the ICSID Convention support the argument that the

8   In the *Yaung Chi OO Trading v. Myanmar* award, a joint press release by the parties was found to constitute an agreement by the parties in connection with the treaty.
9   Spears, *supra* note 6 at p. 275.
10   See Prislan, V., 2012, 'Non investment obligations in investment treaty arbitration – Towards a greater role for states?', in Baetens, F. (ed.), Investment Law Within International Law: An Integrationist Perspective, Cambridge University Press.
11   Franck, S.D., 2005, 'The legitimacy crisis in investment treaty arbitration: Privatizing public international law through inconsistent decisions', Fordham Law Review 73, p. 1521; Sornarajah, M., 2008, 'A coming crisis: Expansionary trends in investment treaty arbitration, in appeals mechanism in international investment disputes', in Sauvant, K.P. (ed.), *Appeals Mechanism in International Investment Disputes*, Oxford University Press, pp. 39–45; see also Brower, C.N. and Schill, S.W., 2009, 'Is arbitration a threat or a boon to the legitimacy of international investment law?', *Chi. J. Int Law* 9, p. 471.

legitimacy of arbitration tribunals is in question and states are becoming increasingly wary of orders and awards of investment tribunals.[12] States see these awards as shrinking the domestic regulatory space of states with the expansion of the scope of investment treaty protection by arbitrators who can exercise interpretive powers that tend to increase the liability of states.[13] Furthermore, the lack of democratic control and accountability of ISDS tribunals, the inability for non-disputing parties to influence proceedings, and the threat that investment protection is accorded preference over competing policy concerns are some of the criticisms levelled against the system.[14] For the investors, they are also affected by some of the concerns surrounding the arbitration system, particularly the potential for inconsistent jurisprudence without institutional mechanisms that can ensure consistency.[15] Schill succinctly describes the various concerns around the BIT regime as:

> the vagueness of investment treaties based on broad standards of protection, the restriction of state sovereignty, the increasing number of conflicting and inconsistent interpretations by arbitral tribunals of standard principles of investment protection, not only under different treaties, but also with identical cases brought under the same treaty; the perception of a built-in bias favouring foreign investors and foreign investments over legitimate non-investment policy choices, the procedural maxims of arbitration, in particular, confidentiality of proceedings, and the idea that dispute settlement under investment treaties constitutes a party-owned process, in which non-parties, even if they are affected, are voiceless.[16]

In light of these problems facing BITs and ISDS, a consideration of the applicable law that should guide not only the interpretation of treaties but also the conduct of tribunals is necessary.[17] In his book *Investment Treaty Arbitration and Public Law*, Gus van Harten argues that while investment treaty arbitration is viewed as a form of reciprocally consensual adjudication between an investor and a state, it should be a mechanism of adjudicative

12 Bolivia and Ecuador have so far withdrawn from the BITs they signed.
13 Schill, S.W., 2011, 'Enhancing investment law's legitimacy: Conceptual and methodological foundations of a new public law approach', *Va J Int'l L* 52, p. 4.
14 A case in point is *Piero Foresti v. South Africa* ICSID Case No. ARB (AF)/07/01, where a group of NGOs came together to oppose an application by foreign mining investors which threatened an empowerment policy of the South African government.
15 Schill, *supra* note 13.
16 *Id*, p. 5.
17 Krommendijk, J. and Morijn, J., 2009, '"Proportional" by what measures? Balancing investors interests and human rights by way of applying the proportionality principle in investor-state arbitration', in Dupuy, P., Petersmann, E. and Francioni, F. (eds), *Human Rights in International Investment Law and Arbitration*, Oxford University Press, p. 425.

review in public law because investment arbitration is established by a sovereign act of the state and it is predominantly used to resolve disputes arising from the exercise of sovereign authority.[18] Van Harten argues that as a public law system, investment treaty arbitration engages the regulatory relationship between the state and individual investors, rather than a reciprocal relationship between juridical equals.[19] Kladermis also identifies the importance of considering the public dimension of disputes as well as the cross-fertilisation from other areas of international law in treaty interpretation.[20] Indeed, after the global financial crisis, the emerging trends in transformation of existing rules have destroyed traditional legal theories that there is a divide between the public and private or the domestic and international and requires a hybrid approach where public law applies in private arbitration and domestic law applies in international arbitration.

The application of other relevant rules of international law

Article 31(3)(c) of the VCLT provides that 'any relevant rules of international law applicable in the relations between the parties' can be a useful way to determine the meaning of broad standards of protection in investment treaties. Reference to relevant rules of international law can help clarify meaning and fill gaps by referring to same words used in other treaties or terms used in treaties on the same subject. The tribunal in *ADF Group Inc v. USA* relied implicitly on article 31(3)(c) in the context of the fair and equitable treatment rule which the tribunal held must be based on 'state practice and judicial or arbitral case law or other sources of customary or general international law'.[21] In *Saluka v. Czech Republic*, the tribunal relied on article VCLT 31(3)(c) for the purpose of importing into the treaty the customary international law exception that a deprivation could be justified if it resulted from the exercise of regulatory actions aimed at the maintenance of public order, in which case the host state was 'not liable to pay compensation to a foreign investor'.[22] In *RosInvest Co UK Ltd v. Russian Federation*, the arbitral tribunal explained the function of VCLT article 31(3)(c), for the purpose of determining the consent of the parties as the basis of the tribunal's jurisdiction. It held:

18   Van Harten, G., 2007, *Investment Treaty Arbitration and Public Law*, Oxford University Press, p. 45.
19   *Id*.
20   Kladermis, D., 2011, 'Investment treaty arbitration as global administrative law: What this might mean in practice' in Brown, C. and Miles, K. (eds), *Evolution in Investment Treaty Law and Arbitration*, Cambridge University Press, p. 158–159.
21   *ADF Group Inc v USA* (ICSID Case No ARB(AF)/00/1, Award of 9 January 2003), para. 184.
22   *Saluka*, Partial Award, PCA (UNCITRAL), 17 March 2006, paras 254–255.

Here the reference is to "any relevant rules of international law applicable in the relations between the parties". "Applicable in the relations between the parties" must be taken as a reference to rules of international law that condition the performance of the specific rights and obligations stipulated in the treaty – or else it would amount to a general licence to override the treaty terms that would be quite incompatible with the general spirit of the Vienna Convention as a whole.[23]

The point made by the tribunal in the *RosInvest* case that article 31 does not allow the blanket override of treaty terms was also emphasised in different terms by the tribunal in *Parkerings Compagniet* which considered the respondent's obligations under the United Nations Educational, Scientific and Cultural Organization (UNESCO) World Heritage Convention in the assessment of whether there was a breach of the national treatment standard.[24] The tribunal held that such relevant rules must however be applicable to both parties to the BIT.[25] Hence, a treaty will not be applicable where there is only one of the BIT parties as a signatory.

Investment tribunals have been reluctant to interpret BITs and their compatibility with other rules, which has led to the approach of interpreting obligations without conflicting with other rules of law.[26] This is achieved by assessing whether a state had alternative means to comply with its BIT obligations without violating the non-investment obligations.[27] Article 31(3)(c) favours the harmonisation of investment and non-investment rules. As a result, it is useful for states to adopt interpretation statements to clarify the scope of substantive investment protection standards in their current BITs.[28] These statements are not meant to amend an existing BIT but to establish a common understanding between the parties and this approach certainly finds force in article 31(3)(a) of the VCLT, which allows for 'any subsequent agreement between the parties regarding the interpretation of the treaty or the application of its provisions'.

23   *RosInvest Co UK Ltd. v. Russian Federation*, Award on Jurisdiction, SCC Case No. V079/2005, 5 October 2007 at para. 39.
24   *Parkerings Compagniet v. Republic of Lithuania*, ICSID No ARB05/8, paras 377–397.
25   Prislan, *supra* note 10 at p. 15.
26   Kladermis, D., 2012 'Systemic integration and international investment law – some practical reflections', working paper No. 2012/46, viewed (6 May 2017) from http://arbitrationlaw.com/files/free_pdfs/2012_-_d_kalderimis_-_systemic_integration_and_iil_-_some_practical_reflections.pdf, pp. 17–18.
27   *Azurix v. Argentine Republic* (ICSID Case No ARB/01/12, Award of 14 July 2006, para. 261; or *Siemens AG v. Argentine Republic* ICSID Case No ARB/02/8, Award of 17 January 2007, para. 354.
28   The Note of Interpretation adopted by the NAFTA Free Trade Commission in 2001 rejected the decision in the Pope and Talbot case that the fair and equitable treatment provision was an autonomous treaty standard that was 'additive' to the minimum standard of treatment, but rather, was equivalent to the international minimum standards of aliens under customary international law.

The public dimension of investment disputes

According to Schill, international investment law constitutes a public law discipline because it imposes restraints on a state's exercise of powers and is functionally analogous to administrative or constitutional judicial review.[29] Furthermore, it escapes classifications into exclusive categories of international law or domestic public law and it is international law as regards its sources, but comparable to administrative or constitutional law in its function to limit government conduct regarding private investors.[30] Schill proposes a comparative public law approach, which draws parallels between international investment law and domestic public law as well as other regimes of public international law.[31] This is a suitable approach because it consists in conceptualising and applying investment law standards by drawing parallels with public law concepts used in both domestic and international law.[32] According to Schill, comparative public law analysis helps:

1 to concretise and clarify the interpretation of the often vague standards of investment protection and determine the extent of state liability in specific contexts;
2 to balance investment protection and non-investment concerns;
3 to ensure consistency in the interpretation and application of investment treaties because the interpretative method would be uniform for all investment treaties;
4 to ensure cross-regime consistency and mitigate the negative effects of fragmentation by stressing commonalities and openness of international investment law towards other international regimes, such as human rights and environmental law;
5 to legitimise existing arbitral jurisprudence by showing that the solutions adopted in investment treaty arbitration are analogous to the ones adopted by domestic courts or other international courts or tribunals; and
6 to suggest legal reform of investment treaty-making or changes to arbitral practice in view of different, or more nuanced, solutions adopted in other public law systems.[33]

In the conceptualisation of a comparative public law approach, considerations of the multilateral nature of investment agreements through obligations such as most favoured nation treatment as well as the opportunity for forum shopping by treaty parties mean that the comparative public

---

29   Schill, S.W., 2011, 'Enhancing investment law's legitimacy: Conceptual and methodological foundations of a new public law approach', *Va J Int'l L* 57, p. 1.
30   *Id.*
31   *Id*, p. 12.
32   *Id*, p. 13.
33   *Id.*

law approach should cut across various regimes and should not be limited to the investment agreements and domestic law only.

There are areas in the domestic law of states that have direct implications for the decisions made in investment arbitrations. For instance, the recognition of the right to access information as a human right is significant given the private nature of investment arbitration that excludes certain transparency imperatives. The right of access to information has attained universal recognition with several regional human rights treaties upholding the recognition of this right. Regional courts such as the Inter-American and the European Courts also recognise this right as well as its linkage to other rights.[34] The application of the principles of information disclosure to investment arbitration is relevant to the public interest because the state party exercises sovereign powers and occupies a sovereign capacity in relation to the dispute and second, the subject of arbitration and the outcome in relation to liability for wrong doing and the award of damages are public interest issues.[35]

Orellana suggests that to the extent that awards in investment arbitration are fast becoming sources of international law, there is a public interest element, which warrants the invocation of the principle of information disclosure.[36] In invoking the human right of access to information, considerations of when, how and what information is to be disclosed are relevant.[37]

While the tribunal in the *Biwater* case[38] favoured the approach of the disclosure of information after the completion of the proceedings, the Inter-American Court in the *Claude Reyes* case favoured the contemporaneous approach to enable the public to 'question, investigate and consider whether public functions are being performed adequately'.[39] In a 2012 judgment by the Polish administrative court, it was held that arbitration awards under investment treaties constitute public information and are eligible for release under Poland's freedom of information law.[40] A local NGO had applied for a yet to be published investment treaty award relating to the *Servier v. Poland* case. The government had raised article 32.5 of the UNCITRAL rules to prevent disclosure of the award, which provided that awards can only be

---

34   *Claude Reyes et al. v. Chile*, Inter-Am Ct HR (ser C) No 151, paras 84–85 (Sept 19, 2006).

35   Orellana, M.A., 2011, 'The right of access to information and investment arbitration', *ICSID Review Foreign Investment Law Journal* 26(2), p. 77.

36   *Id.*

37   *Id.*

38   *Biwater Gauff (Tanzania) Ltd. v. United Republic of Tanzania*, ICSID Case No. ARB/05/22.

39   *Claude Reyes et al. v. Chile*, Inter-Am. Ct. H.R. (ser. C) No. 151, para. 86 (Sept. 19, 2006).

40   Hepburn, J. and Balcerzak, F., 2013, 'Polish court rules on release of investment arbitration awards under Freedom of Information Law', IA Reporter, viewed (17 February 2013) from www.iareporter.com/articles/20130102_3

released subject to the consent of the parties.[41] The court held to the contrary that the award was public information and the respondent that had received the information request was a public authority bound by the freedom of information law.[42]

Most domestic laws on information disclosure have recognised the importance of exemptions to public access to information.[43] Where arbitration tribunals want to restrict access to confidential information of parties, it is important to recognise that 'a state cannot contract out of its human rights obligations, even when ceding authority to international organisations'.[44] A host state that has to comply with a confidentiality order by a tribunal will still have to comply with its domestic obligation to protect the right of access to information of its citizens.

The contrasting objectives in terms of upholding the right of access to information and enforcing confidentiality orders was dealt with by the *Metaclad* and *Biwater* tribunals. In the *Metaclad* case, the tribunal was concerned with the effect of disclosure on the arbitration process but nevertheless recognised the need for respect of obligations relating to public disclosure which will include the right of access to information.[45] The *Biwater* tribunal's attempt to balance what it called the competing interest of transparency and procedural integrity on the one hand and recognition of the right of the parties to conclude any agreement in relation to confidentiality on the other, failed to recognise the importance of transparency as an important element of procedural integrity. The interests in the case did not compete against each other because they complemented each other and the tribunal should not have encouraged derogating from the binding nature of human rights obligations such as the right of access to information.[46]

These problems however persist. A reason for this has been the consistent misunderstanding of the investment arbitration process as a commercial arbitration process that only involves private parties. The role and relevance of public interest issues, the sovereign position of states and the other binding obligations that interfere with compliance with investment treaty norms have not been adequately taken into account. The principle of deference is an important principle that can be used by tribunals to take into account these issues.

---

41   *Id*; see Adeleke F., 2016, 'Human rights and international investment arbitration', *South African Journal of Human Rights* 32(1), p. 66.
42   *Id.*
43   Classification of confidential information by governments is a common phenomenon.
44   Orellana, *supra* note 35 at p. 87.
45   *Id*, pp. 90–91.
46   *Id.*

Deference to domestic law

Deference in ISDS means tribunals have to respect the treaty making power of states, including authoritative interpretations by contracting parties, and tribunals should not rewrite treaty obligations they disagree with for policy reasons.[47] This meaning of deference concerns the limits of a tribunal's power to interpret the governing law.[48] This notion of deference is embedded in the traditional framework that international law and national law are strictly separate spheres and that international dispute settlement bodies are to give effect to the common will of the contracting states parties, of which they are agents.[49] Also, deference can refer to the principle of interpreting investment treaties in a way that recognises the sovereignty of states.[50]

Although deference can be seen as preferring a state's rules over another,[51] 'there is a fine line between disregarding a contracting state's right to enforce and intruding on the policy space of states' and deference should be used as a margin of appreciation within which host state conduct is exempt from fully fledged review by a tribunal.[52]

Factors affecting the standard of review when considering the notion of deference include the text of international treaties, the circumstances of the state conduct under review, the procedural situation in which a tribunal reviews a government's act, the applicable law in a tribunal and the content of the international legal obligation at stake.[53] This assessment can be conducted using the factors identified in Chapter 2 to determine a public interest regulation measure.

States have an inherent right to regulate in the public interest and this inherent right has been the subject of dispute in the case of *Lemire v. Ukraine*, where the tribunal stated that the protection of foreign investors should be 'balanced against the legitimate right of Ukraine to pass legislation and adopt measures for the protection of what as a sovereign it perceives to be its public interest'.[54] The *Lemire* tribunal preferred a deferential standard of review that restrained it from substituting its judgment 'for that of

47 Schill, S., 2012, 'Deference in investment treaty arbitration: Re-conceptualising the standard of review through comparative public law', *Society of International Economic Law* (SIEL), SSRN, p. 5.

48 *Id.*

49 *Id.*

50 *Id.*

51 *Id*, p. 6.

52 *Id*; Adeleke, *supra* note 41 at p. 67.

53 *Id*, pp. 17–20. Adeleke, supra note at p. 68.

54 *Joseph Charles Lemire v. Ukraine*, ICSID Case No. ARB/06/18, Decision on Jurisdiction and Liability (Jan. 14, 2010), para. 273; see also Chen, T., (2012), 'The standard of review and the roles of ICSID arbitral tribunals in investor state dispute settlement', *Contemporary Asia Arbitration Journal* 5(1), p. 23 and 38.

national bodies applying national laws'[55] According to the tribunal, the standard for reviewing the decision of a host state is dependent on the arbitrariness of the decision.[56]

When determining investor protections such as indirect expropriation, a deferential standard of review will allow a tribunal to consider regulations that are intended for non-investment related issues.[57] There is a possibility that the right to regulate could be used as a defence to indirect expropriation if the regulation meets the standards for a public interest measure as set out in Chapter 2 and there is a limited impact on economic interests alongside a strong justification to adopt the measure at issue.[58]According to Henckels, deference[59] on the basis of respect for a state's sovereignty affirms the recognition that national authorities should be the main determinant of the public interest.[60] Related to this is the proximity of the tribunal to the state whose measures are challenged.[61] Henckels suggests that national authorities may be regarded as more competent than adjudicators to discern and evaluate local conditions, as they are often more closely acquainted with local issues, sensitivities and traditions.[62] Therefore, deference is relevant to the question of whether a measure reflects a fair balance between the interests of foreign investors and host states, or whether a measure is reasonable.[63] Deference reflects the rationale that a case will turn on the specific facts and local context and acknowledges the uncertainties inherent in regulation.[64]

In the *Glamis Gold v. USA* case, the arbitral tribunal adopted a deferential standard of review in terms of federal and state legislative measures[65] and stated that it is not the role of the tribunal 'to supplant its own judgment of underlying factual material and support for that of qualified domestic agency' and that 'governments must compromise between the interests of competing parties'.[66]

55   *Id*; *Lemire*, para. 283; Adeleke, *supra* note 41 at p. 67.
56   Chen, *supra* note 54 at p. 39.57   *Id*.
58   Lo, C., 2011, 'Plain Packaging and Indirect Expropriation of Trademark Rights Under BITs: Does FCTC Help Establish a Right to Regulate Tobacco Products?', 2011 *Conference on International Health and Trade: Globalization and Related Health* 24, p. 23.
59   *Id*.
60   Henckels, C., 2013,'Balancing investment protection and the public interest: The role of the standard of review and the importance of deference in investor-state arbitration', *Journal of International Dispute Settlement* 4(1), p. 9.
61   *Id*.
62   *Id*.
63   *Id*. Some tribunals have referred to the concept of reasonableness as delimiting lawful state conduct in the context of fair and equitable treatment. See *Parkerings-Compagniet AS v. Lithuania*, ICSID Case No ARB/05/8, Award, 11 September 2007, para. 332; *Impregilo SpA v. Argentine Republic*, ICSID Case No ARB/07/17, Award, 21 June 2011, para. 291.
64   Henckels, *supra* note 60 at p. 14.
65   *Glamis Gold Award*, above para. 779.
66   *Glamis Gold Award* para 803; Adeleke, supra note 41 at p. 69.

Furthermore, some arbitrators involved in the disputes against Argentina in the aftermath of its economic crisis have argued for tribunals to stop second guessing the policy choices of government.[67] This is a welcome development that recognises the importance of preventing tribunal overreach.

Possible state defences to treaty violation under international law

Necessity

A number of claims against Argentina by investors dealt with the concept of the defence of necessity in international investment law.[68] The tribunals in these cases were required to determine whether the measures adopted by Argentina during the 2001–2002 economic crises complied with the terms of a non-precluded measure (NPM) or self-judging clause in the US-Argentina BIT. NPM clauses determine when a state may promulgate measures that effectively contravene its substantive obligations in a BIT. They allow states to make exceptions to investor protections unilaterally based on a subjective interpretation without incurring liability.

Tribunals hearing the claims against Argentina found that most of Argentina's actions breached the fair and equitable treatment standard because the investors' expectations had been frustrated through a lack of stability in the legal environment upon which the investors had based their decisions to invest or through the operation of an umbrella clause.[69] In the cases of *Suez* and *Inter-Agua v. Argentina* and *Suez, Vivendi* and *AWG v. Argentina*, it was alleged that Argentina had breached the fair and equitable treatment rule through the enactment of decrees to adjust tariffs for drinking water and sewerage services even after Argentina's economic crisis had

---

67 *LG&E v. Argentina*, paras 239–242; *AWG v. Argentina*, ARB/03/19 30 July 2010, paras 37–40.
68 The International Law Commission (ILC), art. 25, is regarded as the representative expression of the necessity doctrine in customary international law. It provides:
    1.   Necessity may not be invoked by a State as a ground for precluding the wrongfulness of an act not in conformity with an international obligation of that State unless the act:
        (a)   Is the only way for the State to safeguard an essential interest against a grave and imminent peril; and
        (b)   Does not seriously impair an essential interest of the State or States towards which the obligation exists, or of the international community as a whole.
    2.   In any case, necessity may not be invoked by a State as a ground for precluding wrongfulness if:
        (a)   The international obligation in question excludes the possibility of invoking necessity; or
        (b)   The State has contributed to the situation of necessity.
69 *CMS v. Argentina* (Award), paras 273–281; *LG&E v. Argentina*, paras 132–139.

ended.[70] Undertaking a necessity analysis, the tribunals found that the measures fell 'outside the scope of its legitimate right to regulate and in effect constituted an abuse of regulatory discretion'.[71]

Other tribunals found breach of expropriation in relation to the emergency measures imposed during the crisis.[72] In determining whether Argentina could rely on the plea of necessity, tribunals considered the NPM clause and referred to the ILC's articles on the responsibility of states for internationally wrongful acts. Article 25 of the ILC provides that necessity may only be invoked to preclude the wrongfulness of an act that does not comply with a state's international obligations where that act is 'the only way for the state to safeguard an essential interest against a grave and imminent peril'.

The outcome of the decision of the tribunals considering the claims against Argentina highlight the importance of having disputes resolved by tribunals that are knowledgeable about domestic contexts and can use the factors identified in Chapter 2 to determine whether a public measure meets the necessity defence. This does not suggest that the decision of tribunals should be politicised. However, it invites tribunals to consider the domestic contexts of states and to expand their assessment of state conduct beyond contractual and investment liabilities to other considerations that are sometimes beyond the control of states.

The international human rights law defence

While article 30 of the VCLT preserves both the International Covenant on the Economic, Social and Cultural Rights (ICESCR) and the investment treaty obligations of the host state, it does not address the question of breach of either treaty. Article 30 applies whenever incompatibility conceptually arises between the treaties that are subject of the comparison. In such instances, the earlier treaty will be applicable to the extent that it is consistent with the subsequent treaty. Where an investment host state is a party to both the ICESCR and a BIT but the state of the foreign investor is only a party to a BIT, it is the BIT that will guide the mutual rights and obligations of both parties.[73] Where only the host state is party to the ICESCR and the BIT, the BIT prevails. This is based on the rule of *pacta tertiis nec nocent nec prosunt* (a party to a treaty cannot be affected by any agreement which other parties of the treaty conclude with other states).[74]

70   *InterAgua v. Argentina*, para. 218 and *AWG v. Argentina*, para. 238.
71   *AWG v. Argentina*, para. 237; *InterAgua v. Argentina*, para. 217.
72   *InterAgua v. Argentina*, paras 215–217; *AWG v. Argentina*, paras. 235–237; *Impregilo SpA v. Argentine Republic*, ICSID Case No ARB/07/17, Award (June 21, 2011), paras. 325–331.
73   Henckels, *supra* note 60 at p. 14.
74   Desierto, D.A., 2012, 'Calibrating human rights and investment in economic emergencies: Prospects of treaty and valuation defences', Manchester, *Journal of International Economic Law* 9, p. 33.

A way to accommodate the ICESCR is to treat it as part of the law of the host state. This depends on 'the extent to which the host state properly informs the investor of the inclusion of the ICESCR in the regulatory fabric governing the investment as well as the host state's rules for incorporation of international law as part of domestic law'.[75] This has to be done before the investment is established.[76] Desierto argues that to the extent that the ICESCR minimum core obligation could be deemed part of a host state's law, the 'in accordance with host state law' clause in an investment treaty could be a basis for ICESCR consideration.[77] This interpretation must be based on the treaty's text, context, object and purpose and the host state would have to demonstrate the extent to which the ICESCR forms a crucial part of its domestic legal system and the extent to which the investor was informed of the requirements of the ICESCR minimum core obligation with respect to the host state during the establishment of the investment.[78] Where the host state cannot rely on the VCLT, the host state will have to make a policy choice where it must determine performance of either the ICESCR minimum core obligation or the investment treaty duty to pay compensation. This is dependent on the will of states.[79]

Some of the newer generations of investment treaties have adopted more direct treaty language explicitly providing for the application of certain human rights treaties as part of the regulatory framework such as the 2012 SADC Model BIT and the USA model BIT.[80]

The ICESCR maintains that because core obligations are non-derogable, they continue to exist in situations of conflict, emergency and natural disaster. The Office of the UN High Commissioner of Human Rights holds the view that:

> there is no express permission under human rights law for states to derogate from their obligations in relation to economic, social and cultural rights during emergencies, disasters or armed conflicts. In fact, in such circumstances, more attention is often required to protect

75 Desierto, D.A., 1998, Interpreting Committee on Economic Social and Cultural Rights, General Comment No. 3 (The domestic application of the Covenant), E/C.12/1998/24, 3 December 1998, at paras 7–8.
76 *Anderson and ors v. Costa Rica*, Award, ICSID Case No. ARB (AF)/07/3, 10 May 2010, para. 58.
77 Desierto, *supra* note 74 at p. 57.
78 *Id*.
79 *Id*, p. 58.
80 The United States Model BIT, 2012, arts 12–13; The Canadian Model FIPA, 2004, art. 11; The Belgium-Luxembourg Economic Union/Serbia and Montenegro BIT, 2005, arts 5–6.

economic, social and cultural rights, in particular those of the most marginalised groups of society.[81]

In actual practice, some domestic constitutional courts have already accepted and interpreted the ICESCR minimum core obligation in their respective jurisdictions.[82]

The development of the host state's economy and of the economic relations between the host and the other state parties are among the objectives of investment treaties. Consequently, it is a deliberate choice of parties to impose obligations on states in favour of foreign investors. With this choice, nothing is inherent in the nature of investment treaties that prevents states when negotiating BITs to also impose substantive obligations for the protection of human rights.[83] However, investment practitioners approach investment disputes from a commercial arbitration perspective and are often unaware of human rights jurisprudence that support or are relevant to the cases they deal with.[84] Hence, it is not surprising that human rights jurisprudence has only been applied in cases such as expropriation and right to property, where human rights jurisprudence is internationally well established in that regard.[85] The vagueness of the content of human rights norms has also led to the reluctance for the transfer of these norms to application in investment disputes.[86] In the instances where human rights norms have been raised as a defence to investment treaty obligations, the successful reliance on human rights norms can only be achieved where the norm itself is not fluid, that is, a human rights obligation must exist and such obligation must conflict with an investment obligation and the human rights obligation should take priority.[87] In *Suez v. Argentina*, the tribunal found that:

> Argentina has suggested that its human rights obligations to assure its population the right to water somehow trumps its obligations under the BITs and that the existence of the human right to water also implicitly gives Argentina the authority to take actions in disregard of its BIT obligations. The Tribunal does not find a basis for such a conclusion either in the BITs or international law. Argentina is subject to both international obligations, i.e. human rights and treaty obligation, and

---

81   UN Office of the High Commissioner for Human Rights, Frequently Asked Question on Economic, Social, and Cultural Rights, Fact Sheet No. 33, 25, viewed (29 March) from www.ohchr.org/Documents/Publications/FactSheet33en.pdf
82   *Government of South Africa v. Grootboom*, 2001 (1) SA 46 (CC), paras 31–32.
83   Gazzini, T. and Radi. Y. 2012, 'Foreign investment with a human face, with special reference to indigenous peoples' rights', in R. Hofmann and C. Tams (eds), *International Investment Law and Its Others*, NOMOS.
84   *Id*, p.5.
85   *Id*.
86   *Id*.
87   *Id*.

must respect both of them equally. Under the circumstances of these cases, Argentina's human rights obligations and its investment treaty obligations are not inconsistent, contradictory, or mutually exclusive. Thus, as discussed above, Argentina could have respected both types of obligations. Viewing each treaty as a whole, the Tribunal does not find that any of them excluded the defense of necessity.[88]

The approach by the tribunal above failed to deal with the issue of conflicting obligations by simply leaving the enquiry at the application of competing obligations where they do not conflict with each other. It is however important to recognise that human rights have a significant role to play in the interpretation of investment treaties and might be contrary to a state's investment obligations towards foreign investors.

Gazzini and Radi argued for a teleological interpretation, which focuses on the object and purpose of treaties based on the preambles of treaties.[89] Investment treaty preambles typically reference economic development as the primary objective without referencing the importance of sustainable development and the relevance of human rights protection as suggested in the SADC mode BIT. While economic development is important for the protection of human rights, preambles also need to recognise human freedoms, which must thrive for economic development to occur. The teleological interpretation can be used to promote either investors or human rights oriented interpretations of investment treaty provisions.[90]

Article 31(3)(c) of the VCLT applies systemic interpretation which brings human rights into the realm of foreign investment. This approach unifies international law and requires tribunals to take into account relevant rules of international law over and above the law chosen by the parties. This complements the applicable law in an investment treaty and does not displace it.

Conclusion

There has been a rapid rise in the consideration of public policy in investment disputes. This rise has been due to several factors, including the increasing reliance by states on their sovereign right to regulate as well as the expansive interpretation that have been given to investment protection in BITs. Recognising the trend of public interest norms being raised in investment disputes and considering the applicable rules for treaty interpretation, the connecting thread between the creation, performance and interpretation of investment obligations is the good faith review of investment treaties based

---

88 *Suez, Sociedad General de Aguas de Barcelona SA, and InterAguas Servicios Integrales del Agua SA v. Argentina*, ICSID ARB/03/17, Decision on Liability, 30 July 2010, para 240.
89 Gazzini and Radi, *supra* note 83 at p. 12.
90 *Id*, p. 13.

on the intention of the parties as reflected in the text, object and purpose of the treaty. The object of treaty interpretation is to establish, fully and fairly, the common intention of the parties. To achieve this, the systemic integration of relevant rules of international law for a coherent approach to interpretation that ensures BIT obligations are interpreted in a manner that does not violate other non-investment obligations is necessary.

Usage of interpretation statements consistent with article 31 of the VCLT, which allows subsequent agreement between parties, is one way of allowing this systemic integration. This allows a direct application of human rights law or the interpretation of investment obligations with a human rights based approach and will have the effect of balancing various elements and interests on a case by case basis. The role and relevance of public interest issues, the sovereign position of states and the other binding obligations that interfere with compliance with investment treaty norms have not been adequately taken into account. If this were to be done, the reception of the notion of deference in tribunals' decision making accompanied by a principled and transparent elaboration of the applicable standards of review will be an ideal route in considering the human rights obligations of host states in investment disputes.

6 Domestic investment regulation and the influence of regional investment agreements

Introduction

Within the last decade, there have been investment regulatory developments in sub-regional institutions such as COMESA and SADC. These developments are aimed at making the Southern Africa and East Africa regions investor friendly with the purpose of developing a harmonised regional approach towards FDI regulation. At the same time these developments are happening at a regional level, regulatory developments are also taking place at a country level in some of Africa's economic hubs, such as South Africa, and ISDS cases are influencing the regulatory space of other African states. This chapter will assess the state of FDI regulatory development at a regional and domestic level by assessing the investment regulatory framework of three African power blocs, South Africa, Nigeria and Kenya, and the extent to which their investment regulation contributes to the main objectives of promoting investment flows, protecting investors and their investment, the depoliticisation of investment disputes and access to remedies.

There are five dimensions for regional integration in Africa. These are trade integration, productive integration, free movement of people, financial and macroeconomic integration and regional infrastructure.[1] These five dimensions are relevant to maximise intra-African investment flows especially in the unique context of African states where there should be high levels of co-dependency on each other for the following reasons.

The African continent has the highest proportion of landlocked countries in the world, which makes the notion of regional integration highly important for individual countries.[2] Furthermore, with the high number of

---

1   Africa Regional Integration index 2016, viewed (26 March 2017) from www.uneca. org/sites/default/files/PublicationFiles/arii-report2016_en_web.pdf, p. 11.
2   Graduate School of Development Policy and Practice (GSDPP) UCT, 2014, 'The Political Economy of African Economic Integration: Strategic Reflections', Unpublished Report, p. 7.

small countries in Africa,[3] regional integration facilitates the enhancement of productivity for countries to industrialise through trade and investment.[4]

One of the economic benefits of regional integration is the increase in exports and access to cheaper imports.[5] While integration allows access to imported products, which compete with domestic production, this promotes healthy competition that will reduce the dominant positions of companies and will promote innovation with producers to eliminate inefficiencies. In a recent survey by UNECA, some challenges identified as hindering equitable distribution of investments across the continent include poor infrastructure, 'tariff and non-tariff trade barriers, limited movement of persons and capital, high transaction costs of doing business, still-high risk perceptions of investing in Africa, limited access to credit and corruption'.[6] As this chapter aims to establish, African BITs have been weak in leveraging and imposing obligations on investors and tend to favour foreign investors without addressing questions of economic sustainability for the continent.[7]

The Pan-African African Investment Code

The objective of this code is based on the sustainable development of member states and intends to ensure consistency between the obligations of states under the code and any other applicable agreement. The code clearly identifies what qualifies as investment through substantial business activity, commitment of capital or other resources, the assumption of risk and a

3   Fourteen African countries are classified as small states. These countries are Botswana, Cape Verde, Comoros, Djibouti, Equatorial Guinea, Gabon, the Gambia, Guinea-Bissau, Lesotho, Mauritius, Namibia, Sao Tome and Principe, Seychelles and Swaziland: Domeland, D. and Sander, F.G., 2007, *Growth in African Small States*, World Bank, viewed (26 March 2017) from http://siteresources.worldbank.org/INTDEBTDEPT/Resources/468980-1206974166266/4833916-1206989877225/Domeland GilSander200704.pdf
4   United Nations Economic Commission for Africa (UNECA), 2015, *Industrializing Through Trade: Economic Report on Africa 2015*, viewed (26 March 2017) from www.un.org/en/africa/osaa/pdf/pubs/2015era-uneca.pdf
5   It is estimated that intra-African trade will rise to 22 per cent and contribute a $1 trillion to the global economy if a continental free trade area is formed. GSDPP report, *supra* note 2 at p. 4.
6   NECA, 2016, *Investment Policies and Bilateral Investment Treaties in Africa Investment Treaties in Africa: Implications for Regional Integration Implications for Regional Integration*, viewed (26 March 2017) from www.uneca.org/sites/default/files/PublicationFiles/eng_investment_landscaping_study.pdf, pp. 37–38.
7   *Id*, p. 39.

significant contribution to the host state's economic development.[8] These considerations are significant given the cases discussed in this book, such as the *Al Kharafi v. Libya* case where the Libyan government was held liable for over $900 million for a cancelled investment project where the investor had only spent $100,000 in fees within Libya.[9]

The code aims to balance the promotion and protection of investments through offering incentives for investment flows while also protecting investments. The code aims to secure an appropriate balance between the regulatory space of states and the protection offered to investors. For instance, the most favoured nation treatment and national treatment protection are guaranteed subject to the assessment of factors to determine like circumstances.[10] It however excludes from both protections, regulatory measures designed to protect or enhance legitimate public welfare objectives, such as public health, safety and the environment.[11] This is similar to the exceptions in Article XX of the General Agreement on Tariffs and Trade (GATT).

The code further allows states to exclude sectors from the MFN standard and to 'grant preferential treatment to qualifying investments and investors in order to achieve national development objectives'.[12] Furthermore, the code excludes the controversial fair and equitable treatment protection but guarantees adequate compensation should expropriation take place. The expropriation formula is based on market compensation before expropriation, however, it allows states to assess compensation based on:

> an equitable balance between the public interest and interest of the investor affected, having regard to all relevant circumstances and taking account of: the current and past use of the property, the history of its acquisition, the extent of previous profit made by the foreign investor through the investment, and the duration of the investment.[13]

What distinguishes the code from traditional BITs currently applicable and in draft includes the introduction of performance requirements,[14] framework

---

8   Art. 4.4, Pan-African Investment Code (the code), viewed (30 March 2017) from http://repository.uneca.org/handle/10855/23009.

9   www.italaw.com/sites/default/files/case-documents/italaw1554.pdf

10   Arts 7, 8 and 9 of the code.

11   *Id*, arts 8.2 and 10.2.

12   *Id*, art. 9.

13   *Id*, art. 11.

14   *Id*, art. 18: It safeguards measures such as preferential treatment to achieve national or sub-national regional development goals; development of local entrepreneurs; to enhance productive capacity, to increase employment, increase human resource capacity and training, research and development including of new technologies, technology transfer, innovation and other benefits of investment through the use of specified requirements on investors; to address historically based economic disparities suffered by identifiable ethnic or cultural groups due to discriminatory or oppressive measures against such groups prior to the adoption of this Code.

for corporate governance,[15] socio-political obligations,[16] mandatory corporate social responsibility,[17] use of natural resources[18] and most importantly, a business and human rights framework.

The code places both negative and positive human rights obligations on foreign investors and provides that investors shall be governed by the principles of support and respect for the protection of internationally recognised human rights; ensure that they are not complicit in human rights abuses; eliminate all forms of forced and compulsory labour; eliminate discrimination in respect of employment and occupation; and ensure equitable sharing of wealth incurred from investments.[19]

In terms of remedies, the preferred mode of dispute settlement is through state–state dispute settlement subject to initial application of consultations, negotiations or mediation.[20] The code prefers the use of any established African public or African private alternative dispute resolution centres, permanent court of arbitration centres in Africa (or the African Union Court of Arbitration) or the African Court of Justice whose decision shall be final and binding. For ISDS, disputes arising between investors and host states are to be resolved through arbitration only if consultation fails, as well as the exhaustion of local remedies.[21] It is also important to note that the code provides for counter claims by member states against investors for damages for any breach in the code and requires the application of domestic, regional and international laws and principles.[22]

The investment framework of South Africa

In 2013, South Africa opted not to renew some of its BITs with EU countries. South Africa's non-renewal of some of its BITs began towards the

---

15　*Id*, art. 19 among other requirements provides that investments shall meet national and internationally accepted standards of corporate governance for the sector involved, in particular for transparency and accounting practices; ensure that timely and accurate disclosure is made on all material matters regarding a corporation, including the financial situation, performance, ownership, and governance of the company, risks related to environmental liabilities, and any other matters in accordance with the relevant regulations and requirements.

16　*Id*, art. 20 requires respect for national sovereignty and observance of domestic laws, regulations and administrative practices; respect for socio-cultural values; non-interference in internal political affairs; non-interference in intergovernmental relations; and respect for labor rights.

17　*Id*, art. 22 requires investors to contribute to the economic, social and environmental progress with a view to achieving sustainable development of host States.

18　*Id*, art. 23 prohibits exploitation or use of local natural resources to the detriment of the rights and interests of the host State and for investors to respect rights of local populations, and avoid land grabbing practices vis-à-vis local communities.

19　*Id*, art. 24.

20　*Id*, art. 41.

21　*Id*, art. 42.

22　*Id*, art. 44.

end of 2012 with Belgium and Luxembourg.[23] Subsequently, other European countries consisting of Finland, Sweden, Austria, Spain, Germany, France, the UK, Denmark, Switzerland, the Netherlands, Italy and Greece were also notified. This decision was taken after the *Piero Foresti v. South Africa*[24] arbitration case. In this case, Italian investors alleged that South Africa breached its investor protection obligations of no expropriation without compensation, fair and equitable treatment protection and national treatment standard.[25] Though the dispute was settled out of court, the development caused a significant policy shift in South Africa, which not only led to the non-renewal of some EU BITs but also led to the development of the Protection of Investment Act 22 of 2015 (PIA). The South African government embarked on a robust defence of its policy shift and argued that constitutional protections such as property rights, the need to protect South Africa's domestic policy space, the emerging discontent with ISDS in relation to arbitrary and inconsistent awards and the lack of sufficient evidence that suggests BITs promote FDI justified the policy shift.[26]

The purpose of the PIA is to protect investment 'in accordance with and subject to the Constitution, in a manner which balances the public interest and the rights and obligations of investors'.[27] The three main objectives of the PIA are to provide equal treatment to foreign and domestic investors, strike a balance between the rights of investors and the government's right to regulate in the public interest and to replace investor–state arbitration with domestic dispute resolution.

The PIA 2015 provides the following investment protections:

- Fair administrative treatment;
- National treatment;
- Physical security of property;
- Legal protection of investment
- Freedom to repatriate profits subject to taxation and other applicable legislation.

23 Carim, X., 2012, 'South Africa's review and new policy on BITs', *South Bulletin* 69(8), p. 31; Rob Davies, 'Speech delivered by the Minister of Trade and Industry Dr Rob Davies at the South African launch of the United Nations Conference on Trade and Development (UNCTAD) Investment Policy Framework for Sustainable Development', University of the Witwatersrand, Johannesburg, 26 July 2012), viewed (26 March 2017) from http:// unctad.org/ meetings/en/Miscellaneous%20Documents/South-Africa-Investment-statement_Rob_Davies.pdf

24 Case No ARB (AF)/07/1.

25 *Id*, paras 58 and 70.

26 Klaaren, J. and Schneiderman, D., 2009, 'Investor–state arbitration and SA's bilateral investment treaty policy framework review: Comment submitted to the dti 10 August 2009', *Mandela Institute*, viewed (31 March 2017) from www.elaw.org/system/files/Comments+on+DTI+BITs+review+FINAL.pdf, p. 3.

27 Section 4 of the Protection of Investment Act (PIA) No. 22 of 2015.

The PIA investor protections listed above, including national treatment protections, security of investments and protection against expropriation, are qualified.[28] The test of 'in like circumstances' applicable to the national treatment protection lists a number of factors which cumulatively, it appears to make it impossible for any two investments to be considered similar. The PIA does not recognise the fair and equitable treatment protection and consistent with recommendations made in the SADC model BIT; the PIA replaces this protection with what is called a fair administrative treatment standard. This standard provides that investors will not be subject to arbitrary treatment or denied access to administrative or procedural justice.[29] It also requires investors to be given a right to reasons and have a right to administrative review of decisions. In terms of section 10, investments are to be protected from expropriation through section 25 of the Constitution which deals with the right to property. This right permits expropriatory measures to redress the results of past racial discrimination and allows a 'just and equitable' compensation model which is different from the market value compensation often found in BITs. However, the constitutional right to property does not recognise indirect expropriations.

The PIA recognises the sovereign right to regulate investments in the public interest and states that the Bill of Rights in the Constitution applies to all investors and their investments.[30] The PIA expands on the meaning of the right to regulate and introduces several policy exceptions to the application of these protections. These include:[31]

- Redressing historical, social and economic inequalities;
- Upholding the democratic values and principles governing public administration recognised in the Constitution;
- Upholding the human rights in the Constitution;
- Promoting and preserving cultural heritage and practices, indigenous knowledge and biological resources related thereto or national heritage;
- Fostering economic development, industrialisation and beneficiation;
- Achieving the progressive realisation of socio-economic rights;
- Protecting the environment and the conservation and sustainable use of natural resources;
- Measures necessary for the maintenance, compliance or restoration of international peace and security, or the protection of the essential security interests, including with respect to the financial stability, of South Africa.

---

28   *Id*, sections 8 to 10.
29   *Id*, section 6.
30   *Id*, section 4.
31   *Id*, section 12.

These exceptions and measures ensure the protection of investment in South Africa and do not hamper the government's legitimate obligation to protect the interests of the vulnerable who are yearning for economic change.

The recognition of the right of states to regulate, as established in South Africa's new domestic law, is one of five systemic reforms recognised by the UNCTAD,[32] which provides that bilateral investment agreements should not be too expansive to limit state sovereignty in public policy making. In terms of dispute settlement, section 13 of the PIA provides that investors can request government to facilitate mediation. Alternatively, investors can approach a national court or domestic arbitration. Subject to the exhaustion of these remedies, investors can lodge a request for state–state arbitration.

The PIA is not yet operational and in the absence of the law, BITs and applicable regional instruments that have been ratified govern South Africa's investment regulatory framework.

South Africa's BIT framework

South Africa has concluded BITs with 16 African countries. All the BITs adopt an asset based definition of investment and contain the traditional investor and investment protections of MFN, national treatment standards as well as fair and equitable treatment of investors. The BITs also recognise protection against expropriation and adopt market value based compensation to expropriation, despite South Africa's Constitution providing for a different model based on just and equitable compensation. The BITs also allow the settlement of disputes through investor–state arbitration without the exhaustion of domestic remedies. Table 6.1 depicts the current framework of South Africa's BITs with other African countries.

South Africa has taken a consistent and standard approach towards the conclusion of its BITs. However, the approach has ignored relevant constitutional principles that safeguard human rights and ensure the supremacy of the Constitution. This anomaly does not only feature in the BITs. It also features in South Africa's ratification of the SADC finance and investment protocol, which still binds South Africa despite the proposed policy shift and which South Africa led in the development of the SADC model BIT.

The SADC Finance and Investment Protocol and model BIT

The SADC Finance and Investment Protocol (FIP) was adopted in 2006 and has been ratified by the required number of states for it to come into force. The investment annex of the FIP aims to ensure consistency and a harmonised investment policy approach by SADC member states. The FIP

---

32 UNCTAD, 2015, *World Investment Report: Reforming International Investment Governance*, viewed (27 March 2017) from http://unctad.org/en/Publications Library/wir2015_en.pdf

Table 6.1 South Africa's BITs with African states

South Africa	Angola	Congo	DRC	E Guinea	Egypt	Ethiopia	Ghana	Guinea
Definition of investment	Asset based[1]	Asset based	Asset based	Asset based	Asset based	Asset based	Asset based	Asset based
Measures to promote investment	Yes	Yes	Yes	Yes	Yes	Yes	Yes	Yes
Treatment of investors	FET MFN NT	FET MFN NT	FET MFN NT	FET MFN NT	FET MFN NT	FET MFN NT	FET MFN NT	FET MFN NT
Exemptions	Free Trade	Free Trade	Free Trade	Free Trade	Free Trade	Free Trade	Free Trade	Free Trade
	Tax	Tax	Tax	Tax	Tax	Tax	Tax	Tax
	Affirmative action	Affirmative action	Affirmative action	Affirmative action	Affirmative action	Affirmative action	Affirmative action	Affirmative action
Payment for expropriation	Market value	Market value	Market value	Market value	Market value	Market value	Market value	Market value
Hull formula	Hull formula	Hull formula	Hull formula	Hull formula	Hull formula	Hull formula	Hull formula	Hull formula
ISDS	Yes (apply domestic law)	Yes (apply domestic law)	Yes (apply domestic law)	Yes (apply domestic law)	Yes (apply domestic law)	Yes (apply domestic law)	Yes (apply domestic law)	Yes (apply domestic law)

1   Standard definition provides that '"investment" means every kind of asset and in particular, though not exclusively, includes
   a) movable and immovable property as well as other rights such as mortgages, liens or pledges; b) shares, stock and debentures of a company and any other form of participation in a company; c) claims to money, or to any performance under contract having an economic value; d) intellectual property rights, in particular copyrights, patents, utility- model patents, registered designs, trade-marks, trade-names, trade and business secrets, technical processes, know-how, and goodwill; and e) rights or permits conferred by law or under contract, including concessions to search for, cultivate, extract or exploit natural resources; and any change in the legal form in which assets are invested or reinvested shall not affect their character as investments under this Agreement' (South Africa/Zimbabwe BIT 2009, viewed (31 March, 2017) from http://investmentpolicyhub.unctad.org/Download/TreatyFile/2281).

Libya	Mauritius	Nigeria	Rwanda	Senegal	Tanzania	Tunisia	Zimbabwe
Asset based	Asset based	Asset based	Asset based	Asset based	Asset based	Asset based	Asset based
Yes	Yes	Yes	Yes	Yes	Yes	Yes	Yes
FET MFN NT	FET MFN NT	FET MFN NT	FET MFN NT	FET MFN NT	FET MFN NT	FET MFN NT	FET MFN NT
Free Trade	Free Trade	Free Trade	Free Trade	Free Trade	Free Trade	Free Trade	Free Trade
Tax	Tax	Tax	Tax	Tax	Tax	Tax	Tax
Affirm-ative action	Affirm-ative action	Affirm-ative action	Affirm-ative action	Affirm-ative action	Affirm-ative action	Affirm-ative action	Affirm-ative action
Market value	Market value	Market value	Market value	Market value	Market value	Market value	Market value
Hull formula	Hull formula	Hull formula	Hull formula	Hull formula	Hull formula	Hull formula	Hull formula
Yes (apply domestic law)	Yes (apply domestic law)	Yes (apply domestic law)	Yes (apply domestic law)	Yes (apply domestic law)	Yes (apply domestic law)	Yes (apply domestic law)	Yes (apply domestic law)

aims to prevent undesirable adjustments in other state parties whenever another state party amends its investment policies.[33] The FIP provides foreign investor protections that are consistent with the traditional protections found in BITs. It guarantees the fair and equitable treatment of investors and treatment no less favourable to that granted to investors from other states.[34] However, this protection exempts treatment by member states in accordance with domestic laws to grant preferential treatment to investors and investments that promote specific national development objectives.[35] The FIP also protects against the nationalisation or expropriation of investments.[36] It recognises the right to regulate in the public interest,[37] provides a closed and exhaustive list of what would constitute an investment[38] and recognises traditional ISDS subject to the exhaustion of domestic remedies.

The SADC model BIT was adopted in 2012 after the FIP came into force and recognises investor protections relating to non-discrimination and expropriation with fair and adequate compensation.[39] However, the model BIT recommends that member states should opt for a 'fair administrative treatment' protection in place of a 'fair and equitable treatment' protection found in most BITs.[40] The fair administrative treatment protection aims to ensure that the principles of justice and accountability favourably apply to foreign investors as well. While the model BIT provides for ISDS subject to the exhaustion of domestic remedies, it also provides for state–state dispute settlement and cautions member states against adopting ISDS in their BITs.[41] The fair administrative treatment standard in the model BIT formed the basis of adoption in South Africa's new investment law.

However, both the model BIT and FIP are inconsistent with each other and given South Africa's adoption of a domestic law on the protection of foreign investment that is more consistent with the model BIT, it is quite likely that a harmonisation process of these two different positions will soon occur. Some recent arbitration cases that have gone against two member states, Lesotho and Swaziland, which were initiated under the FIP, suggest that SADC member states may be inclined to adopt a position that is suited towards the protection of the member states' sovereign right to regulate.

In the case of *Swissbourgh v. Lesotho*,[42] the primary claimant, Swissbourgh Diamond Mines (Pty), was incorporated in South Africa while the respondent

33   SADC FIP, Cooperation on Investment, art. 3, annex 1.
34   *Id*, art. 6.
35   *Id*, art. 7.
36   *Id*, art. 5.
37   *Id*, art. 14.
38   *Id*, art. 1.
39   SADC model BIT, 2012, art. 6.
40   *Id*, art. 5.
41   *Id*, arts 28 and 29.
42   *Swissbourgh Diamond Mines (Pty) Limited, Josias Van Zyl, The Josias Van Zyl Family Trust and Others v. The Kingdom of Lesotho* (PCA Case No. 2013-29).

was the Kingdom of Lesotho. The dispute concerns mining leases with claims arising as a result of the alleged conduct by the Lesotho government over the expropriation of the claimants' mining leases. The investors acquired five mining leases in the mid-1980s, however, Lesotho subsequently cancelled those leases in 1991 to build a World Bank financed dam. The claimants pursued legal actions in Lesotho and later attempted to pressure the South African government to exercise diplomatic protection on their behalf.[43]

In 2009, the claimants initiated a claim against Lesotho before the SADC tribunal. The outcome of the award despite the significant public interest issues addressed is not publicly available and the reporting on the developments have come from third parties. During the dispute settlement proceeding, the claimants alleged that Lesotho, along with other SADC member states, took measures to frustrate the claim because at the start of August 2010, a review of the powers of the SADC tribunal was first initiated. As a result, in 2011, the claimants introduced a new arbitration claim under the FIP.[44]

The claimants alleged that Lesotho's participation in the disbandment of the SADC tribunal constituted an 'actionable international wrong'.[45] The notice of arbitration claimed that Lesotho committed a denial of justice under customary international law, as well as a breach of several substantive investment protections contained in the FIP, including obligations on fair and equitable treatment, access to courts and tribunals, transparency and a general undertaking to fulfil obligations arising from the protocol.[46] The Lesotho government argued that the SADC tribunal was an act of the SADC that did not implicate any obligations of Lesotho as a single state. Furthermore, the FIP does not confer any jurisdiction to challenge the conduct of a state in the decision of an international organisation.[47] The investors in this case sought compensation of $300 million against expropriation of their mining licenses, which at the time represented 13 per cent of Lesotho's GDP of $2.3 billion.

43   Peterson, L.E., 2013, 'Dismantling of Southern African Development Community Tribunal spawns Uncitral arbitration claim for denial of justice', *IA Reporter*, viewed (30 March 2017) from www.iareporter.com/articles/dismantling-of-southern-african-develop ment-community-tribunal-spawns-uncitral-arbitration-claim-for-denial-of-justice/, para. 13.
44   *Id*, paras 14 and 15.
45   Mohamadieh, K. and Uribe, D., 2016, *The Rise of Investor-State Dispute Settlement in the Extractives Sectors: Challenges and Considerations for African Countries*, South Centre Research Paper 65, viewed (31 March 2017) from www.southcentre.int/research-paper-65-february-2016/, p. 14.
46   Peterson, *supra* note 43 at para. 7.
47   Peterson, L.E., 2016, 'Multilateral investment treaty's exhaustion of remedies requirement does not hobble case because local courts couldn't offer same relief available before international tribunal', *IA Reporter*, viewed (30 March 2017) from www.iareporter.com/articles/multilateral-investment-treatys-exhaustion-of-remedies-requirement-does-not-hobble-case-because-local-courts-couldnt-offer-same-relief-availa ble-before-international-tribunal/, para. 9.

The tribunal ruled that the scope of the jurisdiction of the the FIP is open ended, including any obligation relating to an admitted investment. This meant that the tribunal could look at Lesotho's compliance with investment protections written into the FIP, as well as other obligations under other treaties, such as the SADC treaty and the SADC tribunal protocol.[48]

By accepting jurisdiction over the dispute, the arbitral tribunal accepted to hold a state accountable for its participation in an international organisation. This was the first time a tribunal asserted jurisdiction over the conduct of a state participating in the decision of an international organisation.[49] If the reasoning of the tribunal is to be followed by future arbitration panels, states could ultimately be constrained to vote in a certain way at international organisations based on the impact that their vote would have on foreign investors in their country.

As the tribunal assessed its jurisdiction over the dispute, the tribunal sought to determine whether the claimants – whose expropriation claim dated from 1991 – were seeking to arbitrate a pre-existing dispute under a treaty that came into force only in 2010. While the tribunal saw the long-standing dispute over the expropriated mining leases to lie outside of its jurisdiction, the tribunal found that a separate dispute was capable of arising out of a dispute resolution process that had been used to determine the initial dispute to confirm jurisdiction on the tribunal. This position was taken by the tribunal to circumvent the application of the FIP only to disputes arising after the treaty came in 2010.[50]

The claimants had argued that the current dispute before the tribunal arose out of the sudden deprivation of the litigation forum through the suspension and ultimate termination of the SADC tribunal[51] and the tribunal endorsed this position.[52]

In a notable departure for a modern investment protection agreement, the FIP contains an express requirement for claimants to exhaust local remedies before pursuing international arbitration. The majority of the tribunal held that the primary remedy sought by the claimants was the establishment of a new tribunal under the same conditions as the disbanded SADC tribunal to hear the expropriation claim.[53] Since the local courts lacked the power to order this specific type of relief, the tribunal decided that there were no available effective local remedies and as a result, the exhaustion requirement posed no barrier to hearing this case under the FIP.[54]

48   *Id*, para. 12.
49   *Id*, para. 10.
50   *Id*, para. 13.
51   *Id*, para. 14.
52   *Id*, para. 15.
53   Peterson 2013, *supra* note 43, at para. 19.
54   *Id*, para. 20.

Ultimately, Lesotho was found liable but no damages were awarded to the claimants. Instead, the tribunal held that to restore the claimants' position, the expropriation claims were to be initiated in a new case under the 2010 UNCITRAL rules, but 'to be heard by a tribunal operating under a regime that mirrors as closely as reasonably possible that of the SADC Tribunal, at the time it was seized of [c]laimants' claim'.[55]

The tribunal erred in its decision because local courts had the authority to determine the expropriation claim of the claimants and also offer tort compensation in terms of pure economic loss for the disbandment of the tribunal. This case represents one of the most confounding examples of overreach by ISDS tribunals on the sovereignty of states to restrict their powers and bend the will of states towards the investors. In this particular case, despite the presence of the exhaustion of domestic remedies requirement, the tribunal was able to circumvent the rule and allowed the frivolous claim to persist. This shows the importance of states tightening the rules on investor protection to prevent limitless liabilities while still offering regulatory certainty and respect for the rule of law that will be attractive for FDI.

In the Southern Africa region, only five countries (DRC, Mozambique, Namibia, Tanzania and Swaziland) provide for international arbitration in their regulatory framework.[56] Another set of six countries (Botswana, Lesotho, Malawi, Mauritius, Seychelles and Zimbabwe) only provide for investor–state dispute settlement through the local courts.[57] Consequently, to develop a consistent regional framework between the SADC FIP, the model BIT and the policy choices of states at a domestic level, it is necessary for the dispute settlement provisions in the FIP to be revisited including preference for exhaustion of domestic remedies, with transparency provisions. This approach ensures that democratic and rule of law features are applied from a regional perspective to serve as a counter-measure to negative perceptions of judicial independence and transparency in some African countries.[58]

The investment framework of Nigeria

The Nigerian Investment Promotion Commission Act (NIPC) of 1995 was passed to establish an investment commission to encourage, promote and coordinate investments into the Nigerian economy and act as the Nigerian federal government's agency for the coordination, promotion and

---

55 *Id*, Peterson 2016, *supra* note 47, at para. 37.
56 Ngobeni, L. and Fagbayibo, B., 2015, 'The investor-state dispute resolution forum under the SADC Protocol on Finance and Investment: Challenges and opportunities for effective harmonisation', *Law Democracy Dev.* 19, 2015 viewed (26 March 2017) from www.scielo.org.za/scielo.php?script=sci_arttext&pid=S2077-49072015000100009
57 *Id*.
58 *Id*.

monitoring of investments. The law primarily focuses on the promotion of investments and while it protects investments against expropriation and makes provision for international arbitration, the overarching framework for the protection of investors and their investments in Nigeria is through the concluded BITs.

Nigeria currently has 29 BITs and five of these are with African countries. Nigeria's BIT framework provides for an asset based definition of investment and combines promotion and protection objectives. The BITs recognise the fair and equitable treatment protection, MFN protection, as well as market value compensation for expropriation. Some of the BITs concluded by Nigeria with European countries have some other unique provisions. For instance, while the Nigeria-Spain BIT covers the traditional BIT protections including national treatment protection, it provides that domestic courts can be used for dispute settlement. Similar provisions appear in the Nigeria-Germany BIT and the Nigeria-China BIT.[59]

However, Nigeria's most recent BIT, the Nigeria-Canada BIT, which was signed in 2013, is significantly different. This is based on the new investment policy shift in Canada and not a change in policy approach in Nigeria. It contains an enterprise based definition of investment and recognises the traditional investor protections, including the right to establishment which is embedded in the scope of the fair and equitable treatment protection as well as the national treatment protection. However, from a developing country perspective, the exclusion of performance requirements hinders the ability of host states to maximise the benefits of FDI.[60]

The BIT has a detailed provision on transparency, which extends to interested persons and not only the investors and the Nigeria government.[61] However, the BIT exempts information disclosure that is contrary to essential security interests or necessary to protect essential security interests.[62] It also prevents information disclosure that might affect international peace and security, or is protected under domestic competition law.[63]

The BIT also excludes the application of health, safety and environmental measures and imposes corporate social responsibility requirements on investors.[64] Other general exceptions in terms of the BIT include the freedom of states to adopt necessary measures to 'protect human, animal or plant life

---

59   Treaty between the Federal Republic of Germany and the Federal Republic of Nigeria concerning the Encouragement and Reciprocal Protection of Investments 2000 and the Agreement Between the Government of the People's Republic of China and the Government of the Federal Republic of Nigeria for the Reciprocal Promotion and Protection of Investments 2001.

60   *Id*, art. 9; Canada and Federal Republic of Nigeria for the Promotion and Protection of Investments 2013.

61   *Id*, art. 12.

62   *Id*, art. 18, General Exceptions.

63   *Id*.

64   *Id*, art. 15 and 16.

or health, to ensure compliance with domestic law … or for the conservation of living or non-living exhaustible natural resources'.[65] While the BIT allows ISDS,[66] it sets out various requirements to grant public access to hearings and documents and accept submissions by a non-disputing party.[67] Disputes are to be governed through the BIT and applicable international law but not domestic law.[68]

In an ongoing case against Nigeria, *Interocean Oil Development Company and Interocean Oil Exploration Company v. Federal Republic of Nigeria*,[69] the claimants are both incorporated in the US. The subject of dispute is an oil exploration and production joint venture. The claimants allege that in the late 1990s, Nigerian authorities colluded in the illegal seizure of the claimants' interests in a Nigerian company, Panocean, that held certain rights to produce and prospect for oil in Nigeria. The investors are seeking damages of $500 million, as well as other relief including $150 million for aggravated damages and restitution of their rights. In a decision on preliminary objections rendered on 29 October 2014, the arbitration tribunal dismissed certain jurisdictional objections raised by Nigeria. The objections included that the NIPC Act does not express Nigeria's consent to ICSID arbitration, that certain pre-arbitration formalities were not complied with and that the claims are time barred under Nigerian law.[70] The arguments by Nigeria's counsels failed to recognise that the application of BITs effectively suspends the application of domestic regulation in favour of the applicable rules in a BIT. This case illustrates the effect of BITs on the domestic framework of states and the necessity for restricting the ambit of BITs.

Nigeria is also a member of ECOWAS, where an investment supplementary act was adopted in 2008 by member states with a similar investment rule framework to Nigeria's BIT regime.[71]

ECOWAS Supplementary Act[72]

The ECOWAS Supplementary Act contains investment rules that recognise investment protections of national treatment, MFN treatment and minimum

65   *Id*, art. 18.
66   *Id*, art. 38.
67   *Id*, arts. 31 and 32.
68   *Id*, art. 38.
69   Peterson, L.E., 2014,'Arbitrators Dismiss Some Objections In Face Of $650 Million Oil Expropriation Claim Under Nigerian Investment Statute', *IA Reporter*, viewed (29th November 2016) from www.iareporter.com/articles/arbitrators-dismiss-some-objections-in-face-of-650-million-oil-expropriation-claim-under-nigerian-investment-statute/
70   *Id*.
71   A/SA.3/12/08. The ECOWAS community is constituted by 15 member states: Benin, Burkina Faso, Cape Verde, Cote d'Ivoire, Gambia, Ghana, Guinea, Guinea-Bissau, Liberia, Mali, Niger, Nigeria, Senegal, Sierra Leone and Togo.
72   A/SA.3/12/08.

regional standards.[73] The minimum regional standards that the ECOWAS rule stipulates include the fair and equitable treatment, as well as prohibition of discrimination based on customary international law.[74] This is different from the protection against expropriation without compensation protection, which requires investors to be compensated without delay, according to market value.[75]

The ECOWAS rules permit free transfer of assets and performance requirements to promote domestic development benefits from investments.[76] There is also a provision on obligations and duties of investors and investments, which require pre-establishment environmental and social impact assessments that are to be made publicly available.[77] Furthermore, investors are required to protect human rights and respect for fundamental labour standards. The rules also require member states not to compete against each other in terms of investment incentives.[78]

With regard to dispute settlement, disputes are to be resolved at a national court or tribunal or the ECOWAS Court of Justice.[79] The investment rules further urge member states to renegotiate state treaties that are not consistent with the investment rules.[80]

The ECOWAS rule is one of the most progressive agreements that is cognisant of the unique context of African states and adopts a rights based approach to development. This is a regional standard that other member countries of ECOWAS will do well to adopt.

At a continental level, countries have adopted domestic investment laws that do not focus on the protection of investments but like Nigeria, the laws are mainly geared towards the promotion of investment. For instance, Egypt's investment law only concerns investment guarantees, and incentives only cover tax exemptions and the creation of free zones.[81] The Kenyan Foreign Investments Protection Act[82] only creates two essential protections: the transfer of profits and the prompt payment of compensation on compulsory acquisition of property.[83] This is guided by section 75 of the Constitution, which protects unlawful deprivation of property.

73 *Id*, arts 5–7.
74 *Id*.
75 *Id*.
76 *Id*, art. 10.
77 *Id*, the Supplementary Act, Chapter 3.
78 *Id*.
79 *Id*, art. 33.
80 *Id*, art. 31.
81 Investment Guarantees and Incentives Law No. 8 of 1997.
82 Chapter 518, 2012.
83 *Id*, art. 8.

The investment framework of Kenya

Unlike the South African law, Kenya's domestic law covers the promotion of investment only and does not offer protections to investors and their investment.

Kenya has negotiated 15 BITs. However, only six are in force. The Kenya-Netherlands BIT of 1979 recognises the fair and equitable and expropriation protection standards and does not depart from traditional BIT models. The Germany-Kenya BIT, which came into force in 2000 provides an asset based definition. It incorporates the fair and equitable treatment, MFN and national treatment standards, full protection and security and protection against expropriation without compensation. The Kenya-Italy BIT, which came into force in 1999, has similar traditional BIT protections for investors. The same applies to the Kenya-Switzerland BIT of 2009 and the Kenya-UK BIT of 1999. Kenya has only signed BITs with three African countries, namely, Burundi, Libya and Mauritius and none of them is currently in force.

In the only recorded ICSID case against Kenya, *Cortec Mining Kenya Limited, Cortec (Pty) Limited and Stirling Capital Limited v. Republic of Kenya, ICSID Case No. ARB/15/29,*[84] the dispute concerns a mining concession where it was alleged that the Kenyan government unlawfully revoked the claimant's mining license, following the discovery of new rare earths deposits by the claimant valued at $60 billion. The investors alleged that the minister of mineral resources had requested bribes of around $1 million to reverse the cancellation. The investors challenge was unsuccessful in the domestic courts and an international arbitration was launched while the case is still pending at Kenya's Court of Appeal. The failure to provide an exhaustion of domestic remedies in Kenya's BIT framework has led to the problem of multiple actions against Kenya arising from the same dispute. While this anomaly exists, Kenya is a member of COMESA and the East African Community where a robust sub-regional investment framework, which protects sustainable development while maintaining an investor friendly approach, has been developed.

COMESA Investment Agreement and EAC Investment Code

The COMESA agreement was adopted in 2007 shortly after the East African Model Investment Code was adopted in 2006.[85] The aim of the agreement is to harmonise investment laws and policies of member states and includes investor protections such as fair and equitable treatment, national treatment,

---

84   Hepburn, J., 2015, 'An update on investor-state claims against Kenya', *IA Reporter*, viewed (29 November 2016) from www.iareporter.com/articles/an-update-on-investor-state-claims-against-kenya/

85   The Investment Agreement for the COMESA Common Investment Area was adopted in May 2007.

MFN treatment and protection against expropriation without compensation based on due process of law that is prompt, adequate and effective.[86] The aim of the COMESA agreement is to facilitate a competitive investment area, which allows the free movement of capital, labour, goods and services among the member states.

Despite the adoption of the agreement, no country has ratified the agreement and consequently, the agreement is not in force. The agreement only applies to registered COMESA investors who are nationals or judicial persons of member states and requires compliance with domestic measures of member states both in the pre- and post-establishment phase.[87]

In terms of dispute settlement, the agreement prescribes state-to-state disputes constituted under the COMESA Court of Justice.[88] It also allows investors to institute cases in national courts, the COMESA Court of Justice or international arbitration based on the rules agreed to by the parties.[89] The COMESA agreement allows states to adopt their own investment regulations and the use of national courts to settle investment disputes.

Within the COMESA Court of Justice, transparency principles are applied through the public availability of all documents and public hearings.[90] The agreement requires transparency 'in the application and interpretation of national laws, regulations, and administrative procedures'.[91]

Aside from the COMESA agreement, the East African Model Investment Code, which was adopted in 2006, is also applicable to Kenya. The code is meant to serve as a guide for member states to design their national investment policies and laws. The code provides for the right of establishment.[92] It also provides protections of national treatment, non-discrimination and protection from expropriation without compensation.[93] The rest of the code deals with the establishment of investment promotion agencies and the creation of special economic zones. The EAC comprises of six member countries: Kenya, Uganda, Tanzania, Rwanda, South Sudan and Burundi.

The code is similar to the SADC model BIT in terms of its non-binding nature; however, it has been adopted by member states. It is meant to serve as a guide for the adoption of investment regulations by member states. In terms of dispute settlement, the code recommends both the ICSID and national courts. Table 6.2 offers an in-depth comparative analysis of the various regional agreements across the RECs in Africa that have investment provisions.

---

86   *Id*, arts 15–20.
87   *Id*, arts 12 and 13.
88   *Id*, arts 27 and 28.
89   UNECA Investment Report, *supra* note 4 at p. 33.
90   Muchlinski, P., 2008, 'The COMESA Common Investment Area: Substantive Standards and Procedural Problems in Dispute Settlement', viewed (6 October 2016) from http://ssrn.com/abstract=1698209
91   *Id*, COMESA Agreement, art. 4.
92   EAC Investment Code, 2006, Chapter 5.
93   *Id*, arts 5 and 15.

Table 6.2 Regional investment regulation across Africa post 2000

	SADC model BIT	SADC Finance & Investment Protocol (Annex 1)	Investment Agreement for the COMESA Common Investment Area	Supplementary Act A/SA.3/12/08 adopting community rules on investment and the modalities for their implementation with ECOWAS	EAC Investment Code
OBJECTIVE OF THE LAW	This non-binding instrument recommends the harmonisation of the investment laws and policies of member states and to develop an approach for member states to adopt in their national treaties or to serve as a guide for treaty negotiations.	This Protocol aims to foster harmonisation of the financial and investment policies of member states in order to make them consistent with the objectives of SADC.	The objective of this agreement is to establish a competitive common investment area within COMESA. This agreement only protects investors and their investments in the COMESA area.	This law aims to promote investment and support sustainable development of the ECOWAS region.	This text is a guiding instrument for investment related policies or laws for EAC member states.
INVESTMENT PROTECTIONS **Investment Regulatory Measures**	Article 20 recognises the right of states to take measures with the goal of sustainable development, and other social and economic policy objectives. Article 21 permits member states to grant preferential treatment to any enterprise under the domestic law in order to achieve national or sub-national regional development goals.	Article 14 provides that member states shall maintain their right to regulate in the public interest and to enforce any measure to ensure that investment activity is undertaken in a manner sensitive to health, safety or environmental concerns. Article 7 allows member states to grant preferential treatment that achieves national development objectives.	Article 22 provides that regulatory measures are not to be applied in a manner which would constitute a means of arbitrary or unjustifiable discrimination between investors where like conditions prevail.	There are no relevant provisions on regulatory measures.	Article 30 provides for the establishment of special economic zones in the partner state's territory. These zones are subject to special regulations determined by the relevant partner state for the purpose of increasing economic activities of a particular nature.

Table 6.2 (continued)

SADC model BIT	SADC Finance & Investment Protocol (Annex 1)	Investment Agreement for the COMESA Common Investment Area	Supplementary Act A/SA.3/12/08 adopting community rules on investment and the modalities for their implementation with ECOWAS	EAC Investment Code
NATIONAL TREATMENT				
Article 4 recognises the following exceptions: – non-conforming measures and excluded sectors determined on a state-by-state basis; – concessions, advantages, exemptions or other measures that may result from a BIT, multilateral or regional agreement; – special formalities in connection with the investments of investors.	There is no provision on national treatment.	Article 17 provides that the test of 'like circumstances' will be determined through an examination on a case by case basis of circumstances of the investment.	Article 5 recognises the national treatment protection with respect to the management, conduct, operation, expansion and sale or other disposition of investments. The text also clarifies the test of 'in like circumstances' to require an overall examination, on a case by case basis, of all the circumstances of an investment and sets out various factors to be considered.	Article 5(2) provides that foreign investors shall be in no different position than local investors of an EAC partner state for the purposes of the establishment, carrying on of business activity, income taxation and every aspect of the business activity.

Table 6.2 (continued)

SADC model BIT	SADC Finance & Investment Protocol (Annex 1)	Investment Agreement for the COMESA Common Investment Area	Supplementary Act A/SA.3/12/08 adopting community rules on investment and the modalities for their implementation with ECOWAS	EAC Investment Code
MOST FAVOURED NATION TREATMENT				
Article 4.4	There is no provision on MFN.	Article 19	Article 6	There is no provision for MFN.
It excludes the MFN standard.		Member states are to accord COMESA investors and their investments treatment no less favourable than that it accords, in like circumstances, to investors and their investments from any third country with respect to investments in its territory.	Member states must accord investments made by investors of another member state treatment no less favourable than that it accords in like circumstances, to investments made by investors of any other member state of the Community or of a third party with respect to investments.	

Table 6.2 (continued)

SADC model BIT	SADC Finance & Investment Protocol(Annex 1)	Investment Agreement for the COMESA Common Investment Area	Supplementary Act A/SA.3/12/08 adopting community rules on investment and the modalities for their implementation with ECOWAS	EAC Investment Code
FAIR AND EQUITABLE TREATMENT				
Article 5	Article 6	Article 14	Article 7	There is no provision for FET.
It provides two alternatives for the FET:	Investors and their investments enjoy fair and equitable treatment in the territory of any state party which shall be no less favourable than that granted to investors of a third state.	Application of customary international law standard.	Application of customary international law standard.	
– in accordance with customary international law: requires the demonstration of an act by government that are in bad faith, a willful neglect of duty or an insufficiency short of international standards that every reasonable and impartial person would recognise its insufficiency;	Article 20 provides that states must ensure that the least developed countries receive effective preferential treatment.			
– Fair Administrative Treatment: state parties must ensure that their administrative, legislative, and judicial processes do not operate in a manner that is arbitrary or that denies administrative and procedural [justice][due process] to investors of the other state party or their investments [taking into consideration the level of development of the state party].				

Table 6.2 (continued)

SADC model BIT	SADC Finance & Investment Protocol(Annex 1)	Investment Agreement for the COMESA Common Investment Area	Supplementary Act A/SA.3/12/08 adopting community rules on investment and the modalities for their implementation with ECOWAS	EAC Investment Code
FULL PROTECTION AND SECURITY				
Article 9 Provides for state parties to accord investments of a state party protection and security no less favourable than that which it accords to investments of its own investors or of any third state. This includes restitution, indemnification, compensation as a result of losses resulting from the breach of protection.	The text does not make specific reference to full protection and security.	The text does not make specific reference to full protection and security.	Article 7 It prescribes reasonable protection and security under the domestic law to all states. It also provides prompt, adequate and effective compensation where investments are unnecessarily destroyed by the host state's forces or authority.	It is only provided in the context of protection of property rights.

Table 6.2 (continued)

SADC model BIT	SADC Finance & Investment Protocol (Annex 1)	Investment Agreement for the COMESA Common Investment Area	Supplementary Act A/SA.3/12/08 adopting community rules on investment and the modalities for their implementation with ECOWAS	EAC Investment Code
EXPROPRIATION				
Article 6	Article 5 of Annex 1	Article 20	Article 8	Article 14
Recognises indirect or direct expropriation in the public interest; in accordance with due process of law; and on payment of fair and adequate compensation within a reasonable period of time.	Investments shall not be nationalised or expropriated except for a public purpose, under due process of law, on a non-discriminatory basis and subject to the payment of prompt, adequate and effective compensation.	Member states shall not nationalise or expropriate investments except in the public interest; on a non-discriminatory basis; in accordance with due process of law; and on payment of prompt adequate fair market value compensation.	Contains similar provision in the COMESA agreement and SADC model BIT.	It prohibits compulsory deprivation of property or of any interest or right to property except where it is necessary for public use or in the interest of defence, public safety, public order, public morality or public health; and the compulsory taking of possession of property is made under a law which makes a provision for prompt payment of fair and adequate compensation.
The text gives three options for fair compensation:		Bona fide regulatory measures taken to protect or enhance public welfare objectives, shall not constitute an indirect expropriation.		
Option 1: assessment based on an equitable balance between the public interest and interest of those affected.				
Option 2: fair market value of the expropriated investment immediately before the expropriation took place based on an equitable balance between the public interest and interest of those affected.				
Option 3: fair market value of the expropriated investment immediately before the expropriation took place. It excludes public welfare objectives.				

Table 6.2 (continued)

SADC model BIT	SADC Finance & Investment Protocol(Annex 1)	Investment Agreement for the COMESA Common Investment Area	Supplementary Act A/SA.3/12/08 adopting community rules on investment and the modalities for their implementation with ECOWAS	EAC Investment Code
INVESTOR–STATE DISPUTE SETTLEMENT				
Scope of arbitration				
Article 29 provides for arbitration subject to exhaustion of domestic remedies. The arbitration can take place in the SADC tribunal, ICSID or UNCITRAL. It recognises state–state dispute settlement.	Article 28 of Annex 1 provides for arbitration subject to exhaustion of domestic remedies. The arbitration can take place in the SADC tribunal, ICSID, UNCITRAL, any tribunal in the host state's territory. It recognises state–state dispute settlement.	Article 28 provides for standard investor–state arbitration. The arbitration can take place in the court of the host state, COMESA Court of Justice or international arbitration. It recognises state–state dispute settlement.	Provides for standard investor–state arbitration and offers a choice to settle disputes in the courts of state parties. It recognises state–state dispute settlement.	Article 15 provides for standard investor–state arbitration. Otherwise, parties may refer disputes to the local courts of the partner state or the East African Court of Justice.
Intervention by third parties				
Article 29.15. Provides for a tribunal to have the authority to accept and consider *amicus curiae* submissions from a person or entity that is not a disputing party.	No provision for *amicus* participation.	Article 28 An arbitral tribunal must be open to the receipt of *amicus curiae* submissions.	The text does not provide details on *amicus* participation.	No provision for *amicus* participation.

Table 6.2 (continued)

SADC model BIT	SADC Finance & Investment Protocol(Annex 1)	Investment Agreement for the COMESA Common Investment Area	Supplementary Act A/SA.3/12/08 adopting community rules on investment and the modalities for their implementation with ECOWAS	EAC Investment Code
Transparency of proceedings				
Article 28 provides that all documents relating to a notice of arbitration, the settlement or resolution of any dispute, the pleadings, evidence and decisions in them, shall be available to the public, subject to the redaction of confidential information. Procedural and substantive oral hearings shall be open to the public. This may be achieved through live broadcasting of the hearings. An arbitral tribunal may take such steps as are necessary, by exception, to protect confidential business information in written form or at oral hearings.	No provision for transparency.	Article 28 All documents relating to a notice of intention to arbitrate, the settlement of any dispute, the initiation of an arbitral tribunal, or the pleadings, evidence and decisions in them, shall be available to the public. Procedural and substantive oral hearings shall also be open to the public. Confidential business information or information that is privileged or otherwise protected from disclosure under a member state's law shall, if such information is submitted to the tribunal, be protected from disclosure.	Article 34 The text states that all documents relating to a notice of intention to arbitrate, the settlement of any dispute, the initiation of a panel or appeal, or the pleadings, evidence and decisions in them must be available only to the parties to the disputes. Procedural and substantive oral hearings shall be open to the public also.	No provision for transparency.

Table 6.2 (continued)

SADC model BIT	SADC Finance & Investment Protocol(Annex 1)	Investment Agreement for the COMESA Common Investment Area	Supplementary Act A/SA.3/12/08 adopting community rules on investment and the modalities for their implementation with ECOWAS	EAC Investment Code
Governing Law				
No reference to domestic law.	No reference to domestic law.	Article 31 provides for the application of domestic law.	Article 36 provides for the application of domestic law.	Provides for the application of domestic law.
Appeals				
Article 29.20 provides for the possibility of appeals through any future agreements.	No provision for appeals.	No provision for appeals.	The text mentions the redress to appeal procedures but does not give specific details on this issue.	No provision for appeals.

Emerging trends in investment regulation in Africa

Not too many African power blocs have used their economic dominance to their advantage when concluding BITs with other African countries. As a result, the expected public policy exceptions that states are clamouring for in recent times have not featured prominently in intra-African BITs.

The BIT regimes of most African states are distorted because they often reflect the agenda of a developed country treaty party. Such trends are expected to be replicated when more powerful African states are negotiating with less developed states, but this has not necessarily been the case.

The public policy exceptions that are increasingly being seen in BITs with African countries have been as a result of change in treaty policy by countries such as Canada. As a result of these dynamics, it appears that states in Africa that have dominated the negotiation scene in Africa have been those with specific investment policy strategies with the corresponding expertise to negotiate treaties that are to the state's advantage.

The primary aim of BITs is investor protection, especially against policy risks. As a result, developing countries who are the primary recipients of FDI pay for the costs of investor protection through their sovereignty, especially given the restrictions that these investor protections place on the free will of states to develop policies. Certain treaty features such as performance requirements and pre-establishment clauses do not feature prominently in treaties between developing countries because developing countries adopt closely similar agreements that have been adopted between developed and developing countries, which prohibit performance requirements.[94]

It is necessary to understand why these agreements are similar if developing countries are not burdened with the pressures of succumbing to the will of their developed partners. One explanation could be the lack of expertise and knowledge in developing states to recognise the unique advantages they now face in introducing policy that suits the country's domestic economic needs.[95] Another explanation is the lack of recognition by developing states that BITs constitute more than signalling interest in hosting FDI but also shape the nature of the FDI, accruable benefits and the potential liability of the state to treaty violations.[96]

In order to identify which African states have led a deliberate strategy to shape their treaty framework, it is necessary to look at the extent to which states have a consistent or diverse set of treaties with various states.

94   Sachs, L. and Sauvant, K., 2009, 'BITs, DTTs and FDI flows: An overivew', in Sachs, L. and Sauvant, K. (eds), *The Effect of Treaties on Foreign Direct Investment: Bilateral Investment Treaties, Double Taxation Treaties and Investment Flows*, Oxford: Oxford University Press, viewed (26 March 2017) from http://ccsi.columbia.edu/files/2014/01/Overview-SachsSauvant-Final.pdf

95   Alschner, W. and Skougarevskiy, D., 2016, 'Rule-takers or rule-makers? A new look at African bilateral investment treaty practice', Working Paper No. 7, p. 4, viewed (30 March 2017) from https://ssrn.com/abstract=2791474

96   *Id.*

South Africa, Egypt, Nigeria and Kenya have been the dominating power blocs in the Southern, North, West and East African regions. None of these countries, except for South Africa, has a consistent treaty framework. While South Africa has a consistent investment treaty framework with African countries, its African BITs closely resemble features of South Africa's first BIT with the UK. The BITs do not cater for shared interests in investment protection and promotion while balancing foreign investment protection and the sovereign right of states to regulate in the public interest.

However, outside of these power blocs, other countries have been strategic in the utilisation of their BIT framework. For example, a predominant clause in Mauritius BITs exempts the scope of treaties relating to the right of states to act in essential security interests, protection of public health and the environment. This features in 16 Mauritius BITs and originated from the China-Mauritius BIT.[97]

In recent times, Canadian BITs concluded since 2013 with Tanzania, Cameroon, Burkina Faso, Mali, Rwanda, Benin, Ivory Coast, Nigeria, Senegal and Mozambique have all featured a minimum of ten regulatory exemptions, with Tanzania having the highest of 17.[98] There have been less regulatory restrictions in intra-African BITs though and the most recent Mauritius-Egypt BIT contains seven regulatory exceptions.

Egypt, which has the highest number of BITs, has not established its footprint in its investment treaty landscape.[99] In Egypt's 2003 and 2014 BIT with Mauritius, the BITs were more consistent with Mauritius' BITs with Rwanda and Zimbabwe than with any previous Egyptian BIT, which shows Mauritius is the country influencing the BIT framework with other countries. This is despite Egypt having a GDP of $272 billion compared to Mauritius' $11 billion.[100] Mauritius was more proactive in protecting its own investors and regulatory space than Egypt.

Mauritius therefore represents the example of a country that employs 'expert knowledge and long term strategy to build a coherent treaty network'.[101] The transition of Mauritius from a manufacturing based economy to a financial services hub was deliberate and involved strategic negotiation of international investment agreements as well as double taxation treaties. As a result, a significant proportion of FDI heading for India has been channelled through Mauritius.[102]

---

97   *Id*, p. 11.
98   Aside from carving out future areas for measures such as social services, government security and the like, there are exceptions to the MFN treatment protection and exclusions to ISDS: Annex II of Canada-Nigeria BIT 2013.
99   Egypt has signed a total of 112 investment agreements.
100 Alschner and Skougarevskiy, *supra* note 95 at p. 15.
101 *Id*, p. 17.
102 Forty per cent of India's FDI flows went through Mauritius; *Id*, p. 18.

It is important for states to be deliberate about the kind of technical expertise that is used in negotiating BITs. For instance, while South Africa's BITs were consistent, adopting a treaty framework from the UK may not necessarily have been the right framework for South Africa's policy interests towards its regional partners, particularly in terms of favouring performance requirements.

When states fail to conclude BITs without a strategic approach towards what the BIT should achieve, they increase their risk of exposure to treaty claims, especially when domestic regulations adopted by states contravene treaty obligations. For example, Egypt currently has 29 cases registered against it. Egypt adopts a traditional approach to its BITs with ISDS preferred as the method of dispute resolution. It has the third highest number of disputes registered against it under the ICSID and coincidentally, it also has the highest number of BITs by an African country, with over 100 BITs in force.

The various regional investment regulations across Africa allow African states with similar economic interests to determine suitable investment policies that protect the state right to regulate in the public interest as well as define the applicable rules for investment by being rule makers rather than rule takers. The regional investments in Africa adopt favourable rules that protect the interests of African states, such as ensuring the state right to regulate, the use of domestic courts to resolve disputes, the imposition of obligations on investors and adherence to human rights norms. To adopt a BIT without these strategic considerations will result in the potential exploitation of BIT rules by foreign investors. Investors will challenge domestic regulation and interpret rules that favour the abdication of their responsibilities to the detriment of the host state.[103]

103   For example, in the ongoing case of *Total E&P Uganda BV v. Republic of Uganda* (ICSID Case No. ARB/15/11) Total are challenging what they describe as an unlawful tax levied by the government. The investors acquired four oil exploration blocks and the tax revenue authority subsequently imposed a stamp duty after the acquisition. This is one of several tax related disputes brought by foreign investors against Uganda. Also in *Tamagot Bumi SA and Bumi Mauritania SA v. Islamic Republic of Mauritania* (ICSID Case No. ARB/14/23), the claimants companies, Tamagot Bumi SA and Bumi Mauritania SA, are Mauritanian. Their common parent company, Bumi Holding, is also Mauritanian. Bumi Holding is owned by Rubis International, a Mauritanian company, and Bumi Resources is owned by an Indonesian family. The respondent is the Republic of Mauritania. The claimants allege that Mauritanian authorities have improperly withdrawn their mining license. They allege breach of contract as well as breach of a 2002 domestic investment law. It was alleged that the claimant's license was revoked for its failure to award contracts to a local company who helped the investors secure their mining license.

Table 6.3 ICSID cases against African states

Country	Cases against	Cases concluded	Cases pending	Cases concluded based on jurisdiction	Cases concluded based on merits	Cases discontinued/ settled
Algeria	5	4	1	1	1	2
Burkina Faso	1	1	/	/	1	/
Burundi	4	3	1	/	2	1
Cabo Verde	1	/	1	/	/	/
Cameroon	5	4	1	1	1	2
Central African Republic	3	3	/	/	3	/
Republic of Congo	2	2	/	/	/	2
People's Republic of Congo	2	2	/	/	2	/
Democratic Republic of Congo	9	9	/	2	3	4
Egypt	29	20	9	3	9	8
Equatorial Guinea	2	1	1	1	1	/
Gabonese Republic	2	2	/	/	1	1
Republic of Gabon	1	1	/	/	/	1
Gambia	4	3	1	/	/	3
Ghana	3	2	1	1	1	/
Republic of Guinea	6	4	2	2	/	2
People's Revolutionary Republic of Guinea	1	1	/	1	/	/
Republic of Côte d'Ivoire	1	/	1	/	/	/
Côte d'Ivoire	2	2	/	1	/	1
Kenya	3	1	2	/	1	/
Liberia	3	3	/	/	1	2
Libya	1	/	1	/	/	/
Republic of Madagascar	1	1	/	/	/	1
Madagascar	1	1	/	/	/	1
Democratic Republic of Madagascar	1	1	/	/	2	1
Mali	2	2	1	/	/	/
Mauritania	1	/	1	/	/	/

Table 6.3 (continued)

Country	Cases against	Cases concluded	Cases pending	Cases concluded based on jurisdiction	Cases concluded based on merits	Cases discontinued/settled
Kingdom of Morocco	2	2	/	/	2	/
Morocco	1	1	/	/	/	1
Mozambique	1	/	1	/	/	/
Feral Republic of Nigeria	2	1	1	/	/	1
Nigeria	1	1	/	/	/	1
Niger	2	2	/	/	1	1
Rwanda	1	1	/	/	/	1
Senegal	4	4	/	1	1	2
South Africa	1	1	/	/	/	1
South Sudan	1	1	/	/	1	/
Sudan	1	/	1	/	/	/
United Republic of Tanzania	3	1	2	/	1	/
Tanzania Electric Supply Company Limited	1	1	/	/	1	1
Independent Power Tanzania Limited	1	1	/	/	/	1
Togo	2	2	/	/	1	1
Uganda	3	1	2	/	/	1
Zimbabwe	3	1	2	/	1	/

Source: Compiled from ICSID website as on 30 November 2016.

Conclusion

Africa's economy is growing significantly. There is an increase in political stability across the majority of states and there is a modest increase in the diversification in state economies, which bodes well for economic growth.[104] The penetration of mobile telecommunications, rebasing of GDP to expand to other sectors, increase in the discovery of mineral wealth as well as remittances from Africans in diaspora have all contributed to Africa's economic growth.[105]

At the same time, African integration is also happening aided by RECs. Three RECS (COMESA, EAC and SADC) formed a tripartite free trade area (TFTA), which came into force in 2016. The TFTA is expected to make the region more attractive for investment flows.[106] Crucial roles for RECs include coordinated efforts to address the problem of overlapping trade agreements that have different commitments. Several countries belong to multiple RECs that have different trade regimes, which will require countries to apply different trade rules to different regional partners. This increases the cost of trade in meeting these rules and also leads to inconsistencies, which can distort regional markets. The adoption of the TFTA should help to resolve problems like this and should help facilitate cross-border investment, reduce the cost of doing business in the region and create a conducive environment for private sector development.[107]

There is a strong case for regional integration in Africa. Politically, integration gives the African region a better bargaining power with developed countries in trade and investment negotiations.[108] It also promotes the presence of supranational rules that will replace protectionist national policies. While the presence of supranational rules is sometimes regarded as an infringement of the sovereign policy space of states, the ceding of sovereignty in favour of supranational rules is itself an act of sovereignty. More importantly, harmonisation of investment rules at a regional level allows consistency and certainty that serves to benefit regions as a whole.

Economically, integration also enables the liberalisation of trade with a larger export market and access to cheaper imports.[109] Furthermore, integration encourages healthy competition with the reduction in monopoly of companies, as well as the promotion of efficiency.[110] Access to a bigger integrated market can also attract FDI.[111]

---

104 UNECA Investment Report. *supra* note 6.
105 *Id.*
106 UNECA Investment Report, *supra* note 6 at p. 35.
107 Preamble to the Tripartite Free Trade Agreement.
108 UNECA, *supra* note 6 at p. 83.
109 *Id*, p. 115.
110 *Id.*
111 *Id*, p. 151.

Despite these, regional integration has faced many challenges. The large differences in the population, geographic and economic sizes of African states make integration difficult.[112] In addition, the concentration of trade in mineral wealth and increasingly, financial services, also reduces the impact of integration.[113] While the majority of African states have largely removed tariff barriers, the presence of non-tariff barriers remains. The continued presence of rules of origin, export and import permits as well as protectionist measures by states to protect their industries have hindered integration.[114] Infrastructure deficit remains a problem not only in terms of hard infrastructure but also the absence of strong institutions and regulations. Supranational rules are not being domesticated or ratified and model laws developed for guidance are being ignored.[115] Consequently, while there have been attempts to promote multilateralism at a regional level, the conduct of states is still protectionist oriented. To address these concerns, there is a crucial role for RECs to play.

RECs are made up of member states and the effectiveness of a REC is dependent on the level of commitment and strength of the member states to implement REC agreements and to comply with their obligations.[116] Regional integration is a difficult objective to achieve given the diversity of states that aim to integrate towards a common purpose.[117] Understandably, countries have different national priorities to cater for the different levels of development as well as political and economic ideologies.[118] To align this range of interests, it is important for the regional integration agenda to be aligned with national interests and an important way of doing this is through the domestication of regional agreements into national regulatory frameworks. Due to countries having multiple memberships in different RECs with different rules, this can cause ambiguity.

While there is a very strong economic case in support of regional integration, the domestication of regional agreements is not enough. Connecting the continent through infrastructure and technology is necessary to support smaller, landlocked countries that are inherently more disadvantaged than other countries as a result of their geographical

---

112   For instance, there are eight countries (Benin, Burkina Faso, Guinea-Bissau, Ivory Coast, Mali, Niger, Sénégal and Togo) using the Communauté Financière Africaine (CFA) currency in ECOWAS, which has hindered the prospects of ECOWAS developing a common currency with the presence of Nigeria, which is bigger than the combination of all eight countries.
113   World Investment Report 2015, *supra* note 17; GSDPP, *supra* note 2 at p. 17.
114   *Id*, World Investment Report, p. 146.
115   The COMESA Investment Agreement has not been ratified and the recent BITs of Mozambique and do not reflect the proposals of the SADC model BIT.
116   GSDPP, *supra* note 2 at p. 6.
117   *Id*.
118   *Id*.

location.[119] Consequently, investment in infrastructure is necessary and FDI facilitates that. Furthermore, it is necessary to place emphasis on the removal of tariff and non-tariff barriers and the assimilation of informal cross-border trade networks.[120]

While some states are concerned about the loss of their policy space and protective of their sovereignty, it is important to recognise that regional integration promotes inclusion and brings countries together to protect collective interests.[121] Emphasising African identity is therefore crucial to the regional integration project. Bilateral investment agreements that address the individual national interests of states do not achieve this. Multilateral investment agreements should be preferred but such agreements should be aligned with the diverse domestic objectives of the states that ratify these agreements.[122] The current regional investment agreements across Africa provide a solid background to further develop an investment rules framework that places sustainable development and human rights at the centre of investment priorities.

119 *Id*, p. 7.
120 *Id.*
121 *Id*, p. 12.
122 *Id*, p. 15.

7 Conclusion and recommendations

The recommendations made in this book recognise the need for a multifaceted approach to solving problems with investment regulation.

As African RECs move towards the integration of investment rules, developments outside the continent affirms the need for African states to protect their own interests while maintaining a competitive environment for the attraction of FDI. Investment flows to Africa will continue to grow as African economies continue to diversify and the population grows, creating a big workforce attractive to global corporations and global value chains. The continuous discovery of natural resources also means the need for FDI will continue to grow.

However, it is important that African states maximise FDI flows for the benefit of her citizens and to spur economic development. To do this, African states need to be careful about the development of regulation that ensures the attraction of the right kind of investment and sufficient safeguards are in place to maximise the benefits of such investment for the public interest. Consequently, states need to ensure that on the one hand, they adopt regulation that promote the objectives of sustainable and inclusive development, ensures performance requirements are imposed on investors, and there is an obligation to protect human rights. On the other hand, states should refrain from adopting arbitrary measures that erode the rights of investors and the protections for their investments. Without a careful balance of these competing considerations, disputes are bound to arise which exposes the liability of states. The possibility of investor claims against states in ISDS tribunals that are regarded as unaccountable, among several other concerns, has led to the global public opposition towards the system.

Indeed, the opposition to TPP and TTIP, and to ISDS in particular, has led to the USA's withdrawal from TPP and for the European Commission to suspend its trade negotiations with the USA to conduct a public consultation on the investment aspects of TTIP.[1] The European Commission recently

---

1   Reinsch, A., 2016, *The European Union and Investor-State Dispute Settlement: From Investor–State Arbitration to a permanent Investment Court*, Investor-State Arbitration Series Paper No. 2.

tabled a proposal to establish a permanent investment court that would replace the ad hoc ISDS tribunal.[2] Prior to this latest proposal, in 2013, the European Commission released a paper that sought to refute a number of common criticisms about ISDS. The European Commission defended the ISDS regime by asserting that this system does not subvert democracy though it bypasses domestic courts but for legitimate reasons because there are concerns regarding bias and possible lack of independence in the local courts which raises concerns for investors.[3] In a matter of months, public pressure and opposition have led to the reversal of the Commission's policy decision, which shows the incredible power the public can wield in holding public institutions accountable.

In recognition of this backlash against ISDS, the transparency argument made in this book is premised on the idea that transparency benefits not only non-disputing parties who will have better access to information, but it also enables the investor to obtain relevant information affecting its investment. To advance the transparency agenda, various stakeholders have a role to play, including civil society, to actively push on the level of negotiating new BITs or in the review of existing BITs for active public participation.

Arbitrators also have a role to play by recognising procedural integrity is not a competing objective with transparency imperatives and should recognise the importance of adopting interpretations that favour not only information disclosure but also third party participation. Intervening parties should not be prevented from acting as *amicus* because they have a significant legitimate interest in a dispute, as demonstrated in the *von Pezold v. Zimbabwe*[4] dispute discussed in this book. *Amicus* participation should, importantly, not be limited to civil society participation alone but should also include the participation of grassroots movements to represent the interests and voices of the masses.

In some of the cases considered in this book, including *Swissbourgh Diamond Mines (Pty) Ltd v. Lesotho*[5] and *Southern Pacific Properties (Middle East) v. Arab Republic of Egypt*,[6] disputing parties in ISDS, investors and states often resort to domestic courts when attempting to set aside an investment award. This begs the question of why domestic courts are good enough to annul awards but not good enough to adjudicate investment

2   *Id.*
3   European Commission, 2013, 'Incorrect claims about investor-state dispute settlement', viewed (25 March 2017) from http://trade.ec.europa.eu/doclib/docs/2013/october/tradoc_151790.pdf, p. 1.
4   *Bernhard von Pezold and Others v. Republic of Zimbabwe*, ICSID Case No. ARB/10/15.
5   *Swissbourgh Diamond Mines (Pty) Limited, Josias Van Zyl, The Josias Van Zyl Family Trust and Others v. The Kingdom of Lesotho* (PCA Case No. 2013–29).
6   ICSID Case No. ARB/84/3.

disputes. Such a paradox undermines the traditional and perhaps out dated claim that domestic courts are illegitimate dispute settlement forums. Aside from the use of domestic legal systems, other alternatives are offered in this book, which include use of state–state dispute settlement and regional human rights mechanisms. A major backlash against ISDS has been the absence of relevant democratic ideals including procedural integrity, public participation, transparency and rule of law principles that might be sufficient to overcome a democratic deficit.[7] These features exist in the alternatives proposed and some of the emerging trends in new IIAs, including in the new domestic law of South Africa and the pan-African investment code, suggest an increasing preference for state–state dispute settlement.

Two public law scholars, Morison and Anthony, recognise the complex linkages between national, regional and supranational bodies and the need to address democratic deficits in institutions. Their concern largely lies with the lack of elements of democracy that would allow some form of transparency, public participation and the limitation to internal procedures of decision making in global governance institutions.[8] They endorse the proposal that rather than having final decisions based on authority, decisions should rather be a process of negotiation and compromise as well as challenge and concession between the different constituencies.[9]

These proposals clearly express the discontent with the ISDS model and the need for the revision of the system. Supporters of the current investment ISDS system can no longer sustain the tendency to see BITs as purely dealing with investor's rights, isolating them from the influence of other legal systems. A plurality of legal systems that complement each other is one way forward.[10]

ISDS tribunals only have jurisdiction to adjudicate disputes originating from alleged breaches of a treaty provision and BITs do not usually contain any provisions dealing with substantive human rights obligations.[11] Consequently, it is important for tribunals to accord due consideration to other systems of law that impose obligations on disputing parties. For example, host states can raise the defence of human rights to justify actions taken against a claimant investor. However, the allegations of human rights violations must be related to the claim brought by the investor. According to Dupuy, a party to a dispute invoking a human rights argument, whether it is

---

7   Morison, J. and Anthony, G., 2011, 'The place of public interest', in G. Antony et al. (eds), *Values in Global Administrative Law*, Hart Publishing, p. 232.
8   *Id*, p. 237.
9   *Id*, p. 238.
10 *Id*, p. 221.
11 One example is the Norwegian Model BIT, 2007, which reaffirms the 'parties commitment to democracy, the rule of law, human rights and fundamental freedoms in accordance with their obligations under international law, including the principles set out in the United Nations Charter and the Universal Declaration of Human Rights'.

the host state or the investor, must demonstrate that the human rights at issue affects the implementation of the investment at stake.[12] This constraint exists because the arbitrator's jurisdiction is specifically limited to the settlement of disputes arising out of a given investment.[13] As a result of the restrictive jurisdiction of ISDS, the credibility of decisions coming out of investment arbitrations must give due regard to other existing laws, domestic or international.

While African states should adopt domestic investment regulation that protects their relevant public interests, adopting a unified approached in a time of increasing regionalism will be ideal. This will also help smaller countries with weak bureaucracies and technical expertise to ensure they conclude BITs that do not compromise on the objectives of sustainable development. This approach is already being considered at the EU level where FDI for European countries has become an exclusive competence of the EU.[14] As a result, the EU has started to form its own investment policy, including the negotiation of BITs. Although current BITs continue to be binding on the member states as a matter of public international law, member state BITs now have to be evaluated from the perspective of the exclusive competence of the EU.[15] The European Commission has proposed a new European investment policy, which sets the standards for authorising existing BITs, as well as amending or concluding BITs with third countries. The Commission is also expected to review the BITs in order to determine whether the BITs or their provisions are in conflict with the law of the EU, overlap with an agreement of the EU in force with that third country or constitute an obstacle to the development and the implementation of the EU's policies relating to investment.[16]

African regional bodies can take this approach further by imposing consequences such as ensuring that if these conditions are not met and if it trumps common regional interests of a human rights based approach to development, the authorisation for a country's BIT is withdrawn. This approach extends developments already proposed in model BITs at a regional level into a binding legal norm that ensure BITs do not trump other relevant non-investment obligations.

12   Dupuy, P.M., 2009, 'Unification rather than fragmentation of international law? The case of international investment law and human rights law', in Dupuy, P.M., *Human Rights in International Investment Law and Arbitration*, Oxford University Press, pp. 61–62.

13   *Id.*

14   This is a result of the entry into force of the Lisbon Treaty on 1 December 2009. Levashova, Y., 2012, *Public Interest Norms in the European International Investment Policy: A Shattered Hope?*, University of Oslo Faculty of Law, Legal Studies Research Paper Series No. 8, p. 86.

15   *Id*, p. 88.

16   *Id*, p. 90.

In the SADC model BIT, the preamble provides for the recognition of:

> the important contribution investment can make to the sustainable development of the State Parties, ... and the furtherance of human rights and human development; ... reaffirming the right of the State Parties to regulate and to introduce new measures relating to investments in their territories in order to meet national policy objectives...

The model law further provides a specific right of states to regulate, which states that:

> the Host State has the right to take regulatory or other measures to ensure that development in its territory is consistent with the goals and principles of sustainable development, and with other legitimate social and economic policy objectives.
>
> For greater certainty, non-discriminatory measures taken by a State Party to comply with its international obligations under other treaties shall not constitute a breach of this Agreement.[17]

The adoption of provisions such as these prevents 'the predilections of arbitrators to view investment treaties purely as investor rights.'[18] Given the AU integration agenda, this model should be adopted at the AU level as well. The draft pan-African investment code discussed in Chapters 1 and 6 recognises the importance of framing investment regulation within the framework of sustainable development objectives and imposes human rights obligations on investors. The code is a gold standard law for investment regulation and the political commitment from African states is needed to push for the code to be binding.

In light of the recommendations made in this book, it is important that in revising BITs or negotiating new BITs in the future, emphasis should be placed on the modification of the language of BITs rather than developing new international arbitration structures. If the trend towards the rejection of ISDS continues to grow, the new language of BITs allows the development of a system where rule of law principles and human rights norms apply. This will allow the development of ISDS alternatives such as use of domestic legal systems, state–state dispute settlement and regional human rights mechanisms. Modified treaty language should also extend to the preamble of a treaty, which is central to treaty interpretation. Preambles recognise the broader objectives that BITs aim to realise, including protection and promotion of human rights, sustainable development, the application of

---

17   Commentary to article 20 of the SADC model BIT viewed (30 March 2017) from
      www.iisd.org/itn/wp-content/uploads/2012/10/sadc-model-bit-template-final.pdf
18   *Id.*

administrative justice principles including transparency and public participation, access to justice and safeguards for an interpretive approach that
considers domestic and international law.

This book does not suggest that host states should be able to avoid their
investment obligations in favour of non-investment obligations. What is
recommended is the evolution and development of international investment
law through the influence of other legal regimes. The margin of appreciation
and deference doctrine are particularly important in this regard. The international investment law regime is fluid and unlike other existing legal regimes,
it is guided by thousands of BITs. Consequently, a holistic interpretive
approach to investment treaties is proposed. In proposing the application of
the domestic regulation of states, this should not be the only applicable rule
in BIT interpretation. Adopting a comparative public law analysis from other
legal regimes such as customary international law, ICESCR obligations and
WTO rules should be considered. This includes the systemic integration of
relevant rules of international law in the BIT regime, and assessing whether
the objectives of a state measure that limit investor protections are consistent
with the factors proposed in Chapter 2 on what constitutes a public interest
measure.

At a regional level, we have seen regulatory developments in various RECs
which mirror some of the regulation in African states where there has not
been any deliberate strategy in ensuring that investment regulation is not
unduly skewed towards the protection of investors and their investments. A
strategic approach is needed by states at a domestic and continental level to
ensure that investment regulations achieve the objectives of sustainable
development.

The recommendations in this book are not only relevant for and specific
to IIAs as a legal system; they are also relevant for other systems where
integration is pivotal. RECs for instance are moving into a phase where extra-
territorial laws are being proposed for the regulation of various sectors. At
play will be the relevance of the domestic laws of respective states and their
role in the extra-territorial application of regional laws. In the application of
these regional laws, the sovereign right of states to regulate will come into
question. This will be of significant importance for other scholarly works that
are dealing with the systemic integration of laws.

Bibliography

Chapter 1

Books

Ismail, M., 2016, *International Investment Arbitration: Lessons from Developments in the MENA Region*, Routledge.

Ruggie, G. J., 2013, *Just Business: Multinational Corporations and Human Rights*, W. W. Norton & Company.

Sornarajah, M., 2010, *The International Law on Foreign Investment*, 3rd edn, Cambridge University Press.

Vidal-Leon, C., 2015, 'A New Approach to the Law of Foreign Investments: The South African case', in Bjorklund, A. (ed.) *Yearbook on International Investment Law and Policy 2014–2015*, Oxford University Press.

Journal articles

Africa, J.-G. and Ajumbo, G., 2012, 'Informal Cross Border Trade in Africa: Implications and Policy Recommendations', *Africa Economic Brief* 3(10).

Human Rights Council, 2014, 'Elaboration of an internationally legally binding instrument on transnational corporations and other business enterprises with respect to human rights', A/HRC/26/L.22/Rev., Human Rights Council.

Levitt, J. I., 2015, 'African Origins of International Law: Myth or Reality?', *UCLA Journal of International Law and Foreign Affairs* 19.

Miles, K., 2010, 'International Investment Law: Origins, Imperialism and Conceptualizing the Environment', *Colorado Journal of International Environmental Law & Policy* 21(1).

Schlemmer, E. C., 2016, 'An Overview of South Africa's Bilateral Investment Treaties and Investment Policy', *ICSID Review* 31(1).

Wei, D., 2012, 'Bilateral Investment Treaties: An Empirical Analysis of the Practices of Brazil and China', *European journal of Law and Economics* 33(3).

Online sources

African Development Bank, 'Recognising Africa's Informal Sector', viewed (15 March 2017) from www.afdb.org/en/blogs/afdb-championing-inclusive-growth-across-africa/post/recognizing-africas-informal-sector-11645/

Brenton, P. and Hoffman, B. (eds), 2015, 'Political Economy of Regional Integration in Sub-Saharan Africa', World Bank Group, 3, viewed (20 March 2017) from http://documents.worldbank.org/curated/en/601711468010204270/pdf/10 3324-REVISED-WP-P146857-PUBLIC.pdf

Brenton, P. and Isik, G. (eds), 2011, 'De-Fragmenting Africa: Deepening Regional Trade Integration in Goods Services', World Bank, viewed (20 March 2017) from http://siteresources.worldbank.org/INTAFRICA/Resources/Defrag_Afr_Engli sh_web_version.pdf.

Mbengue, M., 2016, 'The Quest for a Pan-African Investment Code to Promote Sustainable Development', Bridges Africa, 5(5), viewed (30 March 2017) from www.ictsd.org/bridges-news/bridges-africa/news/the-quest-for-a-pan-african-investment-code-to-promote-sustainable

UNCTAD, 2015, 'Strengthening The Private Sector to Boost Continental Trade and Interrogation in Africa', viewed (21 March 2017) from http://unctad.org/en/PublicationsLibrary/presspb2015d5_en.pdf

UNCTAD, 2015, 'World Investment Report 2015', viewed (15 March 2016) from http://unctad.org/en/PublicationsLibrary/wir2015_en.pdf

UNCTAD, 2015, 'Key Statistics and Trends in International Trade in Goods 2015', viewed (15 March 2017) from http://unctad.org/en/PublicationsLibrary/ditctab2015d1_en.pdf

UNCTAD, 2005, 'South-South Cooperation in International Investment Agreements', viewed (31 March 2017) from http://unctad.org/en/docs/iteiit20053_en.pdf

UNECA, 2016, 'Investment Policies and Bilateral Investment Treaties in Africa: Implications for Regional Integration', viewed (15 March 2017) from www.uneca.org/sites/default/files/PublicationFiles/eng_investment_landscapin g_study.pdf

WTO, 2015, 'International Trade Statistics', viewed (15 March 2017) from www.wto.org/english/res_e/statis_e/its2015_e/its2015_e.pdf

Chapter 2

Books

Dupuy, P., 2010, 'Unification Rather than Fragmentation of International Law? The Case of International Investment Law and Human Rights Law', in Dupuy, P. (ed.) *Human Rights in International Investment Law and Arbitration*, Oxford University Press.

Francioni, F., 2010, 'Access to Justice, Denial of Justice, and International Invest ment Law', in Dupuy, P. (ed.) *Human Rights in International Investment Law and Arbitration*, Oxford University Press.

Gazzini, T. and De Brabandere, E., 2012, 'Bilateral Investment Treaties', in Gazzini, T. and De Brabandere, E. (eds) *International Investment Law: The Sources of Rights and Obligations*, Martinus Nijhoff Publishers.

Hirsch, M., 1993, *The Arbitration Mechanism of the International Centre for the Settlement of Disputes*, Kluwer-Nijhoff Publishers.

Hirsch, M., 2010, 'Investment Tribunals and Human Rights: Divergent Paths', in Dupuy, P. (ed.) *Human Rights in International Investment Law and Arbitration*, Oxford University Press.

Kulick, A., 2012, *Global Public Interest in International Investment Law*, Cambridge University Press.

Montt, S., 2009, *State Liability in Investment Treaty Arbitration: Global Constitutional and Administrative Law in the BIT Generation*, Hart Publishing.

Morgan, B. and Yeung, K., 2007, *An Introduction to Law and Regulation*, Cambridge University Press.

Petersmann, E. U., 2012, *International Economic Law in the 21st Century*, Hart Publishing.

Poulsen, L., 2012, 'Investment Treaties and the Globalisation of State Capitalism: Opportunities and Constraints for Host States', in Echandi, R. and Sauve, P. (eds) *Prospects in International Investment Law and Policy*, Cambridge University Press.

Reiner, C. and Schreuer, C., 2010, 'Human Rights and International Investment Arbitration', in Dupuy, P. (ed.) *Human Rights in International Investment Law and Arbitration*, Oxford University Press.

Schill, S. W., 2009, *The Multilaterilazation of International Investment Law*, Cambridge University Press.

Schneiderman, D., 2008, *Constitutionalizing Economic Globalization: Investment Rules and Democracy's Promise*, Cambridge Studies in Law and Society.

Sunstein, C., 1993, *After the Rights Revolution: Reconceiving the Regulatory State*, Harvard University Press.

Journal articles

Adeleke, F., 2016, 'Human Rights and International Investment Arbitration', *South African Journal of Human Rights* 32(1).

Bronckers, M., 2015, 'Is Investor–State Dispute Settlement (ISDS) Superior to Litigation Before Domestic Courts?: An EU View on Bilateral Trade Agreements', *Journal of International Economic Law* 8(3).

Cernic, J. L., 2010, 'Corporate Human Rights Obligations under Stabilization Clauses', *German Law Journal* 11.

Choudhury, B., 2009, 'Democratic Implications Arising from the Intersection of Investment Arbitration and Human Rights', *Alberta Law Review* 46.

Desierto, D. A., 2012, 'Calibrating Human Rights and Investment in Economic Emergencies: Prospects of Treaties and Valuation Decisions', *Manchester Journal of International Economic Law* 9(2).

Fry, J. D., 2008, 'International Human Rights Law in Investment Arbitration: Evidence of International Law's Unity', *Duke Journal of Comparative & International Law* 18.

Meyer, G. and Coleman, M., 2009, 'Arbitration in Africa', *Without Prejudice* 46.

Odumosu, I., 2008, 'The Law and Politics of Engaging Resistance in Investment Dispute Settlement', *Penn State International Law Review* 26.

Roberts, A., 2010, 'Power and Persuasion in Investment Treaty Interpretation: The Dual Role of States', *American Journal of International Law* 104.

Simma, B., 2011, 'Foreign Investment Arbitration: A Place for Human Rights?', *International & Comparative Law Quarterly* 60.

Van Harten, G., 2007, 'The Public-Private Distinction in the International Arbitration of Individual Claims against the State', *International & Comparative Law Quarterly* 56.

Yackee, J., 2012, 'Controlling the International Investment Law Agency', *Harvard International Law Journal* 53.

Online sources

Devaney, M., 2012, 'Leave it to the Valuation Experts?: The Remedies Stage of Investment Treaty Arbitration and the Balancing of Public and Private Interests', Society of International Economic Law, 3rd Biennial Conference, Working Paper No. 2012-06, viewed (31 March 2017) from https://papers.ssrn.com/sol3/papers.cfm?abstract_id=2087777&rec=1&srcabs=2088315&alg=1&pos=4

Gibson, D., 2014, 'Will Africa be Lit by "BITS"?', viewed (13 May 2014) from www.gibsondunn.com/publications/Documents/Will-Africa-Be-Lit-By-BITs.pdf

US-Australia Free Trade Agreement (FTA), 2004, Article 11.6, viewed (20 June 2016) from www.ustr.gov/trade-agreements/free-trade-agreements/australian-fta

UNCTAD, 2007, 'Investor-State Dispute Settlement and Impact on Investment Rule Making', viewed (21 March 2017) from unctad.org>docs>iteiia20073_en.pdf

UNCTAD, 2016, 'World Investment Report 2016', viewed (31 March 2017) from http://unctad.org/en/PublicationsLibrary/wir2016_en.pdf

Other sources

Henckels, C., 2012, 'Proportionality and Standard of Review in Fair and Equitable Treatment Claims: Balancing Stability and Consistency with the Public Interest', Society of International Economic Law Conference, unpublished paper.

Suda, R., 2005, 'The Effect of Bilateral Investment Treaties on Human Rights Enforcement and Realization', Global Law Working Paper 01/05 Symposium: Transnational Corporations and Human Rights.

Vadi, V., 2012, 'Culture Clash: Investor's Rights vs. Cultural Heritage in International Investment Law and Arbitration', Society of International Economic Law (SIEL), 3rd Biennial Global Conference, unpublished paper.

Chapter 3

Books

Dezalay, Y. and Garth, B. G., 1996, *Dealing in Virtue: International Commercial Arbitration and the Construction of a Transnational Legal Order*, University of Chicago Press.

Echandi, R., 2013, *Prospects in International Investment Law and Policy, Complementing Investor-State Dispute Resolution: A Conceptual Framework for Investor-State Conflict Management*, Cambridge University Press.

Harrison, J., 2009, 'Human Rights Arguments in Amicus Curiae Submissions: Promoting Social Justice?', in Dupuy, P. (ed.) *Human Rights in International Investment Law and Arbitration*, Oxford University Press.

Kladermis, D., 'Investment Treaty Arbitration as Global Administrative Law: What This Might Mean in Practice', in Brown, C. and Miles, K. (eds) *Evolution in Investment Treaty Law and Arbitration*, Cambridge University Press.

Maupin, J. A., 2013, 'Transparency in International Investment Law: The Good, the Bad, and the Murky', in Bianchi, A. and Peters, A. (eds) *Transparency in International Law*, Cambridge University Press.

Miles, K., 2013, *The Origins of International Investment Law*, Cambridge University Press.

Petersmann, E., 2012, *International Economic Law in the 21st Century: Constitutional Pluralism and Multilevel Governance of Interdependent Public Goods*, Hart Publishing.

Titi, A., 2013, *The Right to Regulate in International Investment Law*, Nomos Publishing.

van den Berg, A., 2010, 'Dissenting Opinions by Party-Appointed Arbitrators in Investment Arbitration' in Mahnoush H. et al. (eds) *Looking to the Future: Essays on International Law in Honor of M. Reisman*, Brill.

Van Harten, G., 2007, *Investment Treaty Arbitration and Public Law*, Oxford University Press.

Journal articles

Bartholomeusz, L., 2005, 'The *Amicus Curiae* before International Courts and Tribunals', *Non-St Actors & International Law* 5.

Franck, S., 2005, 'The Role of International Arbitrators', *ILSA Journal of International & Comparative Law* 12(1).

Gathi, J. T. and Odumosu, I., 2009, 'International Economic Law in the Third World', *International Commercial Law Review* 11.

Magraw, D. and Amerasinghe, N., 2008, 'Transparency and Public Participation in Investor-State Arbitration', *ILSA Journal of International and Comparative Law* 15.

Miles, K., 2010, 'International Investment Law: Origins, Imperialism and Conceptualizing the Environment', *Colombian Journal of International Environmental Law & Policy* 1.

Odumosu, I., 2008, 'The Law and Politics of Engaging Resistance in Investment Dispute Settlement', *Penn St International Law Review* 26.

Puig, S., 2014, 'Social Capital in the Arbitration Market', *The European Journal of International Law* 25(2).

Rogers, C., 2013, 'The Politics of International Investment Arbitrators', *Santa Clara Journal. International Law* 12.

Schultz, T. and Kovacs, R., 2012, 'The Rise of a Third Generation of Arbitrators? Fifteen Years after Dezalay and Garth', *Arbitration International* 28(2).

Sinclair, A., Fischer, L. and Macrory, S., 2009, 'ICSID Arbitration: How long does it take?', *Global Arbitration Review* 4.

Van Duzer, A., 2007, 'Enhancing the Procedural Legitimacy of Investor-State Arbitration Through Transparency and Amicus Participation', *McGill Law Journal* 52.

Online sources

Bastin, L., 2013, 'Amici Curiae in Investor-State Arbitrations: Two Recent Decisions', Australian International Law Journal, viewed (31 March 2017) from www.austlii.edu.au/au/journals/AUIntLawJl/2013/7.pdf

Cappelletti, M. and Garth, R., 1978, 'Access to Justice: The Worldwide Movement to Make Rights Effective, A General Report', viewed (31 March 2017) from www.repository.law.indiana.edu/cgi/viewcontent.cgi?article=2140&context=facpub

Maupin, J., 2015, 'Recurring Problems in Investor-State Disputes & How South Africa Might Respond to Them', Max-Planck-Institut, viewed (31 March 2017) from www.saiia.org.za/doc_download/699-2015-02-10-investor-state-disputes-pres-by-julie-maupin

Mohamadieh, K. and Uribe, D., 2016, 'The Rise of Investor-State Dispute Settlement in the Extractive Sectors: Challenges and Considerations for African countries', Research paper 65, viewed (31 March 2017) from www.southcentre.int/wp-content/uploads/2016/02/RP65_Rise-of-investor-state-dispute-settlement-in-extrative-sectors_EN.pdf

Reeves, E., 2012, 'Oil Revenues Controversy: Country's Obstructionism Threatens War', viewed (31 March 2017) from http://allafrica.com/stories/201201250523.html

Schill, S., 2014, 'Transparency as a Global Norm in International Investment Law', viewed (21 March 2017) from http://kluwerarbitrationblog.com/2014/09/15/transparency-as-a-global-norm-in-international-investment-law

Sudan Tribune, 2013, 'Sudan Drops Demand for Compensation for Confiscated Oil Assets, viewed (31 March 2017) from www.sudantribune.com/spip.php?article45301

Trevino, C., 2015, 'Uganda Faces Investment Treaty Arbitration By Total Oil Company', IA Reporter, viewed (29 November 2016) from www.iareporter.com/articles/uganda-faces-investment-treaty-arbitration-by-total-oil-company/

UNCTAD, 2010, 'Investor–State Disputes: Prevention and Alternatives to Arbitration', viewed (21 March 2017) from http://unctad.org/en/docs/diaeia200911_en.pdf

UNCTAD, 2010, 'Investor–State Disputes: Prevention and Alternatives to Arbitration', viewed (31 March 2017) from http://unctad.org/en/docs/diaeia200911_en.pdf

UNCTAD, 2012, 'Series on Issues in International Investment Agreements II Transparency 2012', viewed (21 March 2017) from unctad.org/en/PublicationsLibrary/diaeia2013d2_en.pdf

UNCTAD, 2012, 'Series on Issues in International Investment Agreements II Transparency', viewed (31 March 2017) from http://unctad.org/en/PublicationsLibrary/unctaddiaeia2011d6_en.pdf

Other sources

Adeleke, F., 2015, 'The Role of Law in Assessing the Value of Transparency and the Disconnect with the Lived Realities under Investor-State Dispute Settlement', Working Paper No. 6, presented at the Law & Society Conference, Seattle May 2015, unpublished paper.

Chapter 4

Books

Alschner, W., 2014, 'The Return of the Home State and the Rise of "Embedded" Investor-State Arbitration', in Lalani, S. and Lazo, R. P. (eds) *The Role of the State in Investor-State Arbitration*, Brill publishing.

de Sena, P., 2009, 'Economic and Non-Economic Values in the Case Law of the European Court of Human Rights', in Dupuy, P. (ed.) *Human Rights in International Investment Law and Arbitration*, Oxford University Press.

Hallward-Driermeier, M., 2009, 'Do Bilateral Investment Treaties Attract FDI? Only a Bit … And They Could Bite', in Sachs, L. and Sauvant, K. (eds) *The Effect of Treaties on Foreign Direct Investment: Bilateral Investment Treaties, Double Taxation Treaties and investment Flows*, Oxford University Press.

Kriebaum, U., 2009, 'Is the European Court of Human Rights an Alternative to Investor-State Arbitration?', in Dupuy, P. (ed.) *Human Rights in International Investment Law and Arbitration*, Oxford University Press.

Marchessault, L. and Jarvis, M., 2013, 'The Trend Towards Open Contracting: Applicability and Implications for International Investment Agreements', in Bjorklund, A. (ed.) *Yearbook on International Investment Law Policy*, Oxford University Press.

Miles, K., 2013, *The Origins of International Investment Law: Empire, Environment and the Safeguarding of the Capital*, Cambridge University Press.

Nikken, P., 2009, 'Balancing of Human Rights and Investment Law in the Inter-American System of Human Rights', in Dupuy, P. (ed.) *Human Rights in International Investment Law and Arbitration*, Oxford University Press.

Pasqualucci, J. M., 2013, *The Practice and Procedure of the Inter-American Court of Human Right*, 2nd ed., Cambridge University Press.

Reiner, C. and Schreuer, C., 2009, 'Human Rights and International Investment Arbitration', in Dupuy, P. (ed.) *Human Rights in International Investment Law and Arbitration*, Oxford University Press.

Sachs, L. and Sauvant, K., 2009, 'BITs, DTTs, and FDI Flows', in Sachs, L. and Sauvant, K. (eds) *The Effect of Treaties on Foreign Direct Investment: Bilateral Investment Treaties, Double Taxation Treaties and investment Flows*, Oxford University Press.

Sachs, L. and Sauvant, K., 2009, 'The Impact on Foreign Direct Investments of BITs', in Sachs, L. and Sauvant, K. (eds) *The Effect of Treaties on Foreign Direct Investment: Bilateral Investment Treaties, Double Taxation Treaties and investment Flows*, Oxford University Press.

Sornarajah, M., 2015, *Resistance and Change in International Law on Foreign Investment*, Cambridge University Press.

Sornarajah, M., 2010, *The International Law on Foreign Investment*, 3rd edn, Cambridge University Press.

Viljoen, F., 2012, *International Human Rights Law in Africa*, 2nd edn, Oxford University Press.

Journal articles

Bekaert, G. et al., 2014, 'Political Risk Spreads', *Journal of International Business Studies* 45(4).

Bekker, P. and Ogawa, A., 2013, 'The Impact of Bilateral Investment Treaty (BIT) Proliferation on Demand for Investment Insurance: Reassessing Political Risk Insurance After the "BIT Bang"', *ICSID Review* 28(2).

Christenson, G. A., 1962, 'International Claims Procedure before the Department of State', *Syracuse Law Review* 13.

Contreras. P., 2012, 'National Discretion and International Deference in the Restriction of Human Rights: A Comparison Between the Jurisprudence of the European and the Inter-American Court of Human Rights', *Northwestern Journal of International Human Rights* 11.

DeLeonardo, J. M., 2004, 'Are Public and Private Political Risk Insurance Two of a Kind-Suggestions for a New Direction for Government Coverage', *Virginia Journal of International Law* 45.

Diebold, N. F., 2011, 'Standards of Non-Discrimination in International Economic Law', *International and Comparative Law Quarterly* 60.

Dulitzky, A., 2011, 'The Inter-American Human Rights System Fifty Years Later: Time for Changes', *Quebec Journal of International Law*, special edn.

Franck, S. D., 2007, 'Foreign Direct Investment, Investment Treaty Arbitration, and the Rule of Law', *Global Business and Development Law Journal* 19.

Horlick, G. N. and Butteron, G. R., 2000, 'A Problem of Process in WTO Jurisprudence: Identifying Disputed Issues in Panels and Consultations', *Law & Policy in International Law* 31.

Khachaturian, A., 2005, 'Are We in Good Hands: The Adequacy of American and Multilateral Political Risk Insurance Programs in Fostering International Development', *Connecticut Law Review* 38.

Kochevar, S., 2013, 'Amici Curiae in Civil Law Jurisdictions', *Yale Law Journal* 122.

Lubambo, M., 2016, 'Is State-State Investment Arbitration an Old Option for Latin America?', *Conflict Resolution Quarterly* 1.

Marceau, G., 2002, 'WTO Dispute Settlement and Human Rights', *European Journal of International Law* 13.

Paparinskis, M., 2013, 'Investment Treaty Arbitration and the (New) Law of State Responsibility', *European Journal of International Law* 24(2).

Pauwelyn, J., 2001, 'The Role of Public International Law in the WTO: How Far Can We Go?', *American Journal of International Law* 95.

Roberts, A., 2014, 'State-to-State Investment Treaty Arbitration: A Hybrid Theory of Interdependent Rights and Shared Interpretive Authority', *Harvard International Law Journal* 55(1).

Rogers, C. A., 2015, 'International Arbitration, Judicial Education, and Legal Elites', *Journal of Dispute Resolution*, 2015.

Ruiz-Chiriboga, O., 2012, 'The independence of the Inter-American judge', *The Law and Practice of International Courts and Tribunals* 11(1).

Sacerdoti, G., 2016, 'Panelists, Arbitrators, Judges: A Response To Joost Pauwelyn', *AJIL Unbound* 19.

Schill, S., 2006, 'Arbitration Risk and Effective Compliance: Cost Shifting in Investment Treaty Arbitration', *Journal of World Investment & Trad*, 7.

Singh, S. and Sharma, S., 2013, 'Investor-State Dispute Settlement Mechanism: The Quest for a Workable Roadmap', *Merkourious: Utrecht Journal of International Law and European Law* 29(76).

Smith, J., 2004, 'Inequality in International Trade? Developing Countries and

Institutional Change in WTO Dispute Settlement', *Review of International Political Economy* 11.

Stiglitz, J. E., 2008, 'Regulating Multinational Corporations: Towards Principles of Cross-Border Legal Frameworks in a Globalized World Balancing Rights with Responsibilities', *American University International Law Review* 23.

Trevino, C. J., 2014, 'State-to-State Investment Treaty Arbitration and the Interplay with Investor-State Arbitration Under the Same Treaty', *Journal of International Dispute Settlement* 5(1).

Online sources

Bernasconi-Osterwalder, N., 2014, 'State-State Dispute Settlement in Investment Treaties', International Institute for Sustainable Development, viewed (31 March 2017) from www.iisd.org/sites/default/files/publications/best-practices-state-state-dispute-settlement-investment-treaties.pdf

Bernasconi-Osterwalder, N. and Dietrich-Brauch, M., 2015, 'Brazil's Innovative Approach to International Investment Law', International Institute for Sustainable Development, viewed (31 March 2017) from www.iisd.org/blog/brazils-innovative-approach-international-investment-law

Bernasconi-Osterwalder, N. and Dietrich-Brauch, M., 2015, 'Comparative Commentary to Brazil's Cooperation and Investment Facilitation Agreements (CIFAs) with Mozambique, Angola, Mexico, and Malawi', International Institute for Sustainable Development, viewed (31 March 2017) from www.iisd.org/sites/default/files/publications/commentary-brazil-cifas-acfis-mozambique-angola-mexico-malawi.pdf

Bernasconi-Osterwalder, N. and Rossert, D., 2014, 'Investment Treaty Arbitration: Opportunities to Reform Arbitral Rules and Processes', IISD, viewed (25 March 2017) from www.iisd.org/pdf/2014/investment_treaty_arbitration.pdf

Cordes K. E., et al., 2016, 'Land Deal Dilemmas: Grievances', Human Rights, and Investor Protections, Columbia Center on Sustainable Investment, viewed (31 March 2017) from http://ccsi.columbia.edu/files/2016/03/CCSI_Land-deals-and-the-law_Briefing.pdf

Davis, C., 2008, 'The Effectiveness of WTO Dispute Settlement: An Evaluation of Negotiation Versus Adjudication Strategies', Annual Meeting of the American Political Science Association, viewed (31 March 2017) from www.princeton.edu/~cldavis/files/WTOeffectiveness_DavisAPSA08.pdf

Drabek, Z. and Payne, W., 2001, 'The Impact of Transparency of Foreign Direct Investment', World Trade Organization, ERAD-99-02, viewed (25 March 2017) from www.wto.org/english/res_e/reser_e/erad-99-02.doc

European Commission, 2016, 'Establishment of a Multilateral Investment Court for Investment Dispute Resolution', viewed (25 March 2017) from http://ec.europa.eu/smart-regulation/roadmaps/docs/2016_trade_024_court_on_investment_en.pdf

European Union, 2015, 'Proposal of the European Union for Investment Protection and Resolution of Investment Disputes, Chapter II: Investment', European Union, viewed (21 March 2017) from http://trade.ec.europa.eu/doclib/docs/2015/november/tradoc_153955.pdf

Gallagher, K. and Shrestha, E., 2011, 'Investment Treaty Arbitration and Developing

Countries: A re-appraisal', Global Development and Environmental Institute, Working Paper No. 11-01, viewed (25 March 2017) from http://ase.tufts.edu/gdae/Pubs/wp/11-01TreatyArbitrationReappraisal.pdf

Gaukrodger, D. and Gordon, K., 2012, 'Investor-State Dispute Settlement: A Scoping Paper for the Investment Policy Community', OECD Working Papers on International Investment, No. 2012/03, viewed (21 March 2017) from http://dx.doi.org/10.1787/5k46b1r85j6f-en

Gordon K., 2008, 'Investment Guarantees and Political Risk Insurance: Institutions, Incentives and Development', OECD Investment Policy Perspectives, viewed (25 March 2017) from www.oecd.org/finance/insurance/44230805.pdf

Hindelang, S., 2014, 'Part II: Study on Investor-State Dispute Settlement ('ISDS') and Alternatives of Dispute Resolution in International Investment Law Study of Investor-State Dispute Settlement ('ISDS') and Alternatives of Dispute Resolution in International Investment Law', European Parliament, EXPO/B/INTA/2014/08-09-10, viewed (21 March 2017) from www.europarl.europa.eu/RegData/etudes/STUD/2014/534979/EXPO_STU(2014)534979(ANN01)_EN.pdf

Jimenez, M. P. et al., 2016, 'Towards a Model of Transparency and Access to Information in the Inter-American Human Rights System', in Reynolds, K. A. (ed.) *The Inter-American Human Rights System Changing Times, Ongoing Challenges*, Due Process of Law Foundation, viewed (31 March 2017) from www.dplf.org/sites/default/files/challenges_iahrs_final_web_08232016pdf.pdf

Johnson, L. and Sachs, L., 2010, 'The Outsized Costs of Investor-State Dispute Settlement', *Academy of Business Insights* 16(1), viewed (25 March 2017) from http://ccsi.columbia.edu/files/2016/02/AIB-Insights-Vol.-16-Issue-1-The-outsized-costs-of-ISDS-Johnson-Sachs-Feb-2016.pdf

Johnson, L., Sachs, L. and Sachs, J., 2015, 'Investor-State Dispute Settlement, Public Interest and US Domestic Law', Columbia Centre on Sustainable Environment.

Multilateral Investment Guarantee Agency (MIGA), World Investment and Political Risk 09, viewed (25 March 2017) from www.miga.org/documents/WIPR13.pdf

Lambach, J., et al., 2003, 'Judicial Independence: Law and Practice of Appointments to the European Court of Human Rights', viewed (31 March 2017) from www.lhr.md/images/appointment.pdf

Marceau, G. and Mikella H., 2012, 'Transparency and Public Participation: A Report Card on WTO Transparency Mechanisms', Trade, Law and Development, viewed (31 March 2017) from www.tradelawdevelopment.com/index.php/tld/article/view/4(1)%20TL%26D%2019%20(2012)

OECD, 2012, 'Government Perspectives on Investor-State Dispute Settlement: A Progress Report', accessed (25 March 2017) from www.oecd.org/daf/inv/investment-policy/ISDSprogressreport.pdf

Rossert, D., 2014, 'The Stakes are High: A Review of the Financial Costs of Investment Treaty Arbitration', IISD, accessed (25 March 2017) from www.iisd.org/sites/default/files/publications/stakes-are-high-review-financial-costs-investment-treaty-arbitration.pdf

Sanchez, N. C. and Ceron, L. L., 2016, 'The Elephant in the Room: The Procedural Delay in the Individual Petitions System of the Inter-American System', in Reynolds, K. A. (ed.) *The Inter-American Human Rights System: Changing Times, Ongoing Challenge*, Due Process of Law Foundation, viewed (31 March 2017) from www.dplf.org/sites/default/files/challenges_iahrs_final_web_08232016 pdf.pdf

UNCTAD, 2014, 'IIA Issues Note: The Impact of International Investment Agreements on Foreign Direct Investment: An Overview of Empirical Studies 1998–2014', Working draft, viewed (25 March 2017), from http://investment-policyhub.unctad.org/Upload/Documents/unctad-web-diae-pcb-2014-Sep%2016.pdf

UNCTAD, 2015, 'World Investment Report 2015 Reforming International Investment Governance', E.15.II.D.5, viewed (21 March 2017) from http://unctad.org/en/PublicationsLibrary/wir2015_en.pdf

Wong, J., 2014, 'The Subversion of State-to-State Investment Treaty Arbitration', *Columbia Journal for Transnational Law* 53, viewed (25 March 2017) from http://jtl.columbia.edu/wp-content/uploads/sites/4/2015/01/Wong-Article-53-CJTL-6.pdf

WTO, 2003, 'Introduction to the WTO Dispute Settlement System', viewed (25 March 2017) from www.wto.org/english/tratop_e/dispu_e/disp_settlement_cbt_e/intro1_e.htm

Other sources

ASEAN Economic Community, 2004, *ASEAN Protocol on Enhanced Dispute Settlement Mechanism*, Appendix I (Covered Agreements). ASEAN.

Brazil-Mozambique Cooperation and Investment Facilitation Agreement, 2015.

Constitution of the Republic of South Africa, 1996.

Investment Agreement for the COMESA Common Investment Area.

SADC, 2012, *Southern African Development Community Model BIT*. SDAC.

Chapter 5

Books

Gazzini, T. and Radi, Y., 2012, 'Foreign Investment with a Human Face, with Special Reference to Indigenous Peoples' Rights', in R. Hofmann and C. Tams (eds) *International Investment Law and Its Others*, NOMOS Publishing.

Kladermis, D., 2011, 'Investment Treaty Arbitration as Global Administrative Law: What this Might Mean in Practice', in Brown, C. and Miles, K. (eds) *Evolution in Investment Treaty Law and Arbitration*, Cambridge University Press.

Krommendijk, J. and Morijn, J., 2009, '"Proportional" by What Measures? Balancing Investors Interests and Human Rights by Way of Applying the Proportionality Principle in Investor-State Arbitration', in Dupuy, P. (ed) *Human Rights in International Investment Law and Arbitration*, Oxford University Press.

Kulick, A., 2012, *Global Public Interest in International Investment Law*, Cambridge University Press.

Prislan, V., 2012, 'Non Investment Obligations in Investment Treaty Arbitration – Towards a Greater Role for States?', in Baetens, F. (ed.) *Investment Law Within International Law: An Integrationist Perspective*, Cambridge University Press.

Sornarajah, M., 2008, 'A Coming Crisis: Expansionary Trends in Investment Treaty Arbitration, in Appeals Mechanism in International Investment Disputes', in Sauvant K. P. (ed.) *Appeals Mechanism in International Investment Disputes*, Oxford University Press.

Spears, S., 2011, 'Making Way for the Public Interest in International Investment Agreements', in Brown, C. and Miles, K. (eds) *Evolution in Investment Treaty Law and Arbitration*, Cambridge University Press.

Van Harten, G., 2007, *Investment Treaty Arbitration and Public Law*, Oxford University Press.

Journal articles

Adeleke, F., 2016, 'Human Rights and International Investment Arbitration', *South African Journal of Human Rights* 32(1).

Brower, C. N. and Schill, S. W., 2009, 'Is Arbitration a Threat or a Boon to the Legitimacy of International Investment Law?', *Chicago Journal of International Law* 9.

Chen, T., (2012), 'The Standard of Review and the Roles of ICSID Arbitral Tribunals in Investor State Dispute Settlement', *Contemporary Asia Arbitration Journal* 5(1).

Desierto, D. A., 2012, 'Calibrating Human Rights and Investment in Economic Emergencies: Prospects of Treaty and Valuation Defences', *Manchester Journal of International Economic Law* 9(2).

Franck, S. D., 2005, 'The Legitimacy Crisis in Investment Treaty Arbitration: Privatizing Public International Law Through Inconsistent Decisions', *Fordham Law Review* 73.

Henckels, C., 2013, 'Balancing Investment Protection and the Public Interest: The Role of the Standard of Review and the Importance of Deference in Investor-State Arbitration', *Journal of International Dispute Settlement* 4(1).

Orellana, M. A., 2011, 'The Right of Access to Information and Investment Arbitration', *ICSID Review Foreign Investment Law Journal* 26(2).

Schill, S. W., 2011, 'Enhancing Investment Law's Legitimacy: Conceptual and Methodological Foundations of a new Public Law Approach', *Virginia Journal of International Law* 52.

Online sources

Hepburn, J. and Balcerzak, F., 2013, 'Polish Court Rules on Release of Investment Arbitration Awards under Freedom of Information Law', *IA Reporter*, viewed (17 February 2013) from www.iareporter.com/articles/20130102_3

Kladermis, D., 2012, 'Systemic Integration and International Investment Law – Some Practical Reflections', working paper No. 2012/46, viewed (6 May 2017) from http://arbitrationlaw.com/files/free_pdfs/2012_-_d_kalderimis_-_system ic_integration_and_iil_-_some_practical_reflections.pdf

UN Office of the High Commissioner for Human Rights, 2008, 'Frequently Asked Question on Economic, Social, and Cultural Rights', Fact Sheet No. 33, 25, viewed (29 March 2017) from www.ohchr.org/Documents/Publications/ FactSheet33en.pdf

Other sources

Bjørge, E., 2012, 'Evolutionary Interpretation and the Intention of the Parties',

University of Oslo Faculty of Law Research Paper No. 2012-33 (October), SSRN 6.

Schill, S., 2012, 'Deference in Investment Treaty Arbitration: Re-Conceptualising the Standard of Review through Comparative Public Law', Society of International Economic Law (SIEL), SSRN.

Chapter 6

Journal articles

Carim, X., 2012, 'South Africa's Review and New Policy on BITs', *South Bulletin* 69(8).

Online sources

Alschner, W. and Skougarevskiy, D., 2016, 'Rule-takers or rule-makers? A new look at African bilateral investment treaty practice', Working Paper No. 7, viewed (30 March 2017) https://ssrn.com/abstract=2791474

Domeland, D. and Sander, F. G., 'Growth in African Small States' 2007, World Bank, viewed (26 March 2017) from http://siteresources.worldbank.org/INTDEBT DEPT/Resources/468980-1206974166266/4833916-1206989877225/ DomelandGilSander200704.pdf

Hepburn, J., 2015, 'An Update On Investor-State Claims Against Kenya', IA Reporter, viewed (29 November 2016) from www.iareporter.com/articles/an-update-on-investor-state-claims-against-kenya/

Klaaren, J. and Schneiderman, D., 2009, 'Investor–State Arbitration and SA's Bilateral Investment Treaty Policy Framework Review: Comment Submitted to the DTI 10 August 2009', Mandela Institute, viewed (31 March 2017) from www.elaw.org/system/files/Comments+on+DTI+BITs+review+FINAL.pdf

Mohamadieh, K. and Uribe, D., 2016, 'The Rise of Investor-State Dispute Settlement in the Extractives Sectors: Challenges and Considerations for African countries', South Centre Research Paper 65, viewed (31 March 2017) from www.southcentre.int/research-paper-65-february-2016/

Muchlinski, P., 2008, 'The COMESA Common Investment Area: Substantive Standards and Procedural Problems in Dispute Settlement', viewed (6 October 2016) from http://ssrn.com/abstract=1698209

Ngobeni, L. and Fagbayibo, B., 2015, 'The Investor-State Dispute Resolution Forum under the SADC Protocol on Finance and Investment: Challenges and Opportunities for Effective Harmonisation', *Law Democracy Dev.* 19, viewed (26 March 2017) from www.scielo.org.za/scielo.php?script=sci_arttext&pid=S2077-49072015000100009

Peterson, L. E., 2013, 'Dismantling Of Southern African Development Community Tribunal Spawns Uncitral Arbitration Claim For Denial of Justice', IA Reporter, viewed (30 March 2017) from www.iareporter.com/articles/dismantling-of-southern-african-development-community-tribunal-spawns-uncitral-arbitration-claim-for-denial-of-justice/

Peterson, L. E., 2014, 'Arbitrators Dismiss Some Objections in Face of $650 Million Oil Expropriation Claim Under Nigerian Investment Statute', IA Reporter, viewed (29 November 2016) from www.iareporter.com/articles/arbitrators-dismiss-some-objections-in-face-of-650-million-oil-expropriation-claim-under-nig erian-investment-statute/

Peterson, L. E., 2016, 'Multilateral Investment Treaty's Exhaustion of Remedies Requirement Does Not Hobble Case Because Local Courts Couldn't Offer Same Relief Available Before International Tribunal', IA Reporter, viewed (30 March 2017) from www.iareporter.com/articles/multilateral-investment-treatys-exhaustion-of-remedies-requirement-does-not-hobble-case-because-local-courts-c ouldnt-offer-same-relief-available-before-international-tribunal/.

Sachs, L. and Sauvant, K., 2009, 'BITs, DTTs and FDI flows: An Overivew', in Sachs, L. and Sauvant, K. (eds) *The Effect of Treaties on Foreign Direct Investment: Bilateral Investment Treaties, Double Taxation Treaties and Investment Flows*, Oxford University Press, viewed (26 March 2017) from http://ccsi.columbia. edu/files/2014/01/Overview-SachsSauvant-Final.pdf

UNCTAD, 2012, 'Investment Policy Framework for Sustainable Development', University of the Witwatersrand, Johannesburg, 26 July 2012, viewed (26 March 2017) from http:// unctad.org/ meetings/ en/ Miscellaneous%20Documents/ South-Africa-Investment-statement_Rob_Davies.pdf

UNCTAD, 2015, 'World Investment Report: Reforming International Investment Governance', viewed (27 March 2017) from http://unctad.org/en/ PublicationsLibrary/wir2015_en.pdf

UNECA, 2015, 'Industrializing through Trade: Economic Report on Africa 2015', viewed (26 March 2017) from www.un.org/en/africa/osaa/pdf/pubs/2015era-uneca.pdf

UNECA, 2016, 'Africa Regional Integration Index 2016', viewed (26 March 2017) from www.uneca.org/sites/default/files/PublicationFiles/arii-report2016_en _web.pdf

UNECA, 2016, 'Investment Policies and Bilateral Investment Treaties in Africa Investment Treaties in Africa: Implications for Regional Integration Implications for Regional Integration', viewed (26 March 2017) from www.uneca.org/ sites/default/files/PublicationFiles/eng_investment_landscaping_study.pdf

UNECA, 2016, 'Pan-African Investment Code', viewed (30 March 2017) from http://repository.uneca.org/handle/10855/23009

Other sources

Graduate School of Development Policy and Practice (GSDPP) UCT, 2014, 'The Political Economy of African Economic Integration: Strategic Reflections', unpublished Report.

Chapter 7

Books

Dupuy, P. M., 2009, 'Unification Rather than Fragmentation of International Law? The Case of International Investment Law and Human Rights Law', in Dupuy, P. M. (ed.) *Human Rights in International Investment Law and Arbitration*, Oxford University Press.

Morison, J. and Anthony, G., 2011, 'The Place of Public Interest', in G. Antony et al. (eds) *Values in Global Administrative Law*, Hart Publishing.

Online sources

European Commission, 2013, 'Incorrect Claims about Investor-State Dispute Settlement', viewed (25 March 2017) from http://trade.ec.europa.eu/doclib/docs/2013/october/tradoc_151790.pdf

Levashova, Y., 2012, 'Public Interest Norms in the European International Investment Policy: A Shattered Hope?', University of Oslo Faculty of Law, Legal Studies Research Paper Series No. 8, viewed (31 March 2017) from https://papers.ssrn.com/sol3/papers.cfm?abstract_id=2083475

Reinsch, A., 2016, 'The European Union and Investor-State Dispute Settlement: From Investor-State Arbitration to a permanent Investment Court', Investor-State Arbitration Series Paper No. 2, viewed (31 March 2017) from www.cigionline.org/sites/default/files/isa_paper_series_no.2.pdf

Index

accessibility: domestic legal systems 82; PRI 98; regional human rights courts 106; state-state dispute settlement 92

administrative law, and public interest regulation theory 27

Africa: 'Africanisation' of international investment law 7; BITs 12; economic diversification 4; fastest growing economies 14; FDI *see* foreign direct investment (FDI); as international law innovator 5; investment disputes *see* investment disputes; investment law and policy *see* investment law and policy in Africa; regional integration *see* regional integration; trade within 3

African Court of Justice 132

African Court on Human and People's Rights (ACHPR): accessibility 107; appeals 104; costs 105; current operation 99; depoliticisation of investment disputes 100; efficiency 106; impartiality 105; limitations 108; and rule of law 101; third party participation 104; transparency rules 103

African Union (AU): continental free trade area (CFTA) 12; Court of Arbitration 132; mediation by 68; regional integration 11

alternative dispute resolution (ADR): advantages and disadvantages of 53; as alternative to ISDS 53; ISDS *see* investor-state dispute settlement (ISDS); ISDS as 47; methods of 53; third party participation 54; transparency 54

amicus participation in dispute settlement 59, 79, 90, 165

Anthony, G. 166

appeals: against awards 165; domestic legal systems 80; PRI 97; regional human rights courts 104; state-state dispute settlement 90

arbitration: African Union Court of Arbitration 132; BIT arbitration and public interest regulation theory 35; choice of 33; distinction between public and private adjudication 34; first BIT arbitration 32

arbitrators: bias and conflict of interest 49; procedural integrity 165

bilateral investment treaties (BITs): African BITs 12; African concerns about 13; arbitration, and public interest regulation theory 35; deference to domestic law 121; between developing countries 5; first BIT 32; first BIT arbitration 32; future negotiation of 168; growth of 1; and human rights 114; ICESCR interaction with 124; if public or private law 32; IISD model BIT 14; introduction to 110; investment dispute cases 12; investment protection 15; investor protection 29; language modification 168; model BITs 4; and neo-liberal ideology 1; object and purpose of 28; and other relevant rules of international law 116; policy, and public interest regulation theory 39; post-colonial period 2; preference for 28; as primary source of law 26; public dimension of investment disputes 118; South Africa's BIT framework 135; sovereignty and 34;

For Product Safety Concerns and Information please contact our EU
representative GPSR@taylorandfrancis.com
Taylor & Francis Verlag GmbH, Kaufingerstraße 24, 80331 München, Germany

www.ingramcontent.com/pod-product-compliance
Ingram Content Group UK Ltd.
Pitfield, Milton Keynes, MK11 3LW, UK
UKHW020954180425
457613UK00019B/675